C000050349

# MURDERABILIA

## A History of Crime in 100 Objects

HAROLD SCHECHTER

WORKMAN PUBLISHING · NEW YORK

Copyright © 2023 by Harold Schechter

All rights reserved. No portion of this book may be reproduced—mechanically, electronically, or by any other means, including photocopying—without written permission of the publisher.

Library of Congress Cataloging-in-Publication Data is available.

ISBN 978-1-5235-1529-5

Design by Janet Vicario and Galen Smith

Cover photos (left to right): Glasses: Chicago History Museum/Getty Images; Blackwell Bathtub: Courtesy of the Author; Lizzie Borden Hatchet: Fall River Historical Society; Skeleton: Countway Library, Harvard; Bonnie and Clyde: Library of Congress/Wikimedia; Postcard: Case Western Reserve University; License Plate: Courtesy of the Author; Gun: Museums of Western Colorado; Cryptogram: Bettmann/Getty Images; Letter: International News Photo/Getty Images; Typewriter: Office of Public Affairs/Flickr; Burke Mold: Lucy Thomas/Alamy; Mugshot: Courtesy of the Author; Wooden Gun: Courtesy of the Author; Book Spine: Valery Evlakhov/Shutterstock.

See page 276 for photo credits

Workman books are available at special discounts when purchased in bulk for premiums and sales promotions as well as for fundraising or educational use. Special editions or book excerpts can also be created to specification. For details, please contact special.markets@hbgusa.com.

Workman Publishing Co., Inc.,
a subsidiary of Hachette Book Group, Inc.
1290 Avenue of the Americas
New York, NY 10104
workman.com

WORKMAN is a registered trademark of Workman Publishing Co., Inc.,
a subsidiary of Hachette Book Group, Inc.

Printed in China on responsibly sourced paper.

First printing August 2023

10 9 8 7 6 5 4 3 2 1

# Contents

## Author's Note

Though he and I feel very differently about the practice of collecting crime memorabilia, I wish to acknowledge Andy Kahan, Director of Victim Services and Advocacy for Crime Stoppers of Houston, as the person the who coined the term "murderabilia."

---

*For Michael, Mihaela, and Fabian*

---

## Acknowledgments

I owe a particular debt of gratitude to: David "The Great Throwdini" Adamovich, Harold Augenbraum, Joe Coleman, Eva Lozano, David Patterson, Rick Staton, and—as ever—my true love, Kimiko Hahn.

# Introduction

*After the discovery of the horrors on Belle Gunness's "murder farm" in 1908, thousands of curiosity-seekers flocked to her burned-down home to gawk at the cellar where her charred corpse and those of her children were found.*

A
s a historian of American crime, I have long been intrigued by a phenomenon that has generated a great deal of controversy over the years: the trafficking in so-called murderabilia, morbid collectibles ranging from John Wayne Gacy clown paintings to Christmas cards signed by Ted Bundy, which are sold and traded on the internet. Though decried by moral crusaders as a symptom of modern cultural degeneracy, the truth is that the impulse to own a grisly memento of a highly publicized murder has existed for centuries.

In 1827, for example, Maria Marten, a young Englishwoman from the village of Polstead, vanished after supposedly eloping with a man named William Corder. The following April—acting on pleas from her mother, who had dreamed that the girl was

buried beneath the floor of a local farm—police discovered the young woman's body just where her mother had said it would be. The case became a nationwide sensation. When Corder was executed three months later, the crowd was so eager for souvenirs that the hangman's noose was cut up and sold for a guinea per inch. Corder's skin was subsequently flayed from his body, tanned like cowhide, and sold piecemeal at auction. One of the larger sections ended up being made into a tobacco pouch.

In the days before police learned to cordon off crime scenes, souvenir hunters swarmed over the sites of sensational murders, carrying off every scrap of potentially important evidence. In the aftermath of the massacre of an entire farm family, the Deerings, by an employee named Anton Probst in 1866, the barn in which the slaughter took place was overrun with sightseers who made off with wooden splinters from the blood-spattered floorboards. Visiting the site, one witness watched as "a man hurriedly got on his knees right down in the dirty straw and manure, gouged out a gory spot the size of a silver five-cent coin, wrapped it carefully in a piece of paper, and deposited it still more carefully in his vest pocket."

Reporting on another ghastly crime that occurred at the tail end of the nineteenth century—the decapitation-murder of a young Kentucky woman named Pearl Bryan in 1896—one journalist described the frenzied scene at the apple orchard where her body was found:

> **Relic hunters were out in great numbers, and they almost demolished the bush under which the body was discovered, breaking off branches upon which blood could be seen. They peered closely into the ground for blood-spotted leaves, stones, and even saturated clay. Anything that had a blood stain upon it was seized upon eagerly.**

The writer's reference to these ghoulish scavengers as "relic hunters" is very much to the point. Blasphemous as it may seem, there is a connection between the grisly "murderabilia" artifacts and traditional saints' relics. One is, in a very real sense, the flip side—the shadow—of the other. If the finger bone, say, of St. Sergius incarnates the mystery of Christian grace, a lock of Charles Manson's hair embodies the opposite: the mystery of sheer malevolence, of inscrutable evil. To those who coveted them, the wooden fragments taken from the Deerings' barn and the apple orchard where Bryan was found were the dark counterparts of the pieces of the True Cross worshiped by the faithful—objects possessed of an unholy power.

When such grim relics weren't available, visitors to the scenes of notorious murders often came away with other mementoes. With the advent of photography, for example, crime scene postcards became popular items. In the spring of 1908, a dozen dismembered corpses were discovered on the Indiana farmstead of Belle Gunness, aka the "Lady Bluebeard." Within days, thousands of sightseers descended on the property, where enterprising hucksters peddled souvenir postcards of the exhumed remains of her victims. Two decades later, so many gawkers showed up at the site of the Bath School Disaster—in which a local madman blew up the primary school in the small farming community of Bath, Michigan, killing thirty-eight children—that one journalist described the village as a "Mecca for the morbidly curious." Happy to profit from his hometown's notoriety, one local photographer printed and sold picture postcards of the massacre, including one that a depicted a line of blanket-shrouded little bodies dug out of the wreckage.

Collectors of such lurid keepsakes are by no means the only people drawn to "murderabilia." Throughout the latter half of the nineteenth century, seedy "dime museums" proliferated in the United States, attracting patrons with everything from two-headed animals to hideously deformed human fetuses to macabre artifacts from infamous crimes. Among the "20,000 Objects of Wonder" advertised by one of these establishments, for example, was Anton Probst's right arm, amputated and preserved after his execution. Even the venerable P. T. Barnum got in on the act, buying the deathbed clothing of Albert Hicks—a notorious lowlife who slaughtered the entire crew of a Virginia-bound sloop and was hanged in 1860—and promptly putting them on display in his Broadway museum.

The tradition continues to this day. A blockbuster exhibit mounted by the Museum of London in 2016 displayed scores of objects from Scotland Yard's legendary collection (popularly known as the "Black Museum"). Among these were the 1890s medicine case belonging to serial poisoner and Jack the Ripper suspect Dr. Thomas Neill Cream; the spade used by Dr. Hawley Harvey Crippen to bury the remains of his butchered wife in the cellar of their home in 1910; and the rubber apron and gloves of John George Haigh, the British "Acid Bath Killer," who murdered six people in the 1940s and dissolved their bodies in a drum of sulphuric acid. The William Burke Museum in Edinburgh offers visitors a close-up look at an especially grisly relic: a calling-card case fashioned from the flayed skin of William Burke, the notorious

nineteenth-century serial killer who, with his partner William Hare, sold his victims' corpses to a local anatomist for dissection.

The ominous significance of some of the objects in this volume—Lizzie Borden's hatchet, for example, and the Luger used by mass murderer Howard Unruh—is obvious. Other items—the ladder used in the Lindbergh baby kidnapping, Augusta Gein's crucifix—are everyday objects that acquired sinister meaning through the association with notorious homicides. In our own true crime–obsessed era, fans of the genre can collect a variety of macabre novelty merchandise: old B-movie posters, serial killer action figures, T-shirts and mugs emblazoned with the likenesses of their favorite homicidal maniacs. Using these objects as a springboard, this volume creates a historic tapestry of the most sensational true crimes, in both the US and abroad, that have captured and held public fascination for more than two centuries.

*License plate of Bonnie and Clyde's "death car."*

# #1 NAOMI WISE'S TOMBSTONE

## The Murder of "Omie" Wise

**(1808)**

*Naomi Wise is long gone, but her tragic tale has been immortalized in one of America's most famous folk songs.*

The oldest form of true crime literature is the one folklorists call "murder ballads," a genre dating at least as far back as the Middle Ages, when these sung or recited verses spread the news about shocking real-life homicides among the illiterate peasantry. By Shakespeare's time, traveling peddlers had figured out a way to profit from the public's love of sensationalism by producing printed versions of murder ballads. Whenever a particularly ghastly slaying occurred, it was immediately translated into a page-long sheet of doggerel called a "broadside" that sold for a pittance—the Elizabethan equivalent of today's tabloid newspaper.

Imported to America, the traditional murder ballad, both in its sung and printed forms, flourished well into the twentieth century. Though the vast majority of these "bloody versicles" (as one crime historian calls them) have long since faded into obscurity, a handful have become a lasting part of America's folklore heritage. One of the most famous is "Little Omie," an example of a subcategory of the genre known as "murdered-girl ballads." During the folk music craze of the late 1950s, the song was a coffeehouse standard and has been recorded by scores of artists, from Bob Dylan to Elvis Costello. Though it exists (like virtually all folk songs) in many versions, the earliest known lyrics go like this:

> Come all good people,
> I'd have you draw near,
> A sorrowful story you
> quickly shall hear;
> A story I'll tell you
> about Omie Wise,
> How she was deluded
> by Lewis's lies.

> He promised to marry
> and use me quite well;
> But conduct contrary
> I sadly must tell,
> He promised to meet me
> at Adams's springs;
> He promised me marriage
> and many fine things.

> Still nothing he gave,
> but yet flattered the case.
> He says we'll be married
> and have no disgrace,
> Come get up behind me,
> we'll go up to town,
> And there we'll be married,
> in union be bound.

> I got up behind him
> and straightway did go
> To the banks of Deep River
> where the water did flow;
> He says "Now, Naomi,
> I'll tell you my mind,
> Intend here to drown you and
> leave you behind."

"Little Omie," while based on an actual crime, takes considerable liberties with the truth.

Born in 1789 and orphaned in childhood, Naomi Wise became a bound servant in the household of Mr. and Mrs. William Adams of Randolph County, North Carolina. Some accounts paint her as a paragon of youthful femininity—a "gentle, confiding creature" with a soft-spoken manner, fetching personality, and "cheerful temperament." The most reliable contemporary record reveals that she bore two children by two different employers while still in her teens and, by 1807, was pregnant with a third by another man, a "sprightly" young clerk named Jonathan Lewis.

Scion of the Randolph family that gave the county its name, Lewis boarded with his employer in the village of Asheboro, returning to his family home each Saturday night, a fifteen-mile journey that took him past the Adams farm. "Once, as Naomi was carrying water to the spring," writes one historian, "Jonathan stopped and asked if he could have a drink. She obliged, then he dismounted and helped her carry her buckets to the house. Naomi fell in love with Jonathan Lewis then, and he seemed smitten as well." Not surprisingly, Wise was soon with child.

Far from displaying the slightest shame at her condition, as would be expected at the time, the young woman openly boasted of becoming pregnant by a "man of so high a rank as Jonathan." Lewis, in the meantime, had turned his attention to his employer's sister, Hettie Elliott, hoping to make a match that would raise him several rungs on the social ladder. When Hettie confronted him about the now widespread stories that he was the father of Wise's unborn child, he insisted that it was a "base, malicious slander, circulated by the enemies of the Lewis family to ruin his character." Wise continued to broadcast his paternity and threatened to sue him for child support—a "bastardy bond," as it was known—if he did not make her an honest woman.

Jonathan appeared to relent, agreeing to elope with her and arranging to meet her at the spring below the Adamses' house a few days thence. On the appointed evening, Wise, taking bucket in hand and pretending to go fetch some water, hurried down to the spring, where Lewis awaited on horseback. Leaving the bucket behind, she mounted the back of the horse and the two rode off, ostensibly on the way to the home of the magistrate who—so Jonathan assured her—would perform the nuptials.

The next morning, upon discovering that Wise had never returned from her errand, her employer, William Adams, headed down

*A trusting young woman meets her tragic end at the hands of her seducer.*

to the spring. From the evidence—the abandoned water bucket, the hoofprints in the mud, the tracks of Wise's boots—he quickly deduced that she had been carried away on horseback. In short order, he had rounded up a search party of half-dozen neighbors who followed the horse's trail along the banks of the river. They found her body in the water among tangled weeds, her throat bearing the marks of manual strangulation, her skirt pulled up over her face, as though to stifle her screams.

From the facts of the case, it seems clear that Jonathan Lewis was an early specimen of the type of malignant narcissist that journalist Marilee Strong calls an "eraser killer": a seemingly upright young man who sees his wife or girlfriend as an impediment to his own gratifications and cold-bloodedly sets out to rid himself of her. Immediately fingered as the prime suspect, Lewis was tracked down and arrested that same day. Hauled back to the scene of the crime and confronted with Wise's corpse, he stoutly maintained his innocence, displaying so little emotion at the sight of his murdered lover that several of his outraged captors had to be restrained from lynching him on the spot.

He was locked up in the Randolph County jailhouse, a rickety building from which he managed to escape. Recaptured in 1811, he was tried and acquitted, apparently for lack of evidence. Exactly where and when he died remains a matter of debate, though some accounts claim that, on his deathbed in 1820, he finally confessed to Wise's murder—a tragedy that, by then, had entered into local legend.

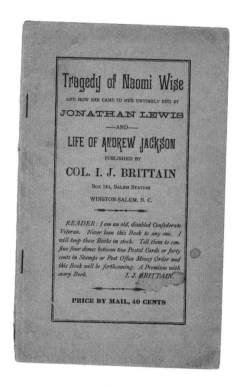

*An early true crime book about the Naomi Wise murder case.*

# #2 WILLIAM BURKE'S DEATH MASK

## Burke and Hare, the British "Anatomy Murders"

**(1828)**

*Photography hadn't been invented at the time William Burke and his accomplice conducted their murder spree, but we know exactly what he looked like thanks to this plaster cast head made immediately after his execution.*

D issecting cadavers has long been a critical part of medical training. Nowadays, thanks to the practice of voluntary body donation, there is a plentiful supply of corpses for med school anatomy classes. Things were different in eighteenth-century Britain, when the only corpses that could be legally used for teaching purposes were those of executed criminals. Despite the staggering number of crimes that could send a felon to the gallows then—everything from pickpocketing to poaching to writing a threatening letter—surgical instructors still found themselves with an acute shortage of freshly dead human specimens.

To meet the demand, a new breed of entrepreneurs sprang up, practitioners of what one scholar has called "the foulest trade in human history." Commonly known as body snatchers or resurrectionists, these enterprising ghouls would sneak into a churchyard at night, dig up a recently buried coffin, pry open the lid, extract the corpse, and—after restoring the grave to its former condition—deliver their plunder to one of their regular medical school customers.

Though the names of virtually all these professional corpse thieves have been lost to history, two men have entered legend as the most infamous of British resurrectionists: William Burke and William Hare. As it happens, they weren't grave robbers at all. They were what we now call serial killers.

A native of County Tyrone, Ireland, William Burke was born into a family of poor but respectable tenant farmers in 1792. At nineteen, he became a soldier, serving as a private in the Donegal militia for five years. At some point during that time, he married and had two children with a woman named Margaret Coleman, only to desert his wife and

offspring a few years later after leaving the army.

Immigrating to Scotland, he found employment as a canal worker and took up with a part-time sex worker named Helen "Nelly" McDougal, who became his common-law wife. Not long afterward, the couple relocated to Edinburgh, where Burke soon made the acquaintance of the man whose name would forever be linked to his own in the annals of infamy.

Born in 1807 and raised (in the words of his earliest biographer) "without any education or proper moral training," William Hare spent his early adulthood as a farm laborer in his native Ireland. In contrast to Burke—who impressed all who knew him with his easygoing charm—Hare, according to one contemporary, possessed "a ferocious, violent, quarrelsome" disposition and was given to particularly brutish behavior when he was drunk, as was often the case. Like Burke, he came to Scotland to work on the new canal linking Edinburgh to Glasgow and ended up boarding at a tenement lodging house run by a man named Logue and his wife, Margaret. When Logue died, Hare lost no time taking his place both in Margaret's bed and as landlord of the squalid doss-house, where, in the autumn of 1827, Burke and McDougal came to live.

The commercial partnership that would earn Burke and Hare everlasting notoriety began in November 1827 with the passing of an elderly lodger named Donald, who died owing Hare £4 of back rent. In those years, Edinburgh was the country's leading center of medical education. To recover the debt, Hare hit upon the idea of selling the old man's corpse to one of the city's many anatomists. Promised a share of the proceeds, Burke helped his friend convey the cadaver to the school of celebrated surgeon, Dr. Robert Knox, where they received the handsome sum of £7 10s—more than $300 in today's currency—and were told that they were always welcome to return "when they had another [body] to dispose of."

Disinclined to engage in the difficult, dirty, and dangerous business of grave robbing, the two reprobates hit on another, less strenuous method of obtaining marketable human corpses: "wholesale murder." Their first victim was an elderly lodger named Joseph who had fallen ill with typhus. Afraid that having the contagious old man on the premises might scare off potential customers, Hare once again enlisted Burke's assistance. After feeding Joseph enough whiskey to put him in a stupor, the two made short work of him, one pressing a pillow to his face while the other lay across his chest. This time, Knox forked over £10 for the corpse. At no point, either then or thereafter, did the doctor inquire as to the provenance of the goods he was paying for.

Though the facts remain murky, another ailing inmate of the boardinghouse, an Englishman in his forties, appears to have been the next victim. Most historians of the case believe that, in dispatching this individual, the two murderers perfected the smothering technique that would come to be known as "burking": Hare would press his hands over the person's mouth and nose while Burke lay across the upper body.

Having exhausted their supply of sick lodgers, the pair went out trawling for victims. The first to fall into their clutches was an elderly peddler, Abigail Simpson. Encountering her in a pub, Hare lured her back to his premises, where he and Burke plied her with whiskey. Once fallen into a stupor, she was smothered, stripped, stuffed into

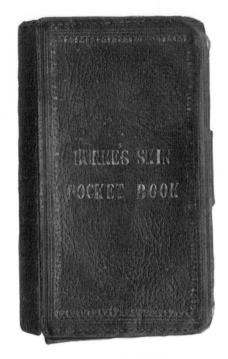

*Pocketbook made from the skin of William Burke following his execution and public dissection.*

a tea chest, and carted off to the offices of the uninquiring Dr. Knox.

Over the next six months—between April and October 1828—the two fiends (as they would soon be branded in newspapers throughout the United Kingdom) would murder an additional thirteen people.

The atrocities of the ghoulish pair climaxed, appropriately enough, on Halloween 1828. By then, Burke and McDougal were residing at a different lodging house, run by a couple named Broggan. That morning, Burke was enjoying his morning dram of whiskey in a neighborhood pub when an elderly beggarwoman wandered in, asking for alms. Sizing her up as easy prey, Burke treated her to a drink and struck up a conversation. Before long, the old lady happily accepted his invitation to come stay at his lodgings.

Leaving her in the company of his wife, Burke sought out Hare at a nearby tavern and informed him that he had found fresh meat for Dr. Knox's dissection table. He then returned to his rooms, where, in preparation for the murder, he persuaded the other lodgers, a couple named Gray and their child, to spend the night elsewhere. Once the Grays were gone and Hare was on the scene, the two dispatched the old lady by their usual method and stuffed her corpse beneath a heap of straw at the foot of a bed.

The following morning, Mrs. Gray returned to the rooms to fetch a pair of her child's stockings, looked under the straw, and was horrified to see the old lady's dead body, stripped of its clothing, blood leaking from her mouth. By the time officers arrived at the Broggans' boardinghouse, however, the two serial murderers had already delivered the corpse to Dr. Knox, where it was later found by police. Burke and Hare were promptly taken into custody.

Betrayed by Hare—who, to save his own skin, agreed to turn King's evidence and testify against his accomplice—Burke was tried for murder, convicted, and condemned to the gallows. Upon his sentencing, it was made clear to Burke that his ultimate fate would be nothing less than an act of poetic justice. His hanged body, the presiding judge declared, would "be publicly dissected and anatomized."

An estimated twenty-five thousand people turned out for his hanging on January 28, 1829. It took Burke about ten minutes to die. In accordance with the court's wishes, his body was then dissected before a standing-room-only audience of medical students. The following morning, the corpse was placed on public exhibition. By the end of the day, thirty thousand eager citizens had filed through the anatomy hall for a glimpse of ghastly remains. The cadaver was then stripped of its flesh and the skeleton given to the University of Edinburgh. Some of the skin was tanned and fashioned into various ghoulish artifacts, including a wallet, a calling-card case, and the binding of a book.

Granted immunity from prosecution, William Hare was set free, much to the outrage of the public. With an infuriated mob clamoring for his blood, he slipped out of Edinburgh, made his way south to Carlisle, and vanished from the historical record.

# #3 CRIME PAMPHLET ENGRAVING

## The Helen Jewett Murder

**(1836)**

*After committing the most sensational American murder of its day—the hatchet slaying of the beautiful sex worker Helen Jewett—the perpetrator fled the crime scene, as depicted in this artst's rendition.*

With no statutes against prostitution, New York City in the 1830s was home to thousands of sex workers. One of these was a twenty-three-year-old beauty who went by the name of Helen Jewett. Born Dorcas Doyen in Temple, Maine, she had gone to work as a domestic in her early adolescence, entering the household of Chief Justice Nathan Weston of the Maine Supreme Judicial Court. Treated less as a servant than as a valued family member, she was educated at a local school, where she distinguished herself as an outstanding student with a deep love of reading, a "remarkable quickness of apprehension," and refined, ladylike manners.

At the age of eighteen—by then a smart, strong-willed young woman with a lively sexuality and a romantic streak—she lost her virginity to someone whose identity has never been established. Under a cloud of disgrace, she left the Weston household and embarked on her life as a sex worker using several aliases, first in Portland, Maine, then in Boston. Sometime between the fall of 1832 and January 1833, she moved to New York City, where—under a fourth and final pseudonym, Helen Jewett—she worked at a succession of brothels before taking up residence at a "house of ill fame" run by a madam named Rosina Townsend.

In the summer of 1835, Jewett—who seemed to have harbored genuinely romantic feelings for some of her clients—became enamored of a nineteen-year-old dry-goods clerk, Richard P. Robinson. Within weeks of their first encounter, she was sending him impassioned letters, proclaiming that she loved him "madly," gushing over his "high, generous, noble" character, and waxing rhapsodic about their lovemaking.

Robinson appeared to be equally smitten with Jewett, declaring in an early letter that "No one can love you more than I do." As their relationship progressed, Robinson would often give vent to a mixture of disgust and self-loathing, treating her with open contempt. Before long, as historian Patricia Cline Cohen writes, their "sweet and all-consuming love" had "degenerated into mutual threats and recriminations."

Still, like countless other lovers locked in toxic relationships, they repeatedly reconciled. Jewett remained ignorant of the darkest aspect of Robinson's personality: He harbored a Jekyll-and-Hyde split that revealed itself in his diaries, where he confessed that, while his mind tended to be calm and rational during the day, "sometimes, at the dead hour of midnight, a thought is aroused out from the deep caverns of the mind, like a startled maniac, which all the energy of reason can scarcely re-cage!"

That maniacal part of Robinson erupted in the early morning hours of Sunday, April 10, 1836, when, during one of his visits to Jewett, he shattered her skull with a hatchet, set her bed on fire to cover up the crime, and fled into the night. Law officers were soon on the scene and quickly doused the fire. Searching the premises, they discovered a bloody hatchet in the backyard and, on the street just outside the fence, a man's blue cloth cloak, evidently dropped by the fleeing killer. Learning the name of the murdered woman's visitor that evening, they tracked Robinson down at his boardinghouse and arrested him. Since both the cloak and hatchet were quickly linked to Robinson, there seemed little doubt as to his guilt. As he would for the remainder of his days, however, Robinson staunchly proclaimed his innocence.

Covered with prurient relish in the *New York Herald*, the crime became an affair of all-consuming public interest. By the time Robinson's trial opened on Thursday, June 2, 1836, it had grown into a national sensation, reported in newspapers across the country. Though the prosecuting attorneys presented overwhelming circumstantial evidence of Robinson's guilt, the jury was quick to dismiss the testimony of their star witness, Rosina Townsend, denounced by the defense as a "common prostitute," an "infamous and abandoned" creature "too corrupt and rotten ever to speak the truth." The twelve men took just fifteen minutes to return a verdict of not guilty.

Adopting the name Richard Parmalee, Robinson headed west, settling in Nacogdoches, Texas. In the years before his sudden death in 1855, he operated a saloon and a stagecoach line, served as clerk of the county court, joined the Masons, invested in real estate, fought and was seriously wounded in a military campaign against the Cherokee Nation, and—after marrying a wealthy widow who had inherited a large estate from her late husband—became a major landowner of a property with more than twenty enslaved people. At his funeral, he was eulogized as "a valiant soldier of the Republic" and "an enterprising citizen of the State" who possessed a "character noble and firm of purpose."

# #4 COVER OF J. H. INGRAHAM'S NOVEL *THE BEAUTIFUL CIGAR GIRL*

## The Murder of Mary Rogers

MARY CECELIA ROGERS,
BETTER KNOWN AS
"THE BEAUTIFUL CIGAR GIRL,"
FOUND MURDERED AT HOBOKEN, ON WEDNESDAY, JULY 28th, 1841.
FOR PARTICULARS SEE SECOND PAGE.

**(1841)**

*The strange death of the "Beautiful Cigar Girl" inspired one of Edgar Allan Poe's famous detective stories, "The Mystery of Marie Rogêt."*

In the early nineteenth century, New Yorkers seeking an escape from the stifling summer heat of the city could take a steamboat from lower Manhattan to an idyllic glade on the New Jersey side of the Hudson River known as Elysian Fields. On the afternoon of Wednesday, July 28, 1841, a young music instructor named Henry Mallin was strolling along the riverbank with a friend. As they gazed into the rippling waters, they received what Mallin later described as an "evil shock." Floating about three hundred yards out was a human body.

The corpse was that of a drowned woman who, to judge by her condition, had been decomposing in the water for several days. She was wearing a torn white frock, a bright blue scarf, "light colored" shoes and gloves, and a leghorn straw bonnet. Despite her grotesque appearance—the purplish-black skin, the bloated face, the frothy blood leaking from her mouth—she was quickly identified as Mary Cecilia Rogers, a young woman who was something of a local celebrity.

Invariably described in contemporary accounts as a young woman of enchanting appearance—"raven-tressed" and possessed of a "dark smile" and a "hypnotically pleasing" figure—Mary Rogers had first come to the public's attention several years earlier while working at a popular Broadway "tobacco emporium" run by a merchant named John Anderson. His customers had one thing in common: They were all men. Calculating that a pretty face behind the counter would be a boon to his business, the canny proprietor had hired the eighteen-year-old Rogers in 1838 to serve less as a salesgirl than as a sexual magnet.

The strategy worked. Anderson's profits soared as male admirers flocked to his shop to "preen and squawk before the young lady."

Dubbed the "Beautiful Cigar Girl," Rogers became a prototype of the modern celebrity, known for being known.

In 1840, Rogers quit the job to manage a boardinghouse leased by her sixty-year-old mother, Phoebe. Located in lower Manhattan, it catered to a clientele of young, single workingmen. A number of them, including a cork cutter named Daniel Payne who had become romantically involved with Rogers, were residing there on Sunday, July 25, 1841, when the young woman left the house at around ten in the morning, announcing her intention to visit an aunt. Her family never saw her alive again.

The results of her autopsy were so shocking that newspapers could only hint at the lurid details. Hoboken coroner Dr. Richard H. Cook concluded that before being dumped in the river, Rogers had been beaten, gagged, tied, and ultimately strangled to death with a strip of fabric torn from her underskirt. Even more appallingly, bruises on her "feminine region" left no doubt in the coroner's mind that the "unfortunate girl" had been gang raped: "brutally violated by no fewer than three assailants."

The case became the talk of the town. Popular novelist Joseph Holt Ingraham published a bestselling fictionalized account of her life and ordeals, titled *The Beautiful Cigar Girl*. Typical of the sites of sensational murders, Elysian Fields became a ghoulish tourist attraction, with crowds picnicking on the spot where Rogers's corpse had been dragged ashore.

In the weeks following the murder, the police focused their attentions on one suspect after another. But in rapid succession, each of these suspects was cleared and released from custody. By the end of August, the police were no closer to a solution.

*Mary Rogers's corpse (portrayed in a highly voyeuristic manner) was found floating on the New Jersey side of the Hudson River.*

In the middle of September there was a sensational development in the case. At its center was a widow named Frederica Loss, proprietor of a popular roadhouse not far from where Rogers's body had been discovered. Several weeks earlier, while out collecting sassafras bark, Loss's two sons, twelve and sixteen years of age, had reportedly come upon some articles of Mary Rogers's apparel within a dense thicket. The little hollow within the thicket "was stamped about, and the branches were broken, and the roots bruised and mashed, all betokening that it had been the scene of a very violent struggle."

The discovery seemed to lend credence to the pet theory that Rogers had been murdered by a gang of "miscreants." Frederica Loss, however, now came forward with a story that she had never shared with the police. According to Loss, Rogers had come to her tavern on July 25 in the company of a "tall, dark-complexioned" man. The two ordered drinks—liquor for the man, lemonade for Rogers—and, after sitting for a while and chatting pleasantly, left arm in arm. Later that night, Loss had heard a scream from the direction of the woods but assumed that the cry had come from an injured animal and put it out of her mind.

One year later, Frederica Loss had a still different story to tell. As she lay dying from a fatally infected wound, Loss reportedly directed her sons "to make known the circumstances attending the death of Mary Rogers, which she had before concealed."

The secret was that Mary Rogers had died during an abortion carried out in Loss's premises by an unidentified "young physician." The child she was carrying had evidently been fathered by her fiancé, Daniel Payne, who, several months after the discovery of Rogers's corpse, had made his way to the riverbank where it had been brought ashore and swallowed a fatal dose of laudanum, leaving a suicide note asking God's forgiveness for his "misspent life."

While much of the public accepted this account, the police had doubts about it, since it so glaringly contradicted much of the physical evidence, including the strangulation marks on Rogers's neck and the coroner's conclusion that she had been gang raped. The investigation was ultimately abandoned, leaving the case of the "Beautiful Cigar Girl" as one of New York City's most famous unsolved murders.

# #5 SHINGLE HAMMER

## The Colt–Adams Affair

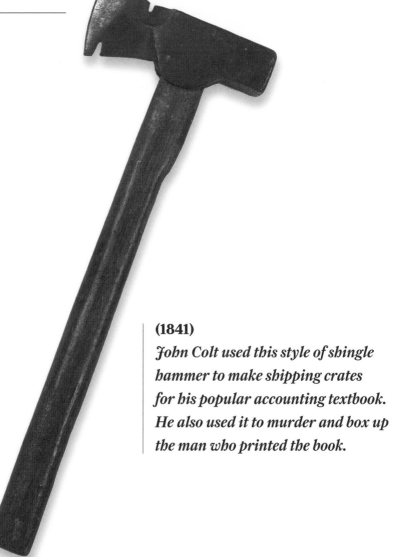

**(1841)**

*John Colt used this style of shingle hammer to make shipping crates for his popular accounting textbook. He also used it to murder and box up the man who printed the book.*

In September 1841, Samuel Adams, a respected printer with a shop in lower Manhattan, disappeared after leaving his office on an unspecified errand. A week later, his naked, putrefying corpse was discovered stuffed inside a wooden packing crate in the hold of a ship. Investigators quickly determined that the crate had been brought to the ship by John Caldwell Colt, a brilliant accountant and older brother of Samuel Colt, legendary inventor of the revolving handgun.

After an initial denial, John Colt admitted to the authorities that he had indeed killed Adams but claimed that he had acted in self-defense. According to his statement, Adams—who had printed the latest edition of Colt's popular textbook—had shown up in his office, demanding immediate payment of an overdue bill for $71.15. Colt's own calculations, however, showed that he owed only $55.85. The two began to argue. Before long they were trading blows. When Adams grabbed him by the necktie and began to choke him, Colt reflexively picked up a shingle hammer lying on his desk and delivered a series of fatal blows to his assailant's head. Then he stuffed the stripped and trussed-up corpse into a packing crate, addressed the box to a nonexistent person, and had it put on a ship bound for New Orleans.

Colt's trial in January 1842 began in a perfectly orderly fashion, but before long it turned into a circus. At one point, Adams's corpse was exhumed and decapitated, and the head displayed to the jury by the coroner, who sat throughout his testimony with the grisly object cradled on his lap. Despite the best efforts of his high-powered defense team, Colt was found guilty and condemned to hang. The denouement of the case would be one of the most bizarre in the annals of American criminal history.

While awaiting execution, Colt received permission to legitimize his relationship with his mistress, Caroline Henshaw. On the afternoon of November 18, 1842—just before he was scheduled to go to the gallows—he and Henshaw were wed in his cell in the Tombs. Afterward, the couple was permitted an hour's conjugal visit alone. When the sheriff returned to fetch John and lead him to the scaffold, he found the condemned man lying dead in a puddle of blood, a clasp knife protruding from his chest. Almost at the same instant, the cupola of the Tombs burst into flames. Though Colt's death was ruled a suicide, many people would forever believe that the corpse found in his cell was actually a medical school cadaver smuggled into the prison during the confusion of the fire and that Colt had been spirited away by his friends. These rumors notwithstanding, there is little doubt that Colt took his own life with a knife provided by a member of his wedding party. His suicide—and the accompanying conflagration—served as a fittingly sensational climax to the case.

THE
SCIENCE
OF
DOUBLE ENTRY
BOOK-KEEPING,
SIMPLIFIED, ARRANGED, AND METHODIZED,
AFTER THE FORMS OF GRAMMAR AND ARITHMETIC;
EXPLAINED BY DEFINITE RULES, AND ILLUSTRATED BY ENTRIES
CLASSED, IN A MANNER MATERIALLY DIFFERENT FROM ANY WORK EVER
BEFORE OFFERED TO THE PUBLIC.

CONTAINING, ALSO,

A KEY,

EXPLAINING
THE MANNER OF JOURNALIZING,
AND THE NATURE OF
THE BUSINESS TRANSACTION OF EACH OF THE DAY-BOOK ENTRIES.

TOGETHER WITH
PRACTICAL FORMS FOR KEEPING BOOKS,
AS CIRCUMSTANCES MAY REQUIRE IN DIFFERENT COMMERCIAL HOUSES.

BY J. C. COLT, ACCOUNTANT.

TWELFTH EDITION.

NEW YORK:
PUBLISHED BY NAFIS & CORNISH,
278 Pearl Street.
PHILADELPHIA—JOHN B. PERRY,
198 Market Street.
1846.

*The title page of John Colt's successful accounting textbook.*

# #6 COURTROOM DIAGRAM OF DR. PARKMAN'S BODY PARTS

## The Parkman–Webster Case

**(1849)**

*The disappearance of prominent Bostonian George Parkman was a citywide mystery—until his dismembered body parts were found in the privy of Harvard professor John White Webster.*

Forensic anthropology has become a vital tool in contemporary law enforcement, practiced by scientific "bone detectives" who are able to determine the identity and cause of death of unknown victims by the close study of their skeletal remains. Though generally regarded as a form of modern-day forensic wizardry, the origins of the field can be traced to one of the most sensational crimes of the nineteenth century, the Parkman–Webster case of 1849.

Trained as a physician, Dr. George Parkman, one of Boston's wealthiest men, was primarily a landlord and moneylender. Among his debtors was the distinguished Harvard chemistry professor John White Webster, who owed Parkman a substantial sum. It was to confront Webster about this matter that Parkman made his way to Harvard one fateful Friday afternoon, never to be seen alive again.

Notified of his disappearance by his wife, police undertook a massive manhunt, pursuing leads that placed Parkman as far away as Cape Cod. During this period, Professor Webster appeared to be his usual amiable self. Only one person detected something peculiar about his behavior: Ephraim Littlefield, janitor at the medical college. Given that Webster had never engaged him in a protracted conversation in all the years they had known each other, it struck Littlefield as strange when the professor grilled him about Dr. Parkman's disappearance. Convinced that Webster had murdered Parkman and was attempting to obliterate the remains, Littlefield chiseled through the brick wall of Webster's privy vault. Lying amidst the muck were a male pelvis with the genitalia still attached, a right thigh, and the lower portion of a dismembered left leg.

Taken into custody, Webster vehemently protested his innocence. His twelve-day trial, which commenced on March 19, 1850, ended in a guilty verdict after less than three hours of jury deliberation. Webster then made a final desperate attempt to escape the hangman's noose by confessing that he had indeed killed Parkman, though without premeditation. Provoked into a fury when Parkman barraged him with insults, Webster had seized a stick of wood and delivered a crushing blow to his creditor's skull, then made a panicked effort to dispose of the body. Despite appeals for clemency, the governor remained unmoved. On the morning of August 30, 1850, Webster was hanged.

Though the Parkman–Webster case has long faded from public memory, it has gone down in US legal history as a forensic milestone, thanks to the involvement of two prosecution witnesses. One was Dr. Parkman's dentist, Nathan C. Keep, who identified the false teeth found in a recovered portion of jawbone as his own handiwork—the first time that forensic dentistry played a role in an American trial. The other was Dr. Jeffries Wyman, professor of anatomy at Harvard. An expert at skeletal analysis, he was called upon to examine the bone fragments recovered from the furnace in Dr. Webster's laboratory. His testimony at the trial was a vital link in the chain of evidence against the defendant. It was also a scientific and legal landmark, the event that launched the field of forensic anthropology.

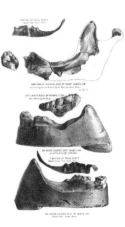

*One of the most damning pieces of evidence against Professor Webster were the false teeth and fragments of jawbone positively identified by dentist Nathan Cooley Keep as belonging to his patient Dr. Parkman.*

# #7 ANTON PROBST TRIAL PAMPHLET

## The Deering Family Massacre

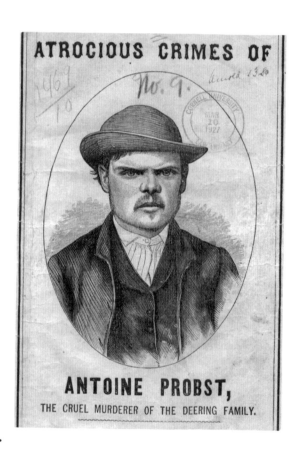

ATROCIOUS CRIMES OF

ANTOINE PROBST,
THE CRUEL MURDERER OF THE DEERING FAMILY.

**(1866)**

*In nineteenth-century America, cheap trial pamphlets served the same function as today's countless true crime podcasts and cable TV shows, feeding the public's insatiable appetite for lurid murder stories.*

On Wednesday, April 11, 1866, Abraham Everett, a resident of a rural, sparsely populated area of South Philadelphia known locally as "The Neck," visited the farm of his neighbor Christopher Deering. He knocked at the door but got no response. Proceeding to the barn, he was shocked to find Deering's horses nearly dead of thirst and starvation.

Once he had taken care of the animals, he returned to the house, peered through a window, and was startled to see the interior in a state of wild disorder, as if it had been ransacked. He alerted other neighbors then returned with them to the farm. Inside the barn, they spotted something that Everett, in his focus on the suffering horses, had missed. Jutting from a pile of hay was a human foot.

One of the men made for the nearest police station. Within a short time, several officers arrived and made a horrifying discovery. Beneath the hay lay the farm owner, Christopher, his skull pulverized, his throat chopped open to the neckbone. Beside him was a young woman, later identified as a visiting cousin, slaughtered in the same way.

In a small corn crib they found the decomposed body of Christopher's wife, Julia, her skull beaten in, her throat gashed. Heaped around and upon her were four of her children, the youngest a fourteen-month-old girl, butchered in the same way. Apart from the oldest child, a ten-year-old boy named Willie—spared only because he was visiting his grandparents—the entire family had been annihilated. Not long afterward, another decaying corpse, that of the Deerings' seventeen-year-old farmhand, Cornelius Carey, was discovered shoved into a haystack.

Suspicion immediately fell upon the Deerings' other employee, Anton Probst, who was nowhere to be found. A brawny German immigrant, Probst had spent most of the Civil War as a "bounty jumper," volunteering for service in one locality, collecting the bonus offered to new enlistees, then promptly deserting and repeating the process elsewhere. Averse to the drudgery and dangers of army life, he had eventually contrived a discharge by "accidentally" shooting off his right thumb. After blowing all his money on liquor and sex workers, he had knocked around the Philadelphia area for a while, seeking work, until he happened upon the Deering farmstead. Though Mrs. Deering was made uneasy by Probst's sullen manner, her husband, an immigrant himself, took pity on him and hired him.

Rather than put as much distance between himself and the crime scene as possible, Probst spent the next five days in various Philadelphia taverns and brothels. When it finally dawned on him that he was the object of a citywide manhunt, he attempted to sneak out of town but was quickly recognized and arrested. A search of his pockets turned up a number of Christopher Deering's possessions, including a pistol and snuffbox. In fact, as the police quickly determined, Probst was wearing Deering's clothes, having exchanged them for his own blood-soaked shirt and pants before fleeing the site of the massacre.

As an enraged mob laid siege to the jailhouse, howling for Probst's blood, he underwent a lengthy interrogation. After making the predictable protestations of innocence, he admitted that he had slain Cornelius Carey but insisted that the other seven victims had been slain by an accomplice.

Probst's five-day trial began on April 25, just two weeks after the murders were discovered. Memorably described by the district attorney as "a monster in the shape of man," Probst was convicted after jury deliberations

*Anton Probst disposes of his victims in this contemporary engraving.*

lasting twenty minutes. He was condemned to hang in five weeks.

While awaiting death, Probst continued to proclaim his innocence of all the murders except Cornelius Carey's, though he eventually confessed to luring Mrs. Deering and her children into the barn, one at a time, then slaughtering each of them with an axe. Mr. Deering, who had gone into town that morning to fetch his visiting relative, was slain upon his return, along with his guest. Asked why he had perpetrated such an atrocity, Probst gave a little shrug. "I only wanted the money," he said. "I had no ill feeling to anyone in the family. They always treated me well."

# #8 DIME NOVEL

## "The Boston Boy Fiend"

**(1871–1874)**
*Like comic books and video games before them, nineteenth-century dime novels, with stories full of graphic frontier violence, were believed to have a corrupting effect on the minds of America's youth.*

One of the youngest serial killers on record, Jesse Harding Pomeroy, born in South Boston in 1859, suffered a hideous boyhood. Along with the frequent horsewhippings he received from his alcoholic father, he was cursed with an appearance that made him the butt of merciless persecution by his playmates: a massive head, heavy jaw, harelip, and—most unsettling of all—a right eye covered with a white film. To what extent these external factors—the brutal physical abuse, the unending humiliation—contributed to his psychopathology is impossible to say. What's certain is that by age eleven, he was already a budding sexual sadist.

Between the winter of 1871 and the following fall, he attacked seven little boys, luring them to secluded outhouses, then stripping, binding, and torturing them. His first victims were subjected to savage beatings. Later, Pomeroy took to slashing his victims with knives or stabbing them with needles. By the summer of 1872, the whole city was on the lookout for the "Boy Torturer" (as the newspapers dubbed him). Three months would pass before he was identified by one of his little victims—who recognized his "marble eye"—and arrested.

Sentenced to six years—"the term of his minority"—in a reformatory, he was released after only eighteen months, partly by putting on a convincing show of rehabilitation, partly as a result of relentless petitioning by his mother, Ruth, who would maintain to her dying day that her darling boy couldn't possibly be guilty of the crimes he was accused of.

No sooner had he been set free, however, than he reverted to his former ways. But this time the teenage psychopath wasn't content merely to inflict injury. In March 1874, just six weeks after his release, a ten-year-old

girl named Katie Curran went missing after visiting Ruth Pomeroy's dressmaking shop while Jesse was alone behind the counter. One month later, he abducted four-year-old Horace Millen and took him to a remote stretch of marshland, where he nearly decapitated the child with a pocketknife and mutilated his genitals.

Suspicion immediately lighted on the recently paroled "Boy Torturer," whose vest pocket contained a bloody jackknife and whose boots exactly matched the prints found in the soggy ground of the murder site. Taken to the funeral parlor to confront Horace Millen's body, Pomeroy was asked why he had killed the little boy. "Something made me," he replied with a shrug. Ten months would pass before workmen, renovating the building that had housed Ruth's dressmaking

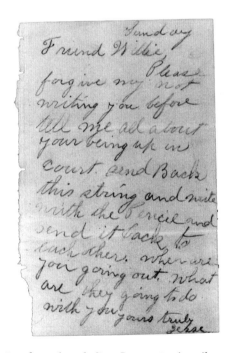

*Page from a letter by Jesse Pomeroy to a juvenile jailmate Willie Baxter, begging for graphic details about floggings the young prisoner received.*

shop, discovered Katie Curran's remains in the cellar. Though the corpse was badly decomposed, doctors were able to determine that her throat had been slashed, her dress and undergarments sliced open, and her genitals mutilated.

Pomeroy's 1874 trial was a nationwide sensation. Seeking to account for the atrocities perpetrated by the "Boston Boy Fiend" (as he was now dubbed), moral reformers pointed their fingers at the "blood-and-thunder" dime novels of the day (very much like those modern-day crusaders who blame violent video games for the plague of mass school-shootings). Declaring that "the reading of dime novels constituted a good share of the boy's mental nourishment," the *Boston Globe* maintained that it was Pomeroy's particular fondness for stories "about Indians and the way they torture prisoners" that "first put it in his mind to torture boys." Unfortunately, this assertion was undermined by Pomeroy's insistence that he had never read a dime novel in his life.

Despite his age, Pomeroy was condemned to death. Before he could be hanged, however, the public outcry over sending a minor to the gallows caused the governor to commute the sentence to life imprisonment, although with a harsh proviso: Jesse Pomeroy would spend the rest of his days in solitary confinement. He lived until 1932, having spent over forty years of his nearly sixty-year incarceration in solitary.

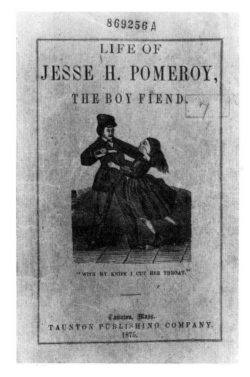

*Exploiting the public's prurient interest in sensational murders, nineteenth-century publishers rushed out luridly illustrated true crime pamphlets like this one.*

# #9 ENGRAVING OF DISCOVERIES AT THE BENDER INN

## The Bloody Benders

**(1873)**

*For weary travelers who stopped at the Bender family's roadside tavern, the property turned into their final resting place.*

As with other frontier legends, the saga of the criminal clan known as the Bloody Benders has become so shrouded in myth that fact is hard to separate from fiction. According to one oral version of the story, transcribed by Midwestern folklorist Vance Randolph in the 1930s, "the Benders was not respectable people, and kind of tough"—an understatement if there ever was one.

The historical record begins in October 1870, when a buckboard drew up at a little trading post in Labette County, Kansas. The driver, John Bender Jr., was a slender young man in his midtwenties, with a pleasant face, a trim mustache, and a way of breaking into sudden, nervous giggles that led some to regard him as a simpleton. Seated beside him was his father, a hulking, heavily bearded man in his sixties. With his powerful frame, sullen mien, and low, growling voice, the elder Bender would be described by more than one neighbor as "like a gorilla." He spoke only German, his entire fund of English consisting of a few profanities.

Within weeks of their arrival, the two men had staked a claim to a 160-acre spread, where they erected a crude dwelling—little more than a one-room log box, sixteen by twenty feet—with a trapdoor in the floor that opened onto a stone cellar, seven feet deep. Once the place was completed, they sent for the two remaining family members, mother and daughter, who arrived by train around Christmastime.

To this day, no one has established with any certitude the first name of the woman known only as Ma Bender. A stout, homely woman in her fifties, with "a tallow-white" face and a temperament every bit as surly as her husband's, she too spoke little English. In later years, after her family's crimes came to light, stories spread that she was a witch who, back in Pennsylvania, had stripped naked in a graveyard and given herself "body and soul" to the devil.

Her supposed partner in this midnight ritual was her twenty-three-year-old daughter, Kate, the figure who, of all the Benders, has always exerted the greatest fascination. Legend describes her as a sylphlike, red-haired beauty who exerted an irresistible attraction on men, though the truth seems to be that she was solidly built, ruddy-faced, and somewhat mannish-looking. Like her mother, she was rumored to be a witch who had sworn unspeakable oaths to Satan. Even more scandalously, it was said that she and her brother John indulged in unnatural relations—that, as Vance Randolph's informant put it, "they slept together just like they wasn't no kin. They didn't care who knowed it, either, and whenever she had a baby, they would just knock it in the head."

Kate's professional activities did nothing to discourage the popular belief in her occult powers. Identifying herself as "Professor Miss Katie Bender," she distributed handbills throughout the region, trumpeting her ability to "cure Blindness, Fits, Deafness, and all such Diseases." She also conducted séances, read palms, told fortunes, and—so it was claimed—"worked spells against evil spirits."

Precisely how much money she earned from these ventures is unknown. In any case, Kate's work as a magical healer and medium was not the primary source of Bender family income. That came from their infamous hostelry.

*＊*

The Bender cabin was situated close by the Osage Trail, the primary thoroughfare for travelers crossing the prairie in that part

*Newspaper portraits of the infamous Bender family, whose fate remains a mystery to this day.*

of the state. Sometime shortly after settling into their new home, the family turned it into a rudimentary inn, dividing the interior in half by hanging a large sheet of canvas across the center. The four Benders lived in the rear. The front room had a dining table where way-farers could enjoy a home-cooked meal, and a straw mattress on the floor for those who wished to bed down for the night.

No one knows how many guests the Benders entertained during the two years they ran their roadhouse, but at least nine of them were never seen alive again. Their dreadful fate was uncovered in the spring of 1873, following the mysterious disappear-ance of a prominent local physician named William York, last seen traveling by buggy along the Osage Trail. A search party led by the doctor's brother, Colonel A. M. York, traced his movements to the Bender home-stead. Questioned by Colonel York, John Jr. confirmed that the doctor had, in fact, spent a night at the inn but insisted that he had departed in good health the following morn-ing. Claiming that he himself had recently escaped an ambush by highwaymen, John suggested that the doctor might have fallen

victim to the gang—a theory Colonel York found highly implausible. After question-ing Kate—who offered to use her clairvoyant gifts to find the missing man—the colonel and his men took their leave. It was clear, how-ever, that their suspicions had been deeply aroused.

Some weeks later, a neighbor of the Benders rode over to the inn and was sur-prised to discover the place deserted. From the mess inside, it seemed that the Benders had abandoned their home in a hurry.

When word of this development reached Colonel York, he lost no time in assembling a group of men and making straight for the inn. According to some chroniclers, it was York who discovered the trapdoor in the floor of what had been the Benders' kitchen. The moment it was lifted, a dreadful odor assaulted his nostrils. Closer inspection revealed the source of the stench: a pool of dried blood caked on the stone floor.

Prying up the entire cabin with stout poles, the men managed to move it clear of its foundation but found nothing beneath. By the light of the late afternoon sun, however, one of the men spotted something suspicious in the soil of the nearby apple orchard: a strange, rectangular depression, like a slightly sunken grave. He called to the others, who grabbed shovels and began digging. In less than a minute, they had unearthed the remains of a partly clothed man lying facedown in the dirt. The base of his skull was bashed in. When the men turned over the body, they saw that the throat had been slashed from ear to ear. Despite the corpse's badly decomposed state, Colonel York had no trouble identifying his missing brother, William.

By then, darkness had fallen. Early the next morning, the men returned to the spot and, using metal rods to probe the soil, conducted a thorough search of the orchard. By the time they were done, they had unearthed eight more bodies, all but one of them adult males, subsequently identified as travelers who had never reached their destinations. They were all known to have been carrying substantial amounts of cash and had all died in an identical manner—the base of their skulls crushed, their throats slit. The single exception was an eight-year-old girl, Mary Ann Loncher, found beside her father's corpse with a silk scarf bound tightly around her neck. A postmortem exam determined that she had been strangled to the point of unconsciousness, then buried alive.

From the physical evidence—the size and shape of the men's head wounds, the matching dimensions of the hammers found in the cabin, certain telltale stains on the canvas curtain—as well as from the testimony of several people who had survived stays at the inn, a picture emerged of the Benders' diabolical MO. When a prosperous-looking traveler showed up, he would be seated at the dining table with his back to the canvas divider. While Kate beguiled him with dinnertime conversation, her father or brother would be lurking on the other side of the curtain, hammer at the ready. When the unsuspecting guest leaned his head back against the curtain, the hammer would come crashing down, shattering the back of his skull. The body would then be dragged to the rear of the cabin, where it would be robbed, stripped, and dumped through the trapdoor into the cellar. There, his throat would be slit for good measure. Later, the body would be buried in the orchard.

In the days following the gruesome discoveries, hordes of sightseers swarmed to the site, completely tearing down the inn and carrying away every bit of it as morbid souvenirs. Three thousand dollars in reward money was offered for the apprehension of the fugitives. Despite a massive manhunt by lawmen, bounty hunters, and assorted vigilantes, however, the Benders were never caught. Rumors about their whereabouts would circulate for years: that John Jr. was working on a railroad gang in Texas, that Kate was running a brothel in San Francisco, that Pa Bender had died by suicide in Michigan, that the whole family had perished while attempting to cross into Mexico via hot-air balloon. But their fate remains a mystery.

# #10 BRICK FROM THE ISLE OF SHOALS LIGHTHOUSE

## The Smuttynose Horror

**(1873)**

*Keeper of the lighthouse on White Island, Thomas Laighton was also the owner of Smuttynose, site of the most well-known American axe-murder before Lizzie Borden wielded her hatchet.*

About ten miles off the coast of New Hampshire lie the Isles of Shoals, a rugged archipelago of nine tiny islands, most of them desolate chunks of rock visited only by gulls. Even those fit for human habitation have never been home to more than a handful of exceptionally hardy souls. In the spring of 1873, the entire population of Smuttynose—the second largest of the isles—consisted of a close-knit clan of six Norwegian immigrants: a fisherman named John Hontvet and his wife, Maren; Maren's older sister, Karen; the two women's adored brother, Ivan, and his new bride, Anethe; and John's brother, Matthew. They were occasionally joined by a boarder named Louis Wagner, a hard-luck Prussian émigré who assisted the three men with their fishing business.

At daybreak on March 5, 1873, the three men of the Hontvet household set sail on a fishing trip. Though they intended to return by dinnertime, circumstances caused them to stay overnight in Portsmouth. While there, they ran into Louis Wagner. When he learned that the women were alone on Smuttynose, Wagner immediately crept down to the wharf, stole a dory, and rowed all the way to the isle, intending to loot the cottage.

He arrived around midnight when the women were asleep. Creeping in through the unlatched front door, he attacked Karen and Anethe with an axe, shattering their skulls. Though wounded herself, Maren managed to climb through a window. Stumbling barefoot over ice and rocks, she made her way toward the farthest end of the island and wedged herself between two rocks at the water's edge. Wagner, meanwhile, had begun a frantic search for the last surviving witness to his atrocities. Unable to find his prey, Wagner eventually set off on his long row back to Portsmouth.

In the morning, Maren waited until the sun was fully risen before crawling from her shelter and making her way on torn and frozen feet to the northernmost tip of Smuttynose, where her frantic shouts brought help from the neighboring island of Appledore. By then the killer had rowed back to Portsmouth, changed his clothing, and boarded a train for Boston. There, he holed up in a room at a sailor's boardinghouse. Word of the Smuttynose atrocities quickly spread via telegraph, and Wagner was arrested that same afternoon, Thursday, March 6, 1873. He was transported back to Portsmouth, where a mob of ten thousand people, bent on a lynching, had to be kept back at bayonet point by a company of marines. Tried and convicted, he went to the gallows on June 25, 1875, before a raucous crowd of spectators.

*Poet Celia Thaxter, here with her two sons, lived on the Isles of Shoals at the time of the atrocity and wrote a pioneering true crime story about the case, "A Memorable Murder" published in the* Atlantic Monthly.

# #11 "BRING BACK OUR DARLING" SHEET MUSIC

## The Kidnapping of Little Charley Ross

**(1874)**

*Ballads about sensational crimes— like this song about the first child ever kidnapped for ransom in the United States— became a staple in the sheet music trade of the late nineteenth and early twentieth centuries.*

ears of child-snatching have plagued parents since the beginning of time. Folktales from around the world feature evil faeries who steal newborns from their cradles, leaving changelings in their place; she-demons, like Lilith and Lamia, who prey on babies in the night; and demonic pipers who lure little boys and girls away from home forever. The historical evidence, too, leaves no doubt that children have always been targets for predators, who have kept them captive, sold them into slavery, or used them as sexual or sacrificial victims.

It wasn't until the late nineteenth century, however, that a shocking new form of child-snatching appeared on the scene, one that forever after would cause mothers and fathers to warn their little ones to "never take candy from a stranger." The victim's name was Charley Ross, and his abduction would represent the first kidnapping for ransom in the history of the United States.

Christian Ross, a Philadelphia dry-goods merchant who lived with his family in the neighborhood of Germantown, arrived home at around six in the evening. His sons were nowhere to be found. A maidservant had last seen them out on the sidewalk, playing with some friends. Assuming, as he later explained, that they "must be somewhere in the neighborhood," Mr. Ross went about his business, feeling "no uneasiness until teatime," when he set off in search of them. All that changed when he spoke to a neighbor, Mary Kidder. A few hours earlier, Kidder, looking out her open window, had noticed a wagon at the curb outside the Ross home and seen Walter and Charley talking to the driver and another man. When she glanced through the window shortly afterward, she saw the wagon drive away with the two boys.

Now "greatly alarmed," Mr. Ross hurried to the police station where he retrieved Walter, who had been found crying and lost in the Kensington neighborhood of Philadelphia. When asked about Charley, Walter told his father that a few hours earlier, a man with a reddish mustache and eyeglasses—the same person who had given the boys candy the previous Saturday—drove up to the Ross house in a buggy. Seated beside him was another, older man, also wearing spectacles, and distinguished by what Walter described as a funny-looking "monkey nose." Offering to buy the brothers firecrackers, the two men helped them into the wagon and drove away. After going some distance, the wagon pulled up in front of a cigar store with fireworks displayed in its window. Walter

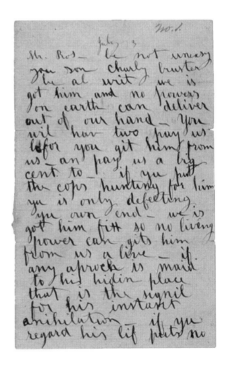

*Ransom note sent to Charley Ross's father demanding $20,000 for the safe return of his son.*

was given twenty-five cents and told to go inside and buy firecrackers for himself and Charley. When he emerged from the store, the wagon was gone. The police assured Ross that his son had undoubtedly been taken for a ride by a pair of drunken fools, who would surely release him once they sobered up. The terrible truth became clear on July 3, when, after placing a newspaper ad offering $300 for his son's safe return, Ross received the first of an eventual twenty-three crudely misspelled ransom letters. "We is got him," read one in part, "and no powers on earth can deliver out of our hand. You will hav two pay us befor you git him from us, and pay us a big cent to." The second letter, which arrived two days later, specified the amount of the "big cent" the abductors were demanding: $20,000 (roughly $400,000 in today's dollars).

Police and other authorities urged Ross not to pay. Doing so would set a dangerous precedent and encourage other kidnappers. Ross reluctantly agreed. In the following weeks, he engaged in negotiations with his son's captors, responding to their letters via personal ads in the newspapers, playing for time while police launched a massive manhunt.

By then, the kidnapping of Little Charley Ross had become a nationwide sensation. One enterprising New York City music publisher rushed out a song with the tear-jerking title "Bring Back Our Darling." The sheet music, adorned with the now-familiar portrait of Little Charley Ross, quickly sold thousands of copies. Even with the whole country on the lookout for Charley's kidnappers, however, they continued to elude capture.

The first significant break in the case occurred in early August, when an informant supplied the New York City police with the names of two likely suspects, a couple of professional thieves named William Mosher and Joeseph Douglass. A fruitless, five-month hunt for the pair ended on the night of December 13, 1874, when the two reprobates were shot while burglarizing a house on Long Island. Mosher died instantly. Douglass, mortally wounded, confessed that he and his cohort had stolen Charley Ross, though he claimed not to know the child's present whereabouts. Brought to New York to view the bodies, little Walter Ross had no trouble identifying Mosher, whose deformed nose, partly eaten away by cancer, made him unmistakable.

Mosher's brother-in-law, a former NYPD cop named William Westervelt, was ultimately tried and convicted for conspiring in the abduction but stoutly maintained his innocence to the end. Shortly before his trial, Pennsylvania became the first state to pass a law changing kidnapping from a misdemeanor into a felony.

Christian Ross would spend the rest of his life and every penny at his disposal in an obsessive search for his lost son. But though people claiming to be Charley continued to pop up for the next fifty years, the stolen boy's fate was never learned.

# #12 *HARPER'S WEEKLY* ILLUSTRATION OF ALFRED PACKER'S VICTIMS

## "The Colorado Cannibal"

**(1874)**

*Readers of* Harper's Weekly *were shocked by this gruesome depiction of the decomposed remains of five missing miners— victims of the Colorado "man-eater," Alfred Packer.*

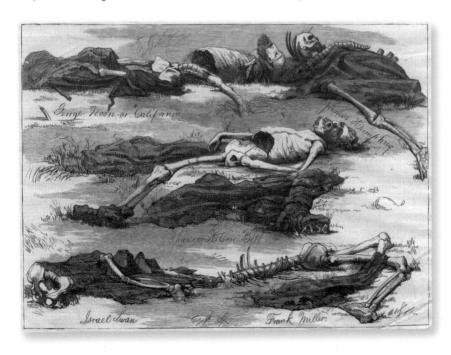

In November 1873, a band of fortune hunters set out from Provo, Utah, for the Colorado Rockies following reports of a massive gold strike near the town of Breckenridge. Among their members was Civil War veteran Alfred Packer, who claimed—falsely—to be familiar with the territory they were heading for and offered his services as a guide.

Three months later, after an increasingly arduous journey, the men arrived at the junction of the Uncompahgre and Gunnison Rivers in the San Juan Mountains of southwest Colorado, where they were promptly surrounded by a band of fifty heavily armed Ute warriors. Brought before renowned tribal leader Chief Ouray, they were extended the full hospitality of his camp and invited to remain until the snow-choked mountain passes opened in the spring. The exhausted men gratefully accepted.

After a few weeks, however, some of the gold-seekers grew restless. On February 9, 1874, equipped with a pair of rifles and enough provisions for a week, six of them, including Alfred Packer, set out for the Los Piños Indian Agency about fifty miles away. Five would never be seen alive again.

On the morning of April 16, a tall, bedraggled figure with long, matted hair and a shaggy black beard staggered into the mess hall of the Indian agency, his shoeless feet wrapped in strips torn from an old blanket. For a man who claimed that he was near starvation, the stranger—Alfred Packer—looked surprisingly well fed.

According to Packer, a few days after he and his companions left Chief Ouray's camp, he had become too snow-blind and footsore to proceed. Leaving him with enough food to last a couple of days, the others had forged ahead to seek the nearest settlement, promising to

come back for him as soon as they were resupplied. They never returned. Having depleted his meager provisions, Packer pushed ahead on his own and, with his ostensible last ounce of strength, had managed to reach the agency.

Packer spent a few days recuperating before traveling to the town of Saguache, where he holed up in a saloon for the next two weeks, drinking, playing cards, and offering constantly shifting accounts of his wilderness ordeal. It wasn't long before his behavior aroused widespread suspicion. He was brought back to the Los Piños Agency, where, following intensive grilling, he finally broke down and offered what came to be known as his "first confession."

According to this version, he and his companions had run out of provisions about ten days after leaving Ouray's camp. Lost in the snow, they had wandered around for several more days until Israel Swan, one of the party members, collapsed and died from hunger, whereupon the others, driven by starvation, had cut up and eaten parts of his body. Taking strips of the sixty-year-old man's calves, thighs, and breast with them, they had set out again. Four or five days later, another member of the party, James Humphrey, died of exposure. He was the next to be dissected and eaten.

One evening a few days afterward, Packer left his three remaining companions at the campfire while he went off to collect wood. Upon his return, he found that Shannon Bell and George Noon had crushed Frank Miller's skull with a hatchet—according to one contemporary account "because of the great amount of soft flesh that he carried." Packer joined the other two in feeding on the corpse.

Eighteen-year-old George "California" Noon was the next to be sacrificed, shot to death by Shannon Bell. A week or so later, having exhausted their supply of Noon's flesh, Packer (so he claimed) killed Bell when the latter, mad from hunger, tried to club him to death with his rifle. Ducking the blow, Packer had gone for his revolver and fired a fatal shot into his attacker. After treating himself to a hunk of Bell's body, he had cut up and "packed away considerable of the flesh," which lasted him another two weeks. The meat had run out just a day before he reached the agency.

Few of those who heard this story accepted it at face value. Arrested on suspicion of murder, he was locked up in a flimsy adobe cabin that served as the Saguache jail.

In August 1874, John A. Randolph, an illustrator for *Harper's Weekly*, was on a sketching tour of the Uncompahgre Valley when he came upon the badly decayed remains of five men, clustered together in their blankets and clothes. Four of their skulls had been broken open with a hatchet. The head of the fifth was missing entirely and was not discovered until a year later, when a prospector stumbled upon it about a mile away from the site of the massacre. It, too, bore hideous gashes clearly produced by a hatchet. From what remained of their features, as well as their scraps of clothing, the five were quickly identified as Packer's companions. All the men had evidently been slain in their sleep, then butchered for their meat.

Randolph produced a macabre drawing of his find that still retains its power to shock. Captioned "The Remains of the Murdered Men," it was published in the October 17, 1874, issue of *Harper's Weekly*, accompanying an account of the "Colorado Tragedy." By then, however, the man who had perpetrated the slaughter had broken out of jail and vanished from sight. Nine years would pass before the world heard of Alfred Packer again.

Among the party of gold-seekers who had set out from Utah with Packer in November 1873 was an immigrant named Jean "Frenchy" Cabazon. By 1883, he had taken up the life of an itinerant peddler. In March of that year, Cabazon stopped for the night at a Cheyenne, Wyoming, roadhouse. Drinking at the bar was a bearded, black-haired prospector. Though he called himself John Schwatrze, Cabazon immediately recognized him as Alfred Packer.

Cabazon informed the local sheriff, who rode out to the cabin where Packer was staying and took him into custody.

Brought back to Denver on March 16, Packer gave his "second confession." According to this account, he and the other five prospectors had left Ouray's camp with only seven days' worth of food and were quickly engulfed by a storm. By their fourth day in the mountains, they were down to their last bit of food. After a futile effort to catch fish in an ice-covered lake, they collapsed in a grove of timber. By then, the men were "praying, shouting, crying"—all except Shannon Bell,

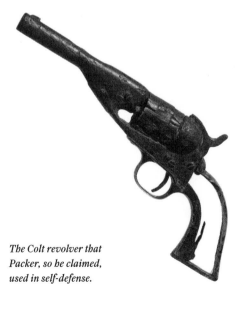

*The Colt revolver that Packer, so he claimed, used in self-defense.*

who "hadn't said a word in two or three days [and] looked wild."

At the urging of Israel Swan, Packer had taken a gun and gone up a hill to see if there was anything edible in sight but saw "nothing but snow all around." When he returned to camp later in the day, he was stunned at the scene that confronted him. Seated near the blazing campfire was Shannon Bell. He was roasting a chunk of meat sliced from of the leg of Frank Miller, whose corpse was lying at some distance from the fire, its skull crushed with the hatchet. The bodies of the other three members of the party were sprawled closer to the fire, their heads similarly split open.

As Packer approached the carnage, Bell sprang to his feet, hatchet in hand, and came at him. "I shot him sideways through the belly," Packer related. "He fell on his face, the hatchet fell forward. I grabbed it and hit him on the top of the head." He stoutly maintained that he "did not kill any of the company except Bell, and that was in self-defense."

The next morning, Packer attempted to find a way out of the mountains, but the snow was too deep. He returned to the spot where the others lay, got the campfire started, finished cooking the piece of meat from Frank Miller's leg, and ate it. For the next sixty days, until he was able to make his way back to civilization, said Packer, "I lived off the flesh of these men."

On April 6, 1883, three weeks after making this statement, Packer was indicted for five homicides. Just three days later—under the theory that a jury would be most likely to convict him for the cold-blooded slaying of an elderly person—he was brought to trial for the murder of Israel Swan. On April 13, 1884, four days after the trial opened, he was found guilty and condemned to the gallows. Legend has it that, in delivering the sentence, Judge M. B. Gerry—speaking in the twangy frontier dialect of a Mark Twain character—declared: "You voracious, man-eating son-of-a-bitch! There was seven Democrats in Hinsdale County and you ate five of them!"

Before Packer could be hanged, his attorneys won a stay of execution while his appeal made its way through the courts. Eventually, the State Supreme Court reversed his conviction on a legal technicality. On August 2, 1886, after three years behind bars, Packer was brought to trial again, this time on five counts of manslaughter. Four days later, he was found guilty and sentenced to forty years of hard labor at the penitentiary at Cañon City.

In early 1900, Polly Pry, a pioneering woman reporter for the *Denver Post*, became convinced that Packer was innocent of homicide. Regarding the cannibalism (for which he was never tried), Pry, like many others, argued that it was the desperate, forgivable act of "a man in the last throes of starvation." Thanks to her campaign, Packer was paroled in January 1901. He died on April 23, 1907, and, because of his Civil War service, was buried with military rites.

# #13 **MURDER PAMPHLET**

## "The Pocasset Tragedy"

**(1879)**
*Nineteenth-century crime pamphlets, under their pious guise, were an early form of tabloid sensationalism.*

By the end of the Civil War, a small group of Second Adventists, believers in the imminent coming of Christ, had set up a church in Cataumet, Massachusetts, a picturesque village on Cape Cod. Among its members was Charles Freeman, a farmer who lived in the neighboring town of Pocasset with his wife, Harriet, and two daughters—six-year-old Bessie Mildred and four-year-old Edith.

During the spring of 1879, Freeman became obsessed by the notion that God required an ultimate sacrifice as a test of his faith. On the evening of April 30, after attending a gathering at the home of a fellow Adventist, he returned to his own cottage, where he tucked his daughters into the bed they shared and kissed them good night. He then retired to his own bed and quickly fell asleep.

At about half past two in the morning, he awoke with a start, shook his wife's arm, and told her that the time had come. "The Lord has appeared to me," he said. "I know who the victim must be—my pet, my idol, my baby Edith."

Singing praises to the Lord, he got a large sheath knife from his toolshed, then returned to the house, lit an oil lamp, and stepped inside his daughters' bedroom. After instructing Bessie, the older child, to go into the other room and get into bed with her mother, he stood over the body of four-year-old Edith and raised the knife high above his head. At that instant, the little girl opened her eyes and gazed up at her father.

"Oh, Papa," she gasped. A moment later, she was dead.

The following day, several dozen of Freeman's neighbors were summoned to his home whereupon he revealed the glorious sacrifice that he had made at God's behest. As his fellow church-members looked on in confusion, Freeman assured them that they need have no concern for the child. In three days, he announced, Edith would rise again.

Despite the silence of Freeman's co-religionists, it didn't take long for word of the atrocity to reach the ears of authorities. By the following day, Freeman and his wife were under arrest and lodged in the Barnstable jail. From his cell, Freeman calmly, even cheerfully, assured visitors that Edith would shortly be "restored to earth-life." His slaughtered child did not reawaken, however. Three days after her murder—on the morning of her promised resurrection—the dead girl was laid to rest in the sod of Pocasset cemetery.

At a special session of the Supreme Court in January 1880, after listening to the testimony of assorted alienists and other medical specialists, the justices ruled that Freeman was insane and incapable of standing trial. He was committed to the State Lunatic Hospital at Danvers "to remain until the further order of the court." Seven years later, he was declared cured and set free.

*Harriet Freeman, mother of the sacrificed child.*

# #14 SUSAN HANCOCK'S AUTOPSY REPORT

## The Servant Girl Annihilator

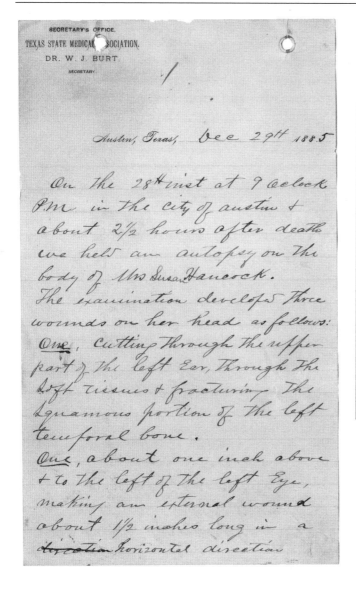

SECRETARY'S OFFICE,
TEXAS STATE MEDICAL ASSOCIATION.
DR. W. J. BURT.
SECRETARY.

Austin, Texas, Dec 29th 1885

On the 28th inst at 9 o'clock P.M. in the city of Austin & about 2½ hours after death we held an autopsy on the body of Mrs Susan Hancock. The examination developed three wounds on her head as follows: One, cutting through the upper part of the left ear, through the soft tissues & fracturing the squamous portion of the left temporal bone. One, about one inch above & to the left of the left eye, making an external wound about 1½ inches long in a horizontal direction

**(1885)**
*The first page of the autopsy report on Susan Hancock hints at the ghastly wounds she received at the hands of the "The Servant Girl Annihilator," named by the writer who would later go by the pen name O. Henry.*

One of the most infamous unsolved serial murder cases in American history began on the last day of 1884. Sometime after midnight, an axe-wielding intruder snuck into the home of Austin, Texas, insurance man William K. Hall and attacked his twenty-five-year-old Black cook, Mollie Smith, along with her boyfriend, Walter Spencer, who was sleeping beside her. Smith's savaged corpse was later found sprawled in the backyard, her head split nearly in two, her face battered almost beyond recognition. Her shredded nightdress and widespread legs left no doubt that she had been raped, perhaps after death. Though Spencer suffered grievous head wounds, he survived.

Austin's entire police force at the time consisted of a dozen officers. Employing the only forensic tools at their disposal—a pack of bloodhounds—they attempted to run down the killer, to no avail. Within weeks, the slaying of Mollie Smith had been largely forgotten.

Five months later the killer struck again. In the early morning hours of May 6, 1885, another Black cook, Eliza Shelly, was slain in her bed at the home of her employer, Dr. Lucien B. Johnson. Her skull had been "cleft . . . to the brain" by the hatchet-wielding assailant. Like Mollie Smith, she had been dragged to the ground and raped, possibly postmortem. Several suspects were arrested but quickly released for lack of evidence.

Just two weeks would pass before the killer's next attack. The victim was Irene Cross, another Black servant, who occupied a tiny two-room cabin behind the house of her employers, the Whitmans. "The unknown fiend" (as the newspapers described him) inflicted two ghastly wounds with a knife, one that nearly severed her right arm, the second that left her partially scalped. She would ultimately bleed to death.

Three months went by without incident, but at around five o'clock in the morning on Sunday, August 30, a livery stable owner named Valentine Weed heard a strange noise emanating from the little backyard cabin where his Black servant, Becky Ramey, lived with her eleven-year-old daughter, Mary. Arming himself with a rifle, Weed went to the cabin, where he found the young woman lying in bed, bleeding profusely from a head wound. Her child was nowhere to be seen.

Weed found the girl in the washhouse, barely alive. Like her mother, whose skull was fractured, Mary had been beaten unconscious. Her attacker had then dragged her outside, raped her, and driven a metal rod through each ear, deep into her brain. Somehow, she managed to survive for another hour after she was found.

Just a few weeks after the Ramey outrage, the "midnight lust-fiend" carried out his most audacious attack yet. The victim was Gracie Vance, a Black servant who occupied a little shanty directly behind the home of her employer, Major William B. Dunham. On Sunday evening, September 27, two of Vance's friends, Lucinda Boddy and Patsy Gibson, had come for an overnight visit. Sometime before midnight, Major Dunham was roused from his sleep by the sounds of a disturbance in the cabin. Grabbing his gun, he hurried to his front door and, flinging it open, saw a woman struggling desperately with a shadowy male figure just outside the front yard gate. Breaking free, the terrified young woman bolted for the house and threw herself at Dunham, preventing him from taking a shot at her assailant, who fled into the darkness.

Inside Vance's cabin, Dunham and his next-door neighbor, Harry Duff, found Vance's live-in lover, a man named Orange Washington, facedown on the floor beside his bed, skull crushed, wheezing out his dying breath. Beside him, Patsy Gibson, her head drenched in blood, brain matter "oozing from the wounds in her skull," sat slumped on the floor in the middle of the room, barely alive. A bloody axe lay nearby. Vance was nowhere to seen.

Hurrying back outside, Dunham and Duff heard a gurgling sound that led them to Vance, who lay "weltering in pools of blood, her head almost beaten to a jelly" with a brick that lay beside her. She had been dragged across the backyard, then raped either before or after her head was turned to pulp. She and Orange Washington died within minutes of each other, becoming victims of the fiend's first double murder.

A dramatic turn in the Annihilator's MO turned the story into a nationwide sensation two months later. On Christmas Eve, the unknown murderer claimed another pair of victims. And this time—in a shocking realization of white Austin's worst racial nightmares—they were not "colored servant girls" but (in the *Statesman*'s words) two of the city's "smooth and fair-skinned wives."

The first woman to be butchered that night was Susan Hancock, the forty-year-old wife of Moses Hancock of 203 East Water Street. Sometime around midnight, Mr. Hancock—who slept in a separate room from his wife—was awakened by the sound of groans. Crossing into Susan's room, he was stunned to see her empty bed clotted with blood, blood-spattered clothing thrown across a chair, and a trail of blood leading across the floor.

Hurrying outside, he found his wife sprawled in the backyard, just barely alive and moaning in agony, her head split open by an axe that lay nearby. Hancock's shouts for help aroused the neighbors. Within fifteen minutes, two physicians and a team of lawmen were on the scene. Even as the officers were scouring the property for clues, word reached them that, half a mile away, another "foul and bloody assault" had taken place.

Seventeen-year-old Eula Phillips lived with her musician husband, Jimmy Phillips, their eighteen-month-old son, and Jimmy's parents in a one-story house near the heart of the city. Sometime after midnight, the elder Mrs. Phillips was awakened by the wailing of her grandson from the room across the hall. Going to investigate, she saw the baby—who typically slept between his parents—"standing up on the bed, his nightclothes crimson with blood." His father lay "on his right side with a deep wound just above the ear made with an axe which lay beside the bed." Eula, whose pillow was saturated with blood, was missing.

She was quickly found in the backyard near the outhouse. Stripped nude, her skull broken open with the butt end of an axe, she lay in a great pool of still-warm blood. Like the killer's other female victims, she had been raped either before or after death.

After a police investigation revealed that both Susan Hancock and Eula Phillips felt trapped in violent, abusive marriages, both husbands were arrested and put on trial. Hancock's case was dismissed after the jury was unable to reach a verdict. Phillips was convicted of second-degree murder after a sensational five-day trial but set free by the Court of Appeals in November 1886.

One year after they began, the murder-rapes ceased, never to resume again. Since that time, various suspects have been identified by local historians, but in the end, the killer's identity would forever remain shrouded in mystery.

# #15 BOTTLE OF HUNYADI JÁNOS MINERAL WATER

## "Jolly Jane" Toppan, Angel of Death

**(Late 1880s–1901)**

*This once-popular mineral water was marketed as an "unsurpassed remedy for constipation, dyspepsia, biliousness, and headaches arising from overloading the stomach." In the hands of serial poisoner Jane Toppan, it became a lethal potion.*

Until 1978, when John Wayne Gacy's house of horrors was discovered (see page 215), America's most prolific serial killer, according to the *Guinness Book of World Records*, was Jane Toppan. Born Honora Kelley in 1854 to a poor Irish couple, she was consigned to a Boston orphan asylum at age six by her alcoholic father following the death of his wife. Indentured as a live-in servant to a widow, Mrs. Ann Toppan—whose last name she adopted as her own—Honora eventually trained as a nurse. Her lively, outgoing personality, which earned her the nickname "Jolly Jane," concealed a profoundly malevolent nature. Over the years, while working first in a hospital, then as a private nurse, she murdered thirty-one people—patients, friends, and family members—deriving perverse sexual pleasure ("voluptuous delight," as she put it) from subjecting them to lingering deaths. Her MO consisted of feeding them carefully doled out measures of atropine and morphine, usually dissolved in Hunyadi János mineral water, a popular drink imported from Budapest. According to her own confession, she achieved her highest ecstasy when she climbed into bed with her victims and held their bodies tight while they suffered their final convulsions.

Her undoing came in the summer of 1901, while she was vacationing in Cape Cod at a cottage owned by an old friend, Alden Davis. Within a six-week span, Toppan murdered Davis, his wife, and two married daughters. The shocking obliteration of the entire family aroused suspicion, and Toppan was soon arrested. Diagnosed as "morally insane"—the Victorian term for a criminal psychopath—she was sentenced to spend the rest of her life in a mental asylum. According to legend, she would occasionally beckon to one of the nurses and, with a conspiratorial smile, say: "Get the morphine, dearie, and we'll go out into the ward. You and I will have a lot of fun seeing them die."

*"Jolly Jane" Toppan, one of America's most prolific serial murderers.*

# #16 SHOVEL USED TO BURY THE BODIES OF ALICE AND NELLIE PITEZEL

## Dr. H. H. Holmes, "The Arch-Fiend"

**(1891–1894)**

*Famed Philadelphia detective Frank Geyer eventually uncovered the nude, decomposed bodies of two young girls buried in the cellar of a Toronto house the "Arch-Fiend" had rented for their murder and disposal.*

**M**any myths have grown around H. H. Holmes. Estimates of his victims range into the hundreds. While these numbers are wildly exaggerated, there is no doubt that he was a prolific serial killer.

Born Herman Webster Mudgett in 1861 in a tiny New Hampshire hamlet, he trained as a physician, eventually making his way to the booming Chicago suburb of Englewood, where, using the alias Henry Howard Holmes, he became the owner of a drug store. Beginning in 1887, he oversaw the construction of a block-long building of his own design. The ground floor housed a number of retail businesses, including his pharmacy. The upper stories supposedly served as a "World's Fair" hotel, where visitors to the great Columbian Exposition of 1893 could find convenient lodging.

According to legend, dozens of them met horrific ends during their stays, asphyxiated in soundproof rooms fitted with lethal gas pipes, then sent down greased chutes into a medieval torture dungeon to be stripped of their flesh so that their skeletons could be sold to medical schools. Titillating as this story is, there are no reported cases of any tourists who went missing during a trip to the "White City." The Gothic-horror descriptions of the building—with its supposed gas chambers, trapdoors, underground surgical lab, and acid vats—appear to have been the concoction of the sensationalistic newspapers of the day.

Still, it seems certain that Holmes dispatched at least five female victims in his "Castle": three of his mistresses, along with the daughter of one and the sister of another. His most heinous crimes, however—and the ones that led to his eventual downfall—involved members of a single family.

While still a pre-med student at the University of Michigan, Holmes had hit on a way to bilk insurance companies of thousands of dollars by taking out an insurance policy for a fictitious person, obtaining a corpse, claiming that the body was the insured individual, and cashing in on the policy. In 1894, Holmes enlisted the aid of a minion, a hard-drinking handyman named Benjamin Pitezel, to pull off one of these scams. With his life insured for $100,000, Pitezel would fake his own death using a cadaver supplied by Holmes, who would collect on the policy and split the proceeds with his accomplice. However, Holmes had no intention of sharing the booty—he simply murdered Pitezel. With diabolical cunning, he then convinced Pitezel's unsuspecting wife to place three of her five children into his care while he arranged for the entire family to be reunited in a secure location. Taking the children on a torturous odyssey, he murdered the two girls, Alice and Nelly, by asphyxiating them in a steamer trunk, and killed their little brother Howard with poison before chopping up his body and burning it in a stove.

Tracked down by Pinkerton detectives, Holmes was arrested in 1894. The trial of the "Arch-Fiend" (as the press quickly dubbed him) became the century's greatest criminal sensation. Following his conviction, Holmes was paid handsomely by newspaper magnate William Randolph Hearst to produce a lurid confession in which he claimed to have murdered twenty-seven people (a significant number of whom subsequently turned up alive) and declared that he was morphing into the devil. He was hanged on May 7, 1896.

# #17 LIZZIE BORDEN'S HATCHET

## The Fall River Murders

**(1892)**

*Though a good number of outlaws, gangsters, and serial murderers are part of American mythology, very few of their weapons have achieved legendary status. One exception is Lizzie Borden's hatchet (replica shown here), with which she allegedly delivered her "forty" and "forty-one" whacks.*

Certainly no other American homicide has generated such an immense body of both serious and crackpot scholarship or inspired such a wide variety of cultural productions as the Lizzie Borden case. There have been ballets, operas, novels, short stories, made-for-TV movies, heavy metal songs, and, of course, the famous nursery rhyme:

**Lizzie Borden took an axe**
**And gave her mother forty whacks.**
**When she saw what she had done,**
**She gave her father forty-one.**

In truth, Lizzie Borden's father suffered eleven wounds, not forty-one; his wife—not Lizzie's mother, but her stepmother—received a "mere" nineteen hatchet blows.

\*\*\*

Fall River, Massachusetts, was a socially segregated factory town dominated by a handful of wealthy families. Their lavish homes stood at the town's highest elevation, the exclusive neighborhood known as The Hill, overlooking the sprawling slums below, home to the mass of immigrant workers who put in fourteen-hour days in the textile mills. As one of Fall River's richest men, seventy-year-old Andrew Borden—a retired casket maker who had made a fortune in real estate and other investments—could certainly have afforded a mansion on The Hill. A notorious skinflint, however, he made his home in a middle class section of town, just a few blocks from its commercial center.

The small wooden house, less than twenty feet wide, lacked such basic amenities as indoor plumbing and anything approaching real privacy. Sharing its confines were Andrew and his second wife, Abby, and his two spinster daughters by a previous marriage, forty-two-year-old Emma and her younger sister, the soon-to-be infamous Lizzie, thirty-two at the time of the murders; and a live-in maid, Bridget Sullivan, a twenty-six-year-old Irish immigrant.

In surviving photographs, Lizzie looks much as she is described by a Fall River acquaintance, the novelist Victoria Lincoln: "stocky, jowly . . . and unremarkable." A devout churchgoer, she taught Sunday school, belonged to the Woman's Christian Temperance Union, and was a member of various charitable organizations. That such a paragon of female respectability could be the perpetrator of so heinous a deed struck her defenders as frankly incredible. Others, however, described Lizzie as "haughty and domineering," "jealous and moody," and of "a sullen and repellent disposition." One modern researcher, applying the diagnostic tools of forensic psychology to the known facts of her behavior—her frequently changing accounts of the crime, her "manipulative cunning," her lack of remorse and "shallow affect"—finds that her "psychopathic personality traits are sufficient to explain the Borden tragedy."

Certainly there is evidence that Lizzie planned to work harm on her stepmother and father. In the weeks leading up to the murders, she appears to have read up on the subject of Prussic acid and made several efforts to purchase the deadly poison in pharmacies in New Bedford and Fall River. On the evening of August 2, 1892, both Andrew and Abby became violently ill after dinner and spent the night throwing up. The next morning—one day before her murder—Abby called on family physician Dr. Seabury Bowen and, as he later testified, "said she was afraid that she had been poisoned." Since the family—at the insistence of their

*As much as anything else, it was Lizzie Borden's social standing, as well as her gender, that saved her from the gallows.*

penny-pinching paterfamilias—had been dining for days on unrefrigerated leftovers, Bowen assumed that Abby and her husband had been stricken with food poisoning and sent her home.

Early on the sweltering morning of Thursday, August 4, Abby, Andrew, and a houseguest, John Vinnicum Morse—brother of Andrew's first wife—sat down for a breakfast of five-day-old mutton, mutton-soup, "johnny cakes," and coffee. At roughly 8:45 a.m., Morse left the house to visit his nephew and niece, who lived across town. He would not return for several hours. By then, his breakfast companions would be dead.

Andrew headed out to attend to some business matters at around nine o'clock. Lizzie's sister, Emma, having left two weeks earlier to stay with friends, there were now three people in the house: Abby, Lizzie, and

Bridget. For the next forty-five minutes or so, Bridget washed the first-floor windows outside, leaving Lizzie alone with her stepmother, who had gone upstairs to make up the bed in the second-floor guest room. Returning from his outing at around 10:40 a.m., Andrew found the doors bolted. Bridget, who had finished her chores and come inside, heard his keys rattle in the locks and hurried to open the front door for him. Once inside, Andrew inquired after his wife. Lizzie told him that she had gone to pay a call on a sick friend. Still feeling somewhat ill himself, Andrew settled onto the sitting room sofa for a nap, while Bridget retired to her attic room for a midmorning rest. She was lying awake at 11:00 a.m. when she heard the city hall clock strike the hour. A few minutes later, she was roused by a shout from below: Lizzie crying out to her to "come down!"

"What's the matter?" Bridget called.

"Father's dead!" Lizzie yelled. "Somebody came in and killed him!"

Neighbors, police officers, and Dr. Bowen were soon on the scene. Andrew half sat, half reclined on the sofa, his usual napping position. Someone had taken a hatchet to his head and face, hacking him beyond recognition. Lizzie—who maintained a remarkable composure in the presence of her father's hideously mangled corpse—suggested that someone inform her stepmother, who, she believed, had returned home and gone upstairs. Bridget and a neighbor went up to get her. They found her in the guestroom, facedown in a pool of coagulated blood, her head crushed, evidently by the same weapon that killed her husband.

After considering—and dismissing—various suspects, investigators began to home in on Lizzie. That such an individual could perpetrate a parricidal double axe-murder seemed so improbable as to defy belief. At the same time, the mounting evidence against her pointed to that conclusion, confirming Sherlock Holmes's famous dictum: "When you have eliminated the impossible, whatever remains, *however improbable*, must be the truth." Lizzie's own explanation—that an intruder had snuck into the house, murdered Abby at 9:30 a.m., then hung around undetected for another ninety minutes, waiting for Andrew to get home—was preposterous. Her inconsistent accounts of her own whereabouts during the time of the killings were not only wildly unconvincing but refuted by the physical evidence. Unlike Bridget Sullivan—the only other person at home when the murders occurred—Lizzie alone had a motive. She was known to resent the financially straitened life her father forced her to lead and bore such animus toward his second wife

that she refused to eat meals with her and bristled whenever someone referred to Abby as her mother.

Arrested on August 11, 1892, Lizzie was incarcerated for nearly a year before being brought to trial on June 3, 1893. The fifteen-day proceedings were the greatest courtroom sensation of the age. Despite overwhelming circumstantial evidence of her guilt, her highly paid legal "dream team" won a prompt acquittal, the jury requiring just over an hour to arrive at its verdict. Most modern historians, however, are convinced of her guilt.

Had Lizzie been "an Irish or Italian immigrant working as a domestic," argues legal scholar Alan Dershowitz, "she surely would have been convicted." Instead, she "was a churchgoing woman of virtue, a product of old New England Puritan stock. She had the support of church and community leaders, who regarded it as inconceivable that one of their own could have done so dastardly a deed."

No sooner was the trial over than Lizzie and Emma—having inherited their father's fortune—moved into a fourteen-room, Queen Anne–style house on The Hill. They named their new home "Maplecroft." For her remaining years, Lizzie—now calling herself Lizbeth—was able to indulge in the kinds of pleasures she had been prevented from enjoying in her former life. She made frequent trips to New York, Washington, and Boston, where she shopped, stayed in fancy hotels, visited museums, and attended the theater. In 1904, she befriended a beautiful young actress, Nance O'Neil, who became a frequent guest at Maplecroft and (according to rumor) Lizzie's lover. Lizzie died in 1927 at age sixty-seven after complications from gallbladder surgery, leaving the bulk of her considerable fortune to the Fall River Animal Rescue League.

# #18 FRONT PAGE OF *THE NATIONAL POLICE GAZETTE*

## "The Demon of the Belfry"

**(1895)**

*An early example of what later was known as a serial killer groupie, a woman would become known in the press as "The Sweet-Pea Girl" for her daily custom of bringing the notorious sex-murderer a bouquet of the flowers during his trial.*

DURRANT'S MYSTERIOUS FRIEND.

THE "SWEET-PEA GIRL" OF SAN FRANCISCO WHO SUPPLIES THE ALLEGED MURDERER WITH FLOWERS.

Pretty twenty-year-old Blanche Lamont, a native of Montana, had moved in 1894 to San Francisco where she lived with a widowed aunt while training to be a teacher. On the morning of April 3, 1895, she left home and boarded a trolley car for school. Her aunt never saw her again. Investigating her disappearance, police learned from several eyewitnesses that a handsome young man had ridden with Lamont on the trolley and, later that afternoon, accompanied her into Emanuel Baptist Church, where she was a member.

The young man was quickly identified as Theodore Durrant, a bright, personable twenty-three-year-old who lived with his parents while studying to be a doctor. He, too, worshipped at Emanuel Baptist Church, where he served as assistant superintendent of the Sunday school. He was also a psychopathic sex-killer, although—like a later clean-cut serial murderer with whom he shared a name, Theodore Bundy (see page 218)—he maintained such a convincing façade of rectitude that he was regarded as above suspicion.

Nine days after Lamont's disappearance, a petite twenty-one-year-old named Minnie Williams, another member of the Emanuel Baptist Church, left her boardinghouse at around 7:00 p.m. to attend a meeting of the church's Young People's Society. She never arrived. The following morning, April 13, 1895, several middle-aged ladies showed up at the church to decorate it for Easter. After completing their task, they repaired to the church library and spotted a reddish-brown trail that led to a closed-off storage room. One of the women opened the door, let out a shriek, and fainted. Inside lay the savaged corpse of Minnie Williams, slashed, stabbed, choked, and—as a coroner later determined—raped after death.

This time, suspicion immediately lighted on Durrant, who had been seen entering the church with Williams on the night of her murder. During a search of his bedroom, police discovered her purse in his overcoat pocket. Any doubts about his guilt were resolved the next morning, Easter Sunday, April 14, when investigators did a systematic search of the church and, in the boarded-up steeple, came upon the "outraged, nude, and bloated remains" of Blanche Lamont. One detail in particular indicated that the atrocity was the work of a medical student like Durrant: The corpse had been placed on its back with a block of wood under the head, the way cadavers were arranged on dissecting tables.

During the three-week trial of the "Demon of the Belfry," as Durrant was dubbed by the press, the courtroom was packed, mostly with young women who couldn't get enough of the accused. Found guilty by a jury that took just five minutes to convict him, Durrant was led to the gallows on January 7, 1898, still protesting that he was "an innocent boy."

# #19 JOHANN HOCH'S WEDDING PORTRAIT

## "The Stockyard Bluebeard"

**(1898–1905)**

*Despite his unassuming appearance, Johann Hoch had no trouble winning the hearts—and stealing the life savings—of dozens of women, at least nine of whom met death at his hands.*

Though he would go by a dozen aliases in the course of his homicidal career, the man who ranks as America's most prolific "Bluebeard" killer (a man who serially marries and murders his wives) was christened Jacob Schmidt at his birth in 1881. A native of Germany who picked up some knowledge of poisons while working in a Berlin drugstore, he fled a fraud charge in his homeland at the age of twenty-six, abandoning a wife and three children. Despite his unappealing looks—bald, bulging dome, double chin, squat physique—he possessed a courtly, cultivated manner that made him attractive to the women he targeted as his prey: middle-aged German widows of comfortable means.

In 1894, under the name Huff, he bigamously married a well-off Chicago widow named Julia Steinbrecher. Four months later, she fell ill with a devastating intestinal ailment, diagnosed by her physician as "gastritis." As she writhed in agony, she told several visitors to her bedside that she had been poisoned, but—attributing the remark to delirium—they paid her no heed. She died within a week. Immediately after her funeral, her husband sold her property for $4,000 and disappeared.

In the early days of 1895, Huff showed up in Wheeling, West Virginia, where he promptly set about searching for a suitable victim. He settled on a thirty-six-year-old German immigrant, Caroline Hoch, whose late husband had left her their house and a healthy bank account. After a courtship lasting less than two weeks, Huff led her to the altar. A month later, at her new husband's prompting, Hoch made out a will, leaving him all her property. Within weeks, she was suddenly afflicted with a mysterious ailment. On a visit to the stricken woman, her minister surprised Huff in the act of giving his wife some white powder—presumably medicine. The next day Hoch was dead. Huff immediately sold the house, claimed his wife's life insurance, then faked his own suicide-by-drowning and disappeared.

Over the next few years, under various names, he traveled around the country, preying on an indeterminate number of women. Some he murdered, others he merely fleeced and abandoned. Eventually he made his way back to Chicago, where he worked briefly in the Chicago stockyards, an occupation that would earn him his nickname: the "Stockyard Bluebeard."

In December 1904, now going by Johann Hoch, he placed a matrimonial ad in a German newspaper and soon received a reply from forty-six-year-old widow Marie Walcker, who owned a small candy store on Chicago's

*The legendary ladykiller "Bluebeard" first appeared in Charles Perrault classic collection of* The Tales of Mother Goose. *The term has since been applied to a type of male psychopath who woos, weds, and murders a succession of wives, often for mercenary gain.*

North Side. They were married within a week. On their way back from the ceremony, the couple stopped at Walcker's bank, where she withdrew her life savings and handed it over to her new husband.

A few days later, she was stricken with excruciating abdominal pains, a violent thirst, and a tingling in her extremities that felt, she said, like ants crawling over her flesh—all classic symptoms of arsenic poisoning. Her physician, however, diagnosed the problem as inflammation of the kidneys and bladder. Hoch, as he always did in such circumstances, hovered at his wife's bedside, doling out her prescribed medications, which he supplemented with his special white powder. Walcker lingered in agony for a few weeks. No sooner had she exhaled her last breath than Hoch proposed to her sister Julia, who had come to tend her dying sibling. Three days later, Hoch and Julia were married. Hoch soon disappeared with all of Julia's money.

Notifying the police, Julia learned that Huff was already under suspicion for swindle and murder. Caroline Hoch's body had previously been exhumed, but examiners were unable to determine if there was poison in her stomach because her organs were too badly decomposed. Authorities had better luck with the body of Marie Walcker. A postmortem examination turned up lethal traces of arsenic in her viscera.

Police immediately distributed the fugitive's photograph. Hoch, who had fled to New York City, was arrested when his landlady recognized his picture in the papers. When police searched him, they found a fountain pen in his possession. Instead of ink, the reservoir contained fifty grains of a powdered white substance that Hoch claimed to be tooth powder but turned out to be arsenic. He was convicted of the murder of Marie Walcker and hanged on February 23, 1906. The number of his victims is unknown; estimates range from nine to fifty.

# #20 ADVERTISING CARD FOR THE A. L. LUETGERT SAUSAGE FACTORY

## The "Sausage Vat Murder"

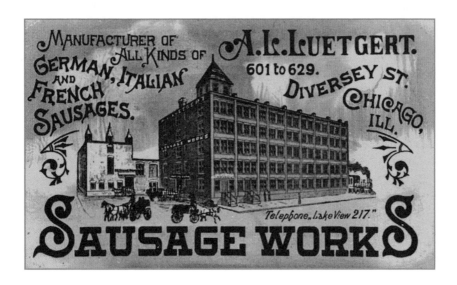

**(1897)**

*Sales of sausages dropped dramatically in Chicago after the public learned how Adolph Luetgert disposed of his wife.*

Though almost entirely forgotten today, the 1897 murder of Mrs. Louisa Luetgert by her husband, Adolph, was not only one of the most widely publicized crimes of its time but a case of genuine historical significance. It was the first time a professional anthropologist was called to testify at a murder trial, a harbinger of the field of forensic anthropology. The Luetgert murder was also an early instance of an "eraser" killing: the elimination of an unwanted wife by a husband who disposes of her corpse so thoroughly that it effectively vanishes. Widely known as the "Sausage Vat Murder," Adolph Luetgert's crime stimulated such primal anxieties in the public's collective imagination that it had a direct impact on the nation's meat-eating habits.

Born in a small German village in 1845, Adolph Lütgert (as his name was originally spelled) immigrated to America at the age of twenty-four. Having apprenticed as a tanner in his native country, he soon found work in a Chicago leather company. Ambitious, industrious, and frugal, he saved enough money within a few years to start his own business. In 1877, his first wife having died in childbirth, he married a recent German arrival to these shores, Louisa Bicknese, a petite, pretty domestic servant nearly ten years his junior. After operating a tavern for a few years, he went into the meat business and, by 1892, was the proud owner of the city's largest sausage manufacturing plant.

In 1897, after falling victim to a swindle, he found himself in dire financial straits. In a desperate attempt to save his business, he went deeply in debt to the bank. Owing partly to their monetary woes, the Luetgert marriage grew increasingly acrimonious. Money, however, was not the only thing they argued about. Despite his coarse appearance (one writer describes him as having "a face of suet, pig eyes, and a large untidy mustache that was a perfect host for beer foam"), Adolph was something of a womanizer. Claiming that he needed to keep a round-the-clock eye on his factory, he had taken to spending his nights in a little room beside his office, equipped with a bed that he frequently shared with his twenty-two-year-old housemaid, Mary Siemering, Louisa's own cousin. He was also conducting a surreptitious courtship of a wealthy widow, Mrs. Christina Feld, sending her amorous letters in which he rhapsodized about their rosy future.

At around 10:15 p.m. on the evening of Saturday, May 1, Louisa was seated in the kitchen, chatting with her twelve-year-old son, Louis, who had attended the circus that evening, when Adolph appeared and told his son to go to bed. Precisely what happened between the two adults after Louis retired to his room is unclear. One fact is beyond dispute: After the boy bid good night to his mother at about 10:30 p.m., she was left alone in the company of her husband. Then she vanished.

In the following days, Adolph casually mentioned to friends and family members that his wife had left him. When her worried brother, Diedrich Bicknese, asked where she had gone, Adolph answered with a shrug, "She might have gone away or wandered away, something like that." Adolph also admitted that he hadn't contacted the police—a striking contrast to his actions a few months earlier when his Great Dane had run off and he hurried to the neighborhood precinct to ask for help in recovering the dog.

His suspicions aroused by his brother-in-law's blasé response to Louisa's disappearance, Bicknese alerted the authorities. Over the following week, detectives conducted a search of the factory and the surrounding neighborhood but turned up nothing. It wasn't until May 15 that Adolph's night watchman, Frank Bialk, approached the police and told them that, on the night Louisa disappeared, his boss had been acting suspiciously, busying himself with one of the large steam-vats in the factory basement. Investigators checked out the vat, which—despite having been cleaned two weeks earlier—still contained a residue of a thick, greasy fluid, reddish-brown in color and giving off a nauseous stink. When the fetid slime was drained from the vat, the detectives discovered tiny pieces of bone along with two gold rings, one of them a wedding band engraved with the initials "L. L." More bone fragments, as well as a false tooth, a hairpin, a charred corset stay, and various scraps of cloth turned up in a nearby ash heap. Adolph was promptly arrested and charged with his wife's murder.

Since Adolph continued to maintain that his wife had run away from home and was, so far as he knew, still alive, prosecutors were faced with the challenge of establishing the *corpus delicti*. For this, they turned to an expert witness, George Dorsey. The first Harvard student to be awarded a PhD in anthropology, Dorsey was assistant curator of anthropology at the Field Museum of Natural History. Shown several small bone fragments found in the boiler room of the sausage factory, Dorsey identified them as burned pieces of a skull and thigh bone, both belonging to "a small adult woman."

When, after three days of deliberation, the jurors were unable to agree on a verdict, the judge declared a mistrial. Two months later, in December 1907, Adolph was brought to trial again. This time, Dorsey was instrumental in securing a conviction. Sentenced to life in prison, the "Sausage King" lasted only slightly more than a year behind bars, succumbing to heart disease in July 1899 at the age of fifty-three.

*Police mug shot of Adolph Luetgert.*

# #21 EMERSON'S BROMO-SELTZER BOTTLE

## The Molineux Poison-Murder Case

**(1899)**

*When two poisoning murders were traced to Manhattan's exclusive Knickerbocker Athletic Club, evidence pointed to former member Roland Molineux, whose trial would become the most sensational courtroom drama of its day.*

Roland Burnham Molineux was a child of celebrity. His father, Edward, was one of the city's leading citizens—a bona fide Civil War hero who had returned home to Brooklyn, earned a fortune in the paint-making business, and became a prominent figure in city politics and public affairs.

Roland was something of a dilettante— a sportsman and playboy who worked for a time as a chemist in his father's paint factory. A champion amateur gymnast, he had a lithe, muscular build and matinee idol looks. In 1895, at age twenty-seven, he became a member of Manhattan's exclusive Knickerbocker Athletic Club.

Not long after the bachelor Molineux had moved into the club, the owner hired a new athletic director, named Harry Cornish. For reasons that remain a mystery, Molineux developed an instantaneous abhorrence of Cornish, accusing him of assorted violations of the club's regulations. Matters came to a head at Christmastime in 1897, when Molineux demanded that Cornish be discharged. When the board of directors voted to retain him, Molineux, overcome with bitterness, resigned.

A year later, on December 24, 1898, Cornish received an anonymous package in the mail containing a small bottle of Emerson's Bromo-Seltzer. Three days later, he brought it back to the apartment he shared with his cousins, Katherine Adams and her daughter, Florence. The next morning, Mrs. Adams arose with a headache, mixed some of the Bromo-Seltzer in water, drank it, and immediately fell dead. A subsequent analysis of the Bromo-Seltzer determined that it was a spiked with cyanide.

Within twenty-four hours of her murder, reporters for the city's "yellow" papers (the Gilded Age precursors of the tabloids) had turned up a startling fact. Harry Cornish was not the first person associated with the Knickerbocker Athletic Club to be sent poisoned medication. Six weeks earlier, a member named Henry Crossman Barnet had received a sample tin of Kutnow's Improved Effervescent Powder (a brand of gaslight-era Alka-Seltzer) from an anonymous sender. The bon vivant Barnet had taken some after a night of carousing and died not long afterward. When the medication was analyzed, it was found to contain cyanide.

It didn't take long for reporters to discover that Cornish and Barnet had something in common: a connection to Roland Molineux. Barnet, it turned out, had been Roland's rival for the affection of an aspiring opera singer and accomplished social climber named Blanche Chesebrough. Mounting evidence against Roland soon led to his arrest. His trial for the murder of Katherine Adams, which began in November 1899, held the nation spellbound. The prosecution's attempts to bring up Henry Barnet's murder led to a judicial landmark still known as the "Molineux rule," which defines the conditions under which evidence of a defendant's previous crimes can be introduced into a trial.

Found guilty and condemned to the electric chair, Molineux was sent to Sing Sing to await execution. Thanks in large part to his father's political clout, however, the verdict was overturned on appeal. Tried again, Molineux was acquitted. He enjoyed some success as an author and playwright before having a mental collapse, apparently from late-stage syphilis. Committed by his father to a state hospital for the insane, he died in November 1917 at the age of fifty-one, having succumbed to complete dementia.

# #22 POSTCARD OF EVELYN NESBIT

## The Murder of Stanford White

**(1906)**

*Evelyn Nesbit's beauty made her the most sought-after model of her day. It also made her the object of a madman's ultimately lethal obsession.*

America's first supermodel, the ravishing Evelyn Nesbit, began her career as an artist's model in Philadelphia, relocating to New York City in 1900 at age fifteen. She swiftly achieved iconic status and was pictured on everything from magazine covers to cigar labels, Coca-Cola calendars to toothpaste ads. In 1901, tiring of the tedium of posing, she became a chorus girl in a popular Broadway musical and soon caught the salacious eye of Stanford White, Manhattan's leading architect and a notorious voluptuary.

Setting out to seduce Nesbit with the cold calculation of the practiced roué, White brought her to his apartment, plied her with champagne, then raped her while she lay unconscious on his canopied bed. After recovering from the initial shock of her violation, she nonetheless became White's pampered mistress.

Nesbit was pursued by other admirers, among them a deeply unstable playboy, Harry K. Thaw of Pittsburgh. Son of a millionaire industrialist, Thaw had shown signs of mental disturbance from earliest childhood.

Driven as much by his hatred of White as by his infatuation with Nesbit, Thaw embarked on a relentless courtship. Though initially put off by his weird intensity and doughy looks, Nesbit slowly came to appreciate his flashes of charm and solicitous attentions. That he was heir to a forty-million-dollar fortune did nothing to detract from his appeal. Taking her on a trip to Europe, Thaw repeatedly proposed to Nesbit, who consistently refused him. Finally, during a stay in Paris, she explained that she could not become his wife because she was not a virgin. Thaw forced her to reveal every sordid detail of White's assault on her. Taking her to a grim, Gothic castle in Bavaria, he entered her room naked one night, beat her with a whip, and raped her, then kept her imprisoned

for two weeks before apologizing and begging her forgiveness.

Back in New York City, Thaw resumed his tenacious pursuit of Nesbit. Concerned about her financial future, she managed to persuade herself that Thaw was at bottom a sweet and generous man. In April 1905, the former chorus girl, now all of twenty, became the wife of the millionaire madman.

Thaw's obsession with his detested rival only grew worse following the marriage. His long-simmering madness finally boiled over on June 25, 1906, when Harry and Evelyn visited the rooftop theater of Madison Square Garden, the entertainment complex that had been designed by White himself. At roughly 11:00 p.m., White took a seat at the table reserved for his exclusive use near the stage. Moments later, Thaw made his way to White's table, drew a pistol, and fired three times. Standing over his victim, he shouted: "He deserved it! He ruined my wife!"

Thaw was sentenced to incarceration for life in a hospital for the criminally insane. After five years that included a brief escape, he was declared sane and released. Shortly after, he was arrested for kidnapping and horsewhipping a nineteen-year-old boy and committed to the mental ward of the Pennsylvania State Hospital, where he remained for the next seven years. Released in 1924, he ultimately died of a heart attack in 1947 at age seventy-six.

Divorced from Thaw and virtually penniless, Nesbit survived for a while by singing in cabarets, acting in low-budget exploitation movies, and writing a pair of tell-all memoirs. She became addicted to alcohol and morphine and made a suicide attempt in the 1930s. Following her recovery, she eventually moved to Los Angeles, where she spent the remainder of her life in relative obscurity. She died in January 1967, at the age of eighty-two.

# #23 CHESTER GILLETTE'S HANDCUFFS

## The "American Tragedy" Murder

**(1906)**

*The story of Chester Gillette and Grace Brown would not only rivet the nation but inspire a literary masterpiece, Theodore Dreiser's* An American Tragedy, *as well its celebrated movie adaptation, George Stevens's* A Place in the Sun.

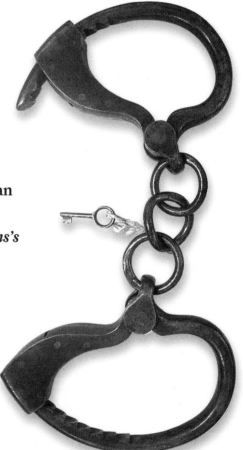

A particularly sensational case of an "eraser killer" (see page 7) occurred in 1906. At its center was twenty-three-year-old Chester Gillette. The son of two Salvation Army missionaries, Gillette rebelled against his strict, religious upbringing, adopting the credo that the true purpose of life was, as he put it, "to have as good a time as you can."

After several knockabout years, he took a job at his uncle's upstate New York skirt factory. Before long, he had embarked on a furtive affair with a young employee, Grace Brown, an attractive, vivacious eighteen-year-old who had grown up on a farm in a nearby village. When Brown discovered she was pregnant in the spring of 1906, she quit her factory job, moved back into her parents' home, and began sending increasingly desperate letters to Gillette, pleading with him to marry her.

With no interest in settling down, Gillette pursued other women, among them a well-to-do beauty named Harriet Benedict, daughter of a prominent attorney. When Brown got wind of her lover's dalliances, her letters took on a threatening tone. The strategy appeared to work. In early July, Gillette invited her to join him on an Adirondacks vacation—a trip that would culminate in their wedding.

On July 11, 1906, the couple checked in at a lakeside hotel in Herkimer County. Then—with Gillette still carrying his suitcase and tennis racket—they went out to enjoy the day in a rented rowboat. When they hadn't returned by the following morning, a search party set off. Coming upon the rowboat floating upside down on the water, they peered into the depths and saw Brown's corpse caught in the weeds. Her death was initially attributed to a boating mishap, though suspicions were aroused when a postmortem revealed that she was pregnant. The discovery of ugly wounds on her face and head—caused by a bludgeoning instrument, very possibly a tennis racket—seemed to confirm that she was the victim of foul play.

Three days would pass before Gillette was tracked down and arrested. At first he insisted that Brown had, in fact, drowned accidentally when the boat overturned. Later, he changed his story, claiming that, in her despair, she had deliberately thrown herself overboard. During his three-week trial, the prosecution bitterly denounced him as a heartless brute who, after defiling an innocent maid and impregnating her, had coldly planned and carried out her murder so that he could be free to pursue his affairs with "girls from a better class of society." Though Gillette's attorney mounted a vigorous defense—arguing that Gillette's actions were not those of a calculating killer but of a scared boy who had panicked when Brown accidentally tipped over the boat—the jury took only a few hours to find him guilty of murder. He was executed in the electric chair on the morning of March 30, 1908.

*Grace Brown had no idea about her lover's nefarious plan when she signed this hotel registration sheet.*

# #24 BELLE GUNNESS'S FALSE TEETH

## "The Female Bluebeard"

**(1908)**

*When the house of Belle Gunness's "Murder Farm" burned down, these dental bridges were all that remained of her missing skull, leading many to believe that she planted them as a decoy and escaped to kill again.*

That serial murderers are always men is a common misconception; the annals of crime contain no shortage of women killers. It is true, however, that murderesses tend not to go in for the extreme forms of violence favored by their male counterparts. When a dismembered corpse turns up in a dumpster, it is safe, by and large, to assume that the perpetrator was a man. Occasionally, however, a woman sociopath comes along who revels in the kind of physical savagery generally associated with the opposite sex. One such woman was Belle Gunness.

She was christened Brynhild Poulsdatter Størset at her birth in 1859. Following a hardscrabble youth on a Norwegian farm, she immigrated to Chicago in September 1881, moving in with a married sister and Americanizing her name to Belle Peterson. Three years later, at age twenty-four, she married a night watchman named Mads Sorensen. For a while, Belle supplemented the family income by working in a butcher shop.

In 1886, Belle and Mads opened a confectionery store in Chicago's Austin neighborhood. Business, slow to begin with, grew progressively worse. Within a year—on a night Belle was alone in the store—it conveniently went up in flames, allowing the Sorensens to collect on their insurance policy. Other misfortunes followed, with similarly profitable results. Within the span of a few years, the couple lost two of their four children. The official cause of death in both cases was acute colitis, whose symptoms, as it happens, are remarkably like those of arsenic poisoning. For Belle, the emotional blow of these tragedies was somewhat softened by the payouts on the insurance policies she'd had the foresight to take out on the little ones. In July 1900, Mads Sorensen followed the children to the grave, dying just one day before his own life insurance policy was scheduled to lapse. Though the timing raised suspicions among relatives and friends—including one neighborhood physician who detected signs of poisoning by Prussic acid—his death was ultimately attributed to heart disease, and his widow came away with a tidy sum.

Belle used the windfall to purchase a forty-eight-acre farmstead in the Indiana town of La Porte. Shortly thereafter, she married a young widower, Peter Gunness. Precisely what attracted him to Belle—aside from her money—is difficult to say. Neighbors recalled her as a massive, powerfully built woman with "square jaws" and "large, grotesque" hands, "ideally suited to slicing up pig carcasses." On butchering days, the men from the adjoining farms would shoot the animal, bleed it, and gut it. Belle, however, performed these messy tasks herself.

Just nine months after the nuptials, Peter was killed when a cast-iron sausage grinder fell from the stovetop and struck him directly between the eyes while he was reaching for a shoe. At least, that was Belle's explanation. So bizarre was this story that neighbors talked openly of murder. The insurance company, however, declared her husband's death an accident, and Belle collected another hefty payment.

*Souvenir postcard of Belle Gunness's "Murder Farm."*

Not one to wallow in her grief, Belle promptly began to place "lonely hearts" advertisements in the *Skandinaven*, a Norwegian-language newspaper. "Comely widow who owns a large farm in one of the finest districts in La Porte County, Indiana, desires to make the acquaintance of a gentleman well provided, with a view of joining fortunes," read the ad. "No replies by letter considered unless sender is willing to follow answer with personal visit. Triflers need not apply." Over the course of the next six years, a steady stream of men made their way to Belle's homestead. Some were well-off, middle-aged suitors, lured by her newspaper come-ons. Others were hired hands, brought in to help with the farm work.

Very few were seen alive again.

Their fate was not discovered until the spring of 1908, when a mysterious fire burned the Gunness farmhouse down to its foundations. Searching the smoldering ruins the following day, a team led by the local sheriff came upon the charred remains of four people—three children and an adult woman—stacked like cordwood in the cellar of the incinerated house. Though badly charred, the murdered children were recognizable as Belle's two daughters and son. The fourth corpse was assumed to be that of Belle herself. Positive identification was impossible, however. The woman had been decapitated, and her head was nowhere to be found.

Suspicion immediately fell on a disgruntled farmhand named Ray Lamphere, who was charged with murder and arson. In the meantime, searchers continued to sift through the ashes in a search for the missing head. They never found it. What they *did* unearth sent shockwaves throughout the nation—and earned Belle Gunness everlasting infamy as one of the most terrifying sociopaths in the annals of American crime.

A dozen butchered corpses lay buried around the property: in a rubbish pit, a privy vault, a chicken yard. Each of the bodies had been carved up like a Thanksgiving turkey—head hacked off, arms removed from the shoulder sockets, legs sawed off at mid-thigh. The various pieces of each body—limbs, head, trunk—had been stuffed into separate grain sacks, sprinkled with lime, then buried.

The discovery of these horrors turned the Gunness farmstead into an instant, macabre tourist attraction. On the Sunday following the discovery of the chopped-up corpses, an estimated ten thousand curiosity seekers descended on the property of the woman now variously known in the national press as "America's Female Bluebeard," the "Indiana Ogress," and the "Mistress of Murder Hill."

Under arrest, Lamphere—who had served not only as Belle's hired hand but also her lover—told a grisly tale. Each of the victims had been murdered for money. But greed wasn't Belle's only motive. Her victims had been treated to home-cooked meals generously laced with strychnine, and Belle watched with pleasure as they were seized with agonized convulsions. Once dead, they were dragged into the basement for dismemberment. Belle did the carving herself.

As to Belle's own fate, questions linger to this day. Many had doubts that the charred, decapitated woman in the cellar was Belle. For one thing, the body weighed just seventy-three pounds—inordinately small. A dental bridge of gold and porcelain teeth found in the cellar was identified as Belle's by her dentist. Lamphere, however, claimed that Belle had staged her death, planting the teeth in the basement to throw off investigators, then absconding with $100,000 in ill-gotten gains.

# #25 **ADVERTISING SIGN FOR MUNYON'S REMEDIES CO.**

## The London Cellar Murder

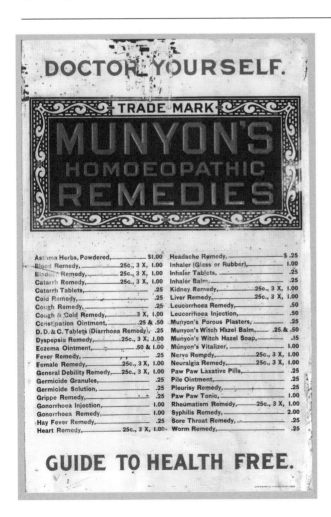

**(1910)**

*Before becoming an international fugitive for the murder of his wife, Harley Hawley Crippen worked as a manager for the Munyon company, purveyor of patent medicines that purported to cure every ailment known to man but typically had no effect at all, beyond inducing a mild state of intoxication.*

orn in Coldwater, Michigan, in 1862, Harley Hawley Crippen was described by one journalist as "one of the mildest-mannered murderers ever to cut up a corpse." Beginning at age twenty, he pursued a career in the field of homeopathy, a branch of medicine then highly popular in the United States.

While interning at a Manhattan hospital Crippen met and married a student nurse, Charlotte Jane Bell. In 1889, the couple had a baby boy, Otto. Less than three years later, Charlotte, age thirty-three and pregnant again, died suddenly of a stroke. Sending three-year-old Otto to Los Angeles to live with the boy's grandparents, Harley joined the practice of a Dr. Jeffrey in Brooklyn. It was there that he met the woman soon to become the second Mrs. Crippen.

Her name—or so she initially said—was Cora Turner. Aged nineteen, she had a generous physique and a booming personality. Even her given name was outsized. It was not Cora Turner but Kunigunde Mackamotzki, bestowed on her by her Russian-Polish father and German mother.

She had extravagant aspirations, too, with dreams of becoming not merely an opera singer but a world-famous prima donna. An operation on her abdomen had left her with a large abdominal scar and rendered her barren, but this did not deter Harley. After a whirlwind courtship, they were married on September 1, 1892.

With the new expense of his wife's voice lessons, along with the lavish wardrobe required by a future star, Harley left his private practice and embarked on a career in the more profitable, if highly fraudulent, field of patent medicines. Within a few years, he was managing the Munyon company's London branch, sailing for England in April 1897.

Four months later, Cora joined him. Upon her arrival, Harley, as he later testified, noted a marked change "in her manner towards me . . . she had cultivated a most ungovernable temper, and seemed to think I was not good enough for her." Nonetheless, he continued to be supportive, paying for the many costly accoutrements—furs, jewelry, elaborate garments—that her flamboyant style demanded and doing what he could to promote her career. Over the next several years, Cora appeared in various music halls, but with no greater success than she had in America.

In November 1899, Harley was called back to America for some months. When he returned, he discovered that his wife had taken up with a "music hall artiste," a former prize-fighter named Bruce Miller. Though they

Beneath Crippen's mild-mannered exterior was a love for his young mistress so passionate that it drove him to commit one of the most famous murders of the twentieth century.

agreed to stay together and keep up appearances, the Crippens' marriage was effectively over.

In 1901, Harley joined the Drouet Institute for the Deaf, purveyors of a special plaster guaranteed to restore hearing. There he met an attractive eighteen-year-old typist named Ethel Le Neve. Two years later, she became his private secretary. Drawn together by what Harley would afterward describe as an "absolute communion of spirit," they grew close. By 1906, they were lovers.

For the next three years, they carried on their affair in assorted hotel rooms, but his home life grew increasingly intolerable, particularly after Le Neve became pregnant, then had a miscarriage, in late 1908. This insupportable state of affairs went on until January 1910. On the fifteenth of that month, Harley visited a chemist's shop and purchased some hyoscine hydrobromide, a drug with sedative properties prescribed for a wide range of conditions, from "maniacal excitement" to insomnia. The standard dose of this substance was a hundredth of a grain; anything more than a quarter-grain could prove fatal. Harley ordered five grains.

Two weeks later, on Monday, January 31, he and his wife played host to a couple named Martinetti, who departed at around 1:30 a.m. after a pleasant evening of dining, conversation, and cards. Cora would never be seen alive again.

In early February, the members of the Music Hall Ladies' Guild, of which Cora was a member, were surprised to receive a notice from Harley, informing them that his wife had been suddenly called to America "by the illness of a near relative" and was resigning from the organization. Several weeks later, at the group's annual charity ball, Harley set tongues wagging when he showed up with

Le Neve, who was wearing one of Cora's favorite pieces of jewelry, a diamond-and-pearl-studded brooch. To the Martinettis, who were also in attendance, their normally quiet little friend seemed "livelier than they had ever known him to be."

Harley had good reason to be in a jovial mood. By the time of this gala, his adoring young lover had moved into his home at 39 Hilltop Crescent and, as she later testified, was "living with [him] as his wife."

During the second week of March, Harley dropped by the Martinettis' home with "worrying news." He had just received a letter from America, saying that Cora had "caught a severe cold" while traveling to Los Angeles and that "it has settled in her lungs." On March 20, the Martinettis learned from Harley that his wife was "dangerously ill with double pleuro-pneumonia." Four days later, the couple got a telegram from Harley: Cora had died.

Over the following months, Cora's friends grew increasingly perplexed by the evasive and often contradictory answers from Harley about the exact circumstances of Cora's death. One couple—theatrical manager John Nash and his wife, Lillian—became particularly suspicious after learning that Los Angeles officials had no record of her death. On June 30, convinced that something was amiss, Nash paid a visit to a friend: Superintendent Frank C. Froest, head of Scotland Yard's Murder Squad.

Froest assigned one of his best men to investigate: Chief Inspector Walter Dew, a seasoned detective who, twenty-two years earlier, had been involved in the hunt for Jack the Ripper. Friendly and accommodating, Harley surprised the detective by revealing that, as far as he knew, his wife was alive and well. She had run off to America to be with her lover, Bruce Miller. Knowing that the truth would scandalize their friends, Harley had invented the story of her death.

After a thorough search of Harley's house, Dew took his leave, satisfied that the mousy little doctor had been telling the truth. Returning to Harley's office a few days later to ask some follow-up questions, Dew was stunned to discover that both the doctor and his mistress "had flown." He further concluded that "the manner of his going pointed to guilt."

Over the following days, Dew and a colleague, Detective Sergeant Arthur Mitchell, made repeated visits to the house on Hilltop Crescent. It wasn't until their fourth visit on Wednesday, July 13, that the shocking truth came to light.

Conducting a painstaking inspection of the coal cellar, Dew came upon something that had previously escaped his notice: a loose brick in the floor. He and Mitchell went to work on the floor, releasing a sickening odor that drove them into the garden for fresh air. Two more trips to the reeking cellar finally exposed the source of the stench: a putrefying mass of human tissue. Though there appeared to be no way to identify the remains—the head, limbs, and sex organs would never be found—a scar on a scrap of abdominal skin still clinging to the viscera left no doubt that this ghastly lump was all that was left of Cora Crippen. Further examination would also reveal traces of hyoscine hydrobromide in the organs.

Within a week, the case was dominating the headlines on both sides of the Atlantic. Reported sightings of the now world-famous fugitives poured into Scotland Yard from around the globe.

Among the millions on the lookout for the couple was Henry George Kendall, captain of the steamship *Montrose*, bound for Quebec City, Canada, via Antwerp. Just hours after the ship embarked on its voyage on July 20, 1910, Kendall—who had read detailed descriptions of the pair on a widely circulated wanted poster—noticed two passengers, who had registered as father and son, were holding hands in a way that struck the captain as "strange and unnatural."

For the next several days, he kept the two under close observation, making note of the teenaged boy's "lady-like" mannerisms and engaging the supposed father in a conversation about seasickness that convinced Kendall of the man's medical expertise. His doubts about their true identity now fully dispelled, he decided to notify Scotland Yard.

As it happened, the *Montrose* was one of only sixty or so ships in the world equipped with a revolutionary new device, Guglielmo Marconi's wireless telegraph. On July 22, Kendall sent out a message, alerting the police of his "strong suspicion" that Harley and a disguised Le Neve were among his passengers. Kendall's transmission—the first time that the wireless would be used to track down a murderer—would earn a place as "one of the most famous messages in maritime history."

Meanwhile Dew embarked on a transatlantic chase on another, speedier steamship and reached Quebec a day ahead of Harley's. On July 1, the detective boarded the *Montrose*, calmly reintroduced himself to his quarry, and took them into custody. Returned to London, Harley was tried in October 1910. At the end of the five-day proceedings, he was convicted and condemned to the gallows, the jury having deliberated for less than thirty minutes. A short time later, Le Neve would be tried as an accomplice but acquitted.

# #26 PAGE FROM CARL PANZRAM'S HAND-WRITTEN CONFESSION

## "The Spirit of Meanness Personified"

**(1906–1930)**

*Unlike most serial killers, Carl Panzram was driven not by sadistic sexual compulsions but by an implacable hatred of society. His campaign to strike back at a world that had offered him nothing but hatred and abuse made him into a kind of all-American antihero in the eyes of his admirers.*

> In my life time I have murdered 21 human beings. I have committed thousands of burglaries, robberies, larcenys, arsons and last but not least I have committed sodomy on more than 1,000 male human beings. for all of these things I am not the least bit sorry. I have no conscience so that does not worry me. I dont believe in Man, God nor devil. I hate the whole damned human race including myself.
>
> Carl Panzram.

**D**uring his final prison stretch in the late 1920s, Carl Panzram confessed to twenty-one murders, countless felonies, and more than one thousand acts of sodomy. "For all these things," he declared, "I am not the least bit sorry." It was a typical statement by one of the most unregenerate criminals in American history.

Born in 1891, Panzram grew up on a hardscrabble Minnesota farm, the son of a violent-tempered father who put the boy to work at an early age and (as Panzram later wrote) doled out a "sound beating every time I looked cockeyed or done something that displeased" him.

He was only eleven when he had his first run-in with the law. Breaking into a neighbor's house, he stole "everything in my eyes that had some value": some apples, a cake, and "a great big pistol." Hopping a westbound freight train with the intention of becoming a cowboy and killing Native Americans, he was caught and shipped to a Minnesota reform school, whose pious superintendent believed in enforcing Christian behavior with a whip. Subjected to frequent beatings and repeatedly sodomized by older inmates, he emerged from his two-year stint having decided "just how I would live my life . . . I would rob, burn, destroy, and kill everywhere I went and everyone I could for as long as I lived."

Paroled to his mother's custody, he promptly ran away to ride the rails across the Midwest. He had just turned fourteen when four "big burly bums" gang-raped him in a boxcar. The experience taught him a lesson that would serve as his lifelong credo: "Force and might make right."

Arrested for burglary in Butte, Montana, he was thrown into another reform school where he earned a reputation as an incorrigible hard case when he used a hardwood board to bludgeon and nearly kill a brutish guard. The following year he and another teenaged inmate managed to escape. They spent the next month, as Panzram wrote, "hoboing our way east, stealing and burning everything we could." His early experience at the Minnesota reform school having left him with a profound hatred of religion, he took particular pleasure in robbing church poor boxes then setting the buildings on fire.

Now going by the alias Jefferson Baldwin, the sixteen-year-old Panzram headed west to Helena, Montana, where—intrigued by a spiel from an army recruiter—he signed up for duty. One month later, after attempting to go AWOL with some stolen army coats and a pocketful of gold collar buttons, he was court martialed and shipped off to Leavenworth Penitentiary. When he emerged from his three-year stint—during which he attempted to burn down one of the prison workshops and spent six months shackled to a fifty-pound iron ball—he was, as he put it, "the spirit of meanness personified. I was a pretty

*A souvenir medal commemorating the man who proudly called himself "the world's worst murderer."*

rotten egg before I went there, but when I left there, all the good that may have been in me had been kicked and beaten out of me."

Over the next few years, he drifted from state to state, committing untold acts of burglary, arson, assault, highway robbery, and sodomy. For a while, he worked as a guard for the Illinois Central Railroad—a job that gave him a prime opportunity for beating practically everyone he could lay his hands on, whether union agitators, scabs, or even other guards. He did several extended spells in various penitentiaries and prison farms, where he was subjected to a host of medieval tortures: hung from posts and whipped with a cat-o'-nine-tails, given a near-fatal jolt of electricity while immersed in a tub of ice water, thrown naked into a freezing dungeon for months, and reduced to subsisting on cockroaches.

In the spring of 1918, during his second stint in the Oregon State Prison, Panzram—now twenty-seven—managed to escape. He headed east, eventually ending up New Haven, Connecticut, where he stole enough loot from the mansion of former US President William Howard Taft to purchase a yacht. "I figured it would be a good plan to hire a few sailors to work for me, get them out to my yacht, get them drunk, commit sodomy on them, rob them and then kill them," he wrote. "This I done." Not long afterward, he journeyed to Portuguese West Africa as a merchant seaman. Making his way down the coast, he hired a canoe and the services of a half dozen locals to help him hunt crocodiles. Panzram ended up shooting all six of the Africans in the back and feeding their corpses to the ravenous reptiles.

Back in the US, he committed another string of outrages, including the rape-murder of several young boys. Arrested in 1922 for sodomy, burglary, robbery, and attempted jailbreak, he was sent to prison, first to Sing Sing, then to Dannemora, a maximum-security hellhole in northern New York. After breaking his legs and injuring his spine while attempting to escape by jumping from a thirty-foot prison wall, he was dumped into an isolation cell where he spent the next agonized months "crawling around like a snake with a broken back, seething with hatred and lust for revenge."

No sooner had he been paroled than Panzram committed another string of burglaries and at least one murder. Arrested in Baltimore, he was extradited to Oregon to serve out his term in Leavenworth, where, a few months later, he killed a guard who had been harassing him and was sentenced to death. He went to the gallows on September 5, 1930, snarling out his final words of contempt as the executioner adjusted the noose: "Hurry it up, you Hoosier bastard! I could hang a dozen men while you're fooling around."

# #27 SCOTLAND YARD DIAGRAM OF BLACKWELL BATHTUB

## "The Brides in the Bath Murders"

**(1912–1914)**

*In a pioneering piece of forensic analysis, a renowned British pathologist, with help from Scotland Yard, was able to prove that the three wives of "Bluebeard" killer George Joseph Smith could not have possibly drowned by accident in their bathtubs.*

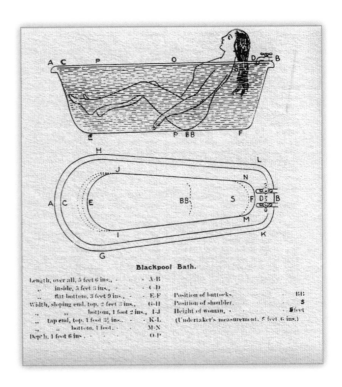

Blackpool Bath.

Length, over all, 5 feet 6 ins., - A-B
" inside, 5 feet 3 ins., - C-D
" flat bottom, 3 feet 9 ins., - E-F Position of buttocks. BB
Width, sloping end, top, 2 feet 3 ins., G-H Position of shoulder. S
" bottom, 1 foot 2 ins., I-J Height of woman, - 5 feet
" tap end, top, 1 foot 3½ ins., - K-L (Undertaker's measurement, 5 feet 6 ins.)
" bottom, 1 foot, M-N
Depth, 1 foot 6 ins., - O-P

George Joseph Smith, one of England's most notorious serial murderers, first ran afoul of the law at the age of nine when he stole some fruit from a street vendor and ended up in a reformatory, emerging seven years later with his criminal tendencies intact. Between the time of his release and the beginning of his homicidal career, he did several stints behind bars for assorted larcenies.

Exploiting his square-jawed good looks and the slick superficial charm typical of psychopathic personalities, he began to prey on women. In 1898, under one of his many aliases, he married a housemaid, Caroline Thornhill, who, under his direction, began stealing items from the homes of her employers, which Smith quickly converted into cash. This racket came to an end two years later when Thornhill, after being caught red-handed and arrested, fingered her husband as the mastermind of the thefts. Consigned to prison for two years, he emerged in 1902 to find that his wife had absconded to Canada.

Over the following decade, Smith bigamously wed, bilked, and abandoned more than a half dozen women, progressing from swindle to murder in 1912. After getting his fourth "wife," Bessie Mundy, to make out a will bequeathing him her own sizable inheritance, he rented a cottage and had a new zinc-and-enamel bathtub installed. A few days later, Mundy was found drowned in the tub. Despite her family's insistence that she didn't have the disease, the coroner ruled that she had died accidentally during an epileptic seizure.

A young nurse named Alice Burnham was the next to go. After leading her to the altar in November 1913, Smith took out a large insurance policy on her life, brought her to a Blackpool boardinghouse, and drowned her by the same method he had used on Mundy: grabbing her by the ankles while she relaxed in the tub and yanking her legs upward, causing her head to slip beneath the water while making it impossible for her to right herself.

Smith's final murder victim was a thirty-eight-year-old spinster, Margaret Lofty. They were wed in December 1914. Having insured his new bride's life for £700, he dispatched her in the bathtub of a London boardinghouse.

The end came for the "Brides in the Bathtub" murderer (as he would soon be dubbed by the press) when Alice Burnham's father read a newspaper account of Margaret Lofty's death. That two of Smith's brides had died in identical "accidents" within days of their weddings struck Mr. Burnham as highly suspicious. He shared his concerns with the police, who launched an investigation. Smith was arrested in February 1915 and charged with the three murders. His nine-day trial in the last week of June drew hordes of spectators, most of them women desperate for a glimpse of the bigamous wife-killer. Despite his vigorous protestations of innocence, the jury took just twenty minutes to convict him. He went to the gallows on August 13, 1915. His final words as the executioner slipped the black hood over his head were: "I am in terror!"

# #28 PETER KÜRTEN'S MUMMIFIED HEAD

## "The Vampire of Düsseldorf"

**(1913–1930)**

*Though a member of the FBI's Behavioral Science Unit took credit
for coining the term "serial killer" in the 1970s, it was first used four
decades earlier by a Berlin investigator to describe Peter Kürten,
a contender for the title of "the worst man who ever lived."*

A t around nine o'clock on the night of February 3, 1929, on a deserted street in the German industrial city of Düsseldorf, an elderly housewife, Apollonia Kühn, was hurrying home when someone came up behind her and grabbed her by the coat sleeve. Spinning her around, the stranger—with a pair of scissors clutched in his free hand—let off a volley of blows to her upper body, stabbing her two dozen times before she could let out a scream. He fled as she fell unconscious to the pavement. It was undoubtedly the thickness of her coat that saved her. Hospitalized for weeks, she ultimately survived, though she was unable to provide any description of her attacker.

Vicious as it was, the assault did not raise any general alarm in the city. However, that circumstance began to change just five days later.

Sometime between 6:00 and 7:00 p.m. on Friday, February 8, eight-year-old Rosa Ohliger, who had spent the afternoon at a friend's house, set off for home, eager to get there before dark. She never arrived. Workmen found her body the following morning. She had been stabbed in the temple and breast more than a dozen times, evidently with a pair of scissors. Her throat also bore signs of strangulation.

Rumors immediately sprang up that a Ripper-like madman was on the loose.

Early on the morning of February 13, a man's corpse was found in a ditch in the same neighborhood where the two earlier crimes had occurred. He was quickly identified as Rudolph Scheer, a forty-five-year-old mechanic last seen alive the previous night at around 11:30 p.m., when he'd drunkenly left a local beerhouse. The powerfully built Scheer had been stabbed twenty times in his temples and neck.

The police were immediately summoned. As one detective hurried to the spot, a well-groomed gentleman came up beside him and struck up a conversation about the murder. Casting a suspicious glance at the fellow, the detective asked how he knew about the crime. "I heard of it by telephone," the man calmly replied. By then, they had reached the cordoned-off crime scene. Ducking under the barrier, the detective joined some colleagues, while the handsomely dressed fellow kept back, watching the proceedings with keen interest.

His name was Peter Kürten. Born in 1883, he was one of ten children. The entire family inhabited a single-room apartment, an arrangement that gave Kürten ample opportunity to observe his parents' sex life. His alcoholic father brutalized his wife and children during his frequent drunken rages. In 1897, when Kürten was fourteen, his father was sentenced to eighteen months of hard labor for committing incest with his eldest daughter.

In addition to the vicious beatings he received from his father—and the sexual savagery he witnessed at home—the young Kürten received an education in sadism from the neighborhood dogcatcher, a degenerate who taught him how to masturbate and torture dogs. By the time he reached early adolescence, Kürten had developed a keen appetite for bestiality, deriving intense pleasure from stabbing, beheading, or slitting the throats of creatures—pigs, sheep, goats, even barnyard fowl—while (as he put it) "forcing his member" into the animal.

Kürten's first documented murder occurred in the summer of 1913 in Cologne. He broke into a tavern and began searching the upstairs living quarters but found nothing worth stealing. In the final room, however, he discovered a nine-year-old girl asleep in bed.

Without a moment's hesitation, he throttled her, tore at her genitals, then slit her throat with a pocketknife, ejaculating as her blood splattered onto his hand. According to his confession, Kürten committed several other murders that summer, sneaking up behind unsuspecting men and women and cleaving their skulls with a small hatchet. His homicidal spree ended abruptly when he was arrested for military desertion and sent away for seven years.

Released from prison in 1921, he met and wooed a "raw-boned, broad-shouldered" woman three years his senior. The future Frau Kürten was a one-time sex worker who had spent five years in jail for shooting a faithless lover. Sometime after her release, she opened a candy shop in the city of Altenburg. She met Kürten through his married sister, one of her customers. Like many other young women, she was impressed with his

dapper looks and courtly manners. His suits were always carefully brushed, his trousers sharply creased, his shoes polished. They were wed in 1923.

Kürten found work in a factory and became actively involved in his trade union. For a while, he managed to keep his bloodlust in check.

It began to reassert itself in 1925, when he and his wife moved to Düsseldorf. Taking up with various young women, he attempted, on at least four occasions, to strangle them to death during sex. All managed to break free and escape. Whatever self-restraint he had achieved gave way entirely in February 1929, when, in rapid succession, he attacked Frau Kühn and murdered both little Rosa Ohliger and Rudolph Scheer. For the next fourteen months, the populace of Düsseldorf lived in terror of the demon who had turned their home into his stalking grounds.

*Peter Kürten's courtly, well-groomed appearance concealed one of the world's most monstrous serial sex-killers.*

On the evening of Wednesday, August 21, 1929, a young housewife, Frau Mantel, was walking home from a county fair when a well-dressed stranger suddenly appeared at her side and asked if he might accompany her. She ignored him and kept walking, and soon felt two sharp blows in her back, both inflicted—as it turned out—by a dagger. Within the span of thirty minutes, two more victims, eight-year-old Anna Goldhausen and thirty-eight-year-old Gustav Kornblum, were also set upon and stabbed, Goldhausen in the breast, Kornblum in the back. Though badly wounded, they all survived.

Responding to the public outcry, the chief of the Düsseldorf homicide division assigned extra officers to patrol the area where the latest crimes had occurred. The increased vigilance did nothing to prevent the horrors that occurred just a few days later.

On Saturday evening, August 24, two girls, five-year-old Gertrude Hamacher and her fourteen-year-old adopted sister, Louise Lenzen, failed to return home after visiting the county fair. It wasn't until six the next morning that their bodies were found lying in a bean patch only two hundred yards from their home. Autopsies revealed that both had been strangled before having their throats slit. The older girl had also been stabbed repeatedly in the back.

That same day—Sunday, August 25—a twenty-six-year-old servant named Gertrude Schulte was on her way to the fair when she was accosted by a nicely dressed, well-mannered man who politely asked if he might accompany her. After a few pleasant hours together, the two repaired to a grassy spot on the banks of the river, where they began to exchange kisses. Suddenly, the man pushed Schulte backward and ripped off her knickers. Grabbing her by the hair with one hand,

he pulled out a dagger with the other and sliced at her throat. Her screams alerted some people nearby and sent him running. Though Schulte survived, she was in such dire condition that she was unable to provide any useful information to the police.

Ida Reuter, another servant on a Sunday outing in Düsseldorf, was not as fortunate. Reuter, too, was picked up by a suave, well-dressed gentleman, who treated her to a beer, then took her for a stroll to a deserted spot near the Rhine. Her body, naked from the waist down and sprawled obscenely in the grass, was found early the following morning, Monday, September 30. A postmortem examination confirmed that she been raped, most likely after her death from a series of hammer blows to her head.

Over the next few weeks, three more women were attacked in the same way. On October 11, a servant, Elizabeth Dörrier, had both sides of her skull crushed by a hammer-wielding assailant, who then raped her inert body. On the evening of October 25, a thirty-four-year-old woman, Frau Meurer, was hurrying home along a lonely street, when a man came up beside her and felled her with two savage hammer blows to her head, one of which ripped open her scalp, laying bare her skull. Later that same evening, a sex worker named Frau Wanders approached a nicely dressed man in the Hofgarten—the central park that lies in the heart of Düsseldorf—and propositioned him. He responded by pulling out a hammer and striking her so savagely on the skull that the tool's wooden handle snapped. Miraculously, both Dörrier and Wanders survived.

Horrors continued to pile upon horrors. On Saturday, November 9, the body of five-year-old Gertrude Albermann was found lying in a patch of nettles beside the wall of

*Fritz Lang's classic 1931 movie* M, *which made an international star of actor Peter Lorre, was based on the atrocities of Peter Kürten.*

The revelation that the Düsseldorf butcher was now writing taunting letters to his pursuers aroused widespread outrage and alarm. A team of crack detectives from the central criminal investigation department at the Alexanderplatz—"Berlin's Scotland Yard"— was dispatched to Düsseldorf to conduct a massive manhunt. In the end, however, the case was broken not by the efforts of the police but—as so often happens—by a momentary lapse of caution on the part of the killer.

On May 14, 1930, an unemployed young woman, twenty-year-old Maria Budlick, a native of Cologne, traveled by train to Düsseldorf, where she hoped to find work. That evening, as she searched for lodgings, she crossed paths with Kürten and was invited to stay overnight in one of his spare rooms. When they reached their destination shortly after 11:00 p.m., she was dismayed to discover that, far from being the spacious apartment described by her new friend, it consisted of a single cramped attic room. When she made it clear that she had no intention of sharing the room's only bed with him, he said that he would be happy to take her to a hostel.

Following a short tram ride, they began to walk along the deserted streets. As the houses thinned out, it became clear to Budlick that, far from taking her into the heart of the city, as he had promised, her companion was leading her toward its wooded outskirts. As they approached a secluded dell, he suddenly came to a halt, seized her by the throat, and began to choke her. She managed to gasp out that she was willing to let him have her if only he would not harm her. He agreed. Afterward—prompted by a rare merciful impulse—he decided not to kill her. Before letting her go, however, he asked if she recalled where he lived. She assured him she did not. This was not a complete lie, since she

an isolated factory. She had been sexually molested, strangled, and stabbed three dozen times—twice in the head, thirty-four times in the breast.

That same day, a local newspaper received an anonymous letter, postmarked November 8—twenty-four hours before searchers came upon Albermann's corpse. The letter, containing details that could only have been known by her killer, identified the exact location of the body. It also contained a crudely drawn map, marking the spot in a meadow on the outskirts of the city where, according to the writer, another body lay buried. A team of investigators proceeded to the specified area and uncovered the naked corpse of a woman bearing more than a dozen stab wounds in her temple and breast.

had paid no attention to the house number. She had, however, noticed the name of the block on a sign illuminated by a streetlamp: *Mettmännerstrasse.*

With the detectives at her side, she walked up and down *Mettmännerstrasse* until she recognized the building. The landlady confirmed that a man matching her assailant's description occupied the attic room, and Kürten was soon under arrest.

Freely confessing to nine killings and thirty-one attempted murders, Kürten calmly explained that he derived his highest sexual pleasure from the sight, smell, sound, and taste of gushing blood. In 1913, while throttling a sixteen-year-old named Gertrude Franken, he claimed he "saw the blood come from her mouth and I then had an orgasm." With Maria Hahn, Kürten "stabbed her throat and . . . drank the blood that gushed out. I probably drank too much because I vomited." This revelation earned him a new nickname in the press: the "Vampire of Düsseldorf."

His trial took place in April 1931. Convicted on all counts, he was condemned to die by the guillotine, a prospect that filled him with pleasure. "Tell me," he excitedly asked the prison doctor as his execution approached, "after my head has been chopped off, will I still be able to hear, at least for a moment, the sound of my own blood gushing from the stump of my neck?" He found out at daybreak, July 2, 1932.

Afterward, his head was bisected and the brain removed for examination. The split, mummified head would eventually become a popular display at the Ripley Believe It or Not! Museum in Wisconsin Dells, Wisconsin.

# #29 CHLOROFORM BOTTLE

## Frederick Mors

**(1914–1915)**

*The gross mishandling of the Frederick Mors serial murder case led to a breakthrough in crime forensics: the establishment of New York City's medical examiner office, headed by Dr. Charles Norris, widely credited as the father of modern crime scene investigation.*

The term "serial murderer" wasn't coined until the 1930s, but if it had existed fifteen years earlier, it certainly would have been applied to Frederick Mors. From his boyhood in Vienna—where he was born Carl Milnarik in 1899—he dreamed of becoming a doctor. Unable to afford medical school, he would sneak into hospitals where he gleaned a rudimentary knowledge of pharmacology. In 1914, he immigrated to America, taking the name Mors because, as he would later explain, it was the Latin word for "death."

Not long after his arrival in New York City, he found work as an orderly in a combination foundling hospital and old-folks home in Yonkers, New York, where he insisted on being addressed as "Herr Doktor" and paraded around in a white lab coat with a stethoscope around his neck. At some point, according to his later confession, a cost-cutting superior requested his help in disposing of some of the sicklier inmates whose upkeep was putting a drain on the charity home's finances. Mors was happy to oblige, feeling that, as he put it, "it was a kindhearted thing to do."

At first he tried arsenic but was put off by the vomiting and diarrhea it induced. He had more satisfying results with chloroform. Between September 1914 and January 1915, he did away with seven victims, four men and three women ranging in age from sixty-five to seventy-eight. His "painless, scientific" method, as he calmly explained to the police, was to:

**pour a drop or two of chloroform on a piece of absorbent cotton and hold it to the nostrils of the old person. Soon my man would swoon. Then I would close the orifices of the body with cotton, stuffing it in the ears,**

**nostril, and so on. Next I would put a little chloroform down the throat and prevent the fumes from escaping in the same way.**

He had no qualms about these cold-blooded murders, seeing himself as an angel of mercy who was sparing his victims needless suffering. "When you give an old person chloroform, it's like putting a child to sleep," he declared. Witnesses at the home, however, saw things differently, reporting that Mors had frequently threatened to eliminate elderly residents who "annoyed him."

Authorities learned of these murders from Mors himself, who strolled into the district attorney's office one January day and calmly confessed. Suspecting he might be delusional, the police wanted solid proof of his alleged crimes before they charged him with homicide. One obvious solution was to exhume the corpses of his purported victims and autopsy them for chloroform. They were discouraged from pursuing this course, however, by the city's supposed forensic expert, coroner Patrick Riordan, who declared that it was impossible to find evidence of chloroform in a corpse, especially after burial.

At the time of the Mors case, the office of coroner was a political plum, handed out to individuals with no medical—or any other—qualifications. Riordan was notorious for showing up drunk at crime scenes and making authoritative pronouncements that had no basis in scientific fact. Everything he told police about chloroform poisoning, for example, was the opposite of the truth.

With no hard evidence to bring him to trial, Mors was consigned to a state hospital for the insane in upstate New York. In May 1915, he simply walked off the grounds and vanished forever.

# #30 HENRI LANDRU'S OVEN

## "The Bluebeard of Paris"

**(1915–1919)**

*With the male population of France decimated by World War I, Henri Landru had no trouble winning the hearts of lovelorn women, at least ten of whom would never be seen again.*

Like his American counterpart Johann Hoch (see page 56), Henri Désiré Landru—with his spiky beard, bristling eyebrows, and hairless dome—was a conspicuously unhandsome man. But he possessed a seductive charm that made him irresistible to women, and at least ten of them would die at his hands.

Born to respectable, devoutly religious parents in 1869, he was a pious, churchgoing youth, an outstanding student, and, following graduation, an exemplary employee who worked for a number of architects. Conscripted into the army, he quickly rose to the rank of sergeant and was married after his discharge in 1891.

Landru's criminal proclivities surfaced in the following years. While engaged in a series of reputable businesses—toy-maker, bicycle manufacturer, used furniture dealer—he committed a steady stream of frauds that earned him seven prison sentences between 1901 and 1914.

With the outbreak of the Great War, he abruptly made the leap from petty con man to diabolical killer. With nearly nine million young men off to the battlefields, the country was full of lonely women. Though still married and living sporadically with his family, he began placing a matrimonial ad in newspapers, describing himself as a well-off widower with two children and a warm, affectionate nature. When a sufficiently wealthy prospect nibbled at this bait, Landru would sweep her off her feet and whisk her to a rented villa outside Paris. After she had signed over all her worldly possessions to him, his new bride would never be seen or heard from again.

Precisely how Landru dispatched his victims has never been established. Poison seems likely, though it is also possible that they were drugged, then strangled or suffocated. What *is* known is that their corpses ended up dismembered and incinerated in an oven constructed specifically for that purpose.

Over the next four years, employing different aliases, Landru lured a string of women into his clutches. In addition to the ten he is known to have killed, he did away with the adolescent son of one victim. All the women were middle-aged widows except one, a nineteen-year-old servant he picked up at a train station and lived with for ten days before murdering. That this penniless woman met the same fate as his other victims makes it clear that—like other "Bluebeard" killers—Landru was driven not just by greed but by homicidal compulsion.

A chance encounter brought his murderous career to a close. On April 11, 1919, as Landru and his latest mistress entered a Paris china shop, he was recognized by a woman whose sister had gone missing nineteen months earlier after announcing her engagement to Landru, then going under the name Frémyet. The woman immediately notified the police, who lost no time in tracking down Landru at his apartment. On April 12, the infamous lady-killer was arrested.

Landru steadfastly protested his innocence throughout his three-week trial, which commenced on November 7, 1921. Mistakenly believing he could not possibly be convicted without physical evidence, he repeatedly challenged the prosecution to "Produce your corpses!" In the end, the overwhelming mass of circumstantial evidence was more than enough to convince the jury of his guilt. Condemned to the guillotine, the "Bluebeard of Paris" went to his death on February 22, 1922, still declaring that he was "innocent and at peace."

# #31 SHEET MUSIC TO GALLOWS SONG SUNG BY CARL WANDERER

## "The Ragged Stranger"

**(1920)**
*Some condemned prisoners go to their deaths with words of repentance. Others snarl last words of defiance. Carl Wanderer went to the gallows singing a popular sentimental ditty, evidently addressed to the young wife he murdered in a diabolical plot.*

O n the drizzly evening of Monday, June 21, 1920, Carl Wanderer suggested to his wife that they go to the movies. A decorated veteran of the Great War, Wanderer had settled down to a seemingly contented domestic life, going to work in his father's Chicago butcher shop and marrying twenty-year-old Ruth Johnson, his childhood sweetheart. The newlyweds moved in with Ruth's parents in a house on North Campbell Avenue.

The movie they settled on was the newly released adaptation of Jack London's *The Sea Wolf*, showing at a nearby cinema. The convenient location was important since Ruth was eight months pregnant at the time.

They left the show at around 9:30 p.m. En route home they passed a shabby-looking man with a shapeless felt cap pulled low on his head. The stranger fell in behind them.

When they reached their house—so Carl later told the police—"Ruth went up ahead of me. . . . She opened the outer door and I heard her fumbling with the keys to the inner door of the hall."

"Just then," Carl reported, "we heard a man's voice in the outer doorway saying, 'Don't turn on that light.'"

Carl immediately reached for his gun, a .45 semiautomatic pistol he had started carrying after his father's shop was robbed. Before he could draw it, the stranger opened fire. A split second later, Carl "jerked out" his own gun and "shot it out with the fellow."

Hearing the gunfire, a passing beat cop named George Nape rushed to the scene. By the light filtering in from a streetlamp, he could make out a woman's body crumpled on the floor and two men, one lying unconscious, the other bending over him and pounding his skull against the floor.

"You shot my wife!" the enraged man was shouting. Nape grabbed him by an arm before he could deliver another blow and yanked him off the seemingly lifeless figure—a tramp, by the look of him. Shot three times in the chest, the man was past saving. On the vestibule floor, police found his pistol: an army .45 Colt semiautomatic.

Ruth had been shot twice, once in her right thigh, once in her abdomen, and soon died.

The following day, June 22, newspaper readers from coast to coast thrilled to the exciting story: the pregnant young bride of ten months, slain in the darkened entranceway of her parents' home, her death then avenged by her war-hero husband. Few questioned Carl's version of events.

On the morning after the incident, Ben Hecht, at that time a star reporter for the *Chicago Daily News*, paid Wanderer a visit at his home on North Campbell Avenue. Much to his surprise, as he wrote, he found Carl "freshly shaved, pressing his pants, and whistling 'It's a Long Way to Tipperary.'" Questioned about the tragedy, Carl expressed no grief at Ruth's violent death, only a grim satisfaction in having dispatched her killer.

Hecht wasn't the only journalist to have doubts about Carl. Walter Howey, managing editor of William Randolph Hearst's *Chicago American*, had gotten hold of official photographs of the handgun used by the alleged perpetrator—the "Ragged Stranger," as he would be labeled by the press. Howey couldn't help wondering what a man dressed "like a tramp out of the gutter" was doing with such an expensive weapon. Putting in a call to his contacts at police headquarters, Howey learned the serial number of the gun and immediately transmitted it via telegram to the Colt firearms company in Hartford,

Connecticut. He learned the gun was part of a shipment sold in 1913 to a Chicago sporting goods store.

A check of the store's records revealed that the gun had been purchased by a mailman named Peter Hoffman. Hoffman readily admitted that he had once owned the gun but explained that he had sold it several years earlier to his brother-in-law, Fred Wanderer.

Like Howey, police sergeant John W. Norton was bothered by certain peculiarities in the case. Police had found five bullet holes in the vestibule where the crime took place—one in the floor, four in the walls. Added to the two bullets that had struck Ruth and the three in the tramp, that made a total ten shots fired during the blazing gun battle in the cramped entranceway. And yet, Carl had escaped without a scratch.

And then there was the matter of money. Shortly after the shooting, Eugenia Johnson, Ruth's mother, had discovered $1,500 in cash in her daughter's bedroom dresser. The bankbook revealed that Ruth had withdrawn the money just hours before she was killed. Norton found that circumstance more than bit suspicious.

Once informed about the provenance of the gun, Norton lost no time in sending a squad car to pick up Fred Wanderer, who turned out to be a cousin of Carl's. Fred confirmed that the gun was his but said he hadn't seen it in a couple of weeks—not since he had loaned it to Carl two weeks ago, on June 21.

On Tuesday afternoon, July 6, Carl Wanderer was taken into custody for questioning. Detective Sergeant Norton began by revealing what the police had discovered about the second gun: that it was Fred Wanderer's and that Carl had borrowed it on the day of the shootings. Why had Carl claimed that the Ragged Stranger had been carrying it?

Carl quickly came up with a far-fetched explanation, claiming he was actually carrying two handguns, his own service pistol and Fred's Colt .45, which Carl picked up earlier in the evening after offering to fix it when Fred complained that it had jammed. He said there was a scuffle and the Ragged Stranger ended up with his service pistol, which got fired in the process, but Carl drew Fred's gun and began shooting.

Norton wasn't buying this improbable tale. Over the next seventy-two hours, Carl was subjected to a relentless "sweating," as the third degree was called in those days. Finally, at around six o'clock on the evening of Friday, July 9, he let out an exhausted sigh and told the truth.

Just ten months after his wedding, Carl had already grown tired of married life. He longed to get back into the army. "I didn't want to be married, and I didn't want to be a father. I wanted to be a soldier—free to go where I will and do what I will," he said.

Why, Carl was asked, didn't he simply divorce his wife?

"I loved her too much to let another man have her," he replied.

Prompted by his interrogators, Carl spilled the details of his nefarious scheme. On the morning of the murder, after running an errand, he had encountered a young panhandler and offered him a job driving a delivery truck for twenty-five dollars a week. When the man—whose name Carl never bothered to learn—accepted, he was told to meet Carl at 6:30 p.m. that evening not far from the butcher shop.

They met at the agreed-upon time, and proceeded by trolley to Fred Wanderer's house, where Carl borrowed his cousin's pistol while the other man waited outside. The two then rode the trolley to Carl's neighborhood, where

Carl asked the man if he wanted to make even more money. The man affirmed that he did.

Sometime "between nine and half past nine," Carl explained, he and his wife would be returning from the movie theater. When the man saw them, he was to follow them home and pretend to hold them up in the vestibule.

If the tramp was puzzled by this bizarre request, he kept it to himself. After handing the man a dollar for a meal, Carl returned home and—as the *Chicago Daily News* reported— "ate his own supper with the woman he was to kill two hours later." When Carl left for the movie with Ruth, he was carrying his own gun and Fred's, each loaded with a full clip of seven rounds. On their way home after the show, they passed the tramp loitering on a corner. When Carl nodded to him, the man followed, and when the couple entered the vestibule, he stepped in behind them.

As soon as he did, Carl drew both his guns and started firing at his wife and the stranger—seven shots from Fred's gun, three from his own.

"I wanted it to appear as if he shot my wife and I shot him," Carl calmly explained. Asked about the $1,500 Ruth's mother had discovered in her daughter's bureau, Carl said he "intended to take what money was left after Ruth's burial and go back to the army."

Public antipathy toward the "zero-blooded slayer" (as the tabloids described him) was ferocious and grew even more so when newspapers revealed that getting back to the "free and easy" life of a soldier wasn't Carl's only reason for slaying his wife. He had gone out on a half dozen dates with a pretty seventeen-year-old named Julia Schmitt, who was unaware that he was married.

Tried for the murder of his wife that October, Carl was found guilty. The jury, however, fixed the punishment at just twenty-five years—a sentence which meant that, with time off for good behavior, Carl might serve as little as thirteen years and nine months and be a free man at forty-six. So intense was public outrage that he was put on trial again, this time for the murder of the "Ragged Stranger." On March 18, 1921, after just twenty-two minutes of deliberation, the jury found him guilty and sentenced him to death.

The death march to the gallows began at 7:14 a.m. on September 30. As Carl mounted the scaffold, he suddenly burst into song—a sentimental ditty about lost love called "My Gal Sal." His singing only came to a halt when one of the deputies slipped the white hood over his head. A moment later the trap was sprung and Carl plunged into space. Fifteen minutes passed before he was pronounced dead.

*Postcard of the neighborhood where Carl Wanderer met the Ragged Stranger.*

# #32 NURSE MARJORIE MOVIE POSTER

## The Mysterious Murder of William Desmond Taylor

**(1922)**

*Mary Miles Minter was one of the biggest motion picture stars of her day. She was also at the center of one of the greatest scandals in Hollywood history, the unsolved murder of the man she loved, director William Desmond Taylor.*

I n the early months of 1922, the movie industry was rocked by a sex-and-celebrity scandal destined to become the most celebrated unsolved murder case in Hollywood history. Its central figure was known as William Desmond Taylor. Like many other denizens of Hollywood, he had undergone a radical reinvention. Scion of an eminent Anglo-Irish family, he was born William Cunningham Deane-Tanner in County Carlow, Ireland, in 1872 and led a life as colorful and adventurous as anything shown on the big screen. He was shipped off at seventeen to a dude ranch in Kansas for "manhood training," then knocked around the US, working as everything from a door-to-door salesman to a railroad yardman to a waiter before ending up as a partner in a fashionable Fifth Avenue antiques shop in Manhattan.

At the age of twenty-nine, he married Ethel Hamilton, a young dancer known as "New York's prettiest chorus girl," only to abandon her and their young daughter five years later. He tried his hand at prospecting in the Yukon, then joined a traveling theatrical company, eventually making his way to Los Angeles, where—with his matinee idol looks—he quickly found work in the fledgling motion picture business, first as an actor, then as a director.

Following a military stint during World War I—when (as a British citizen) he enlisted as a private in the Canadian Expeditionary and returned home as a major in the Royal Army Service Corps—he resumed his Hollywood career, becoming one of the movie industry's leading directors. One of his greatest successes was the 1919 screen adaptation of the children's classic, *Anne of Green Gables*. Its star was the seventeen-year-old ingenue Mary Miles Minter.

An actress since the age of five, she grew up under the tyrannical rule of her mother, Charlotte Shelby, who kept her on an exceptionally tight leash. That stranglehold only made Minter desperate to break free. Seeing her dashing director as a potential savior, she developed an obsessive infatuation with him, barraging him with gushing love letters and making it clear that—despite the thirty-year age gap between them—she would stop at nothing to become his wife. Terrified that she might lose control over the high-earning child she had invested so much in, Shelby showed up at Taylor's home one night with a pistol and threatened to "blow [his] goddamned brains out" if he didn't stop "hanging around" her daughter.

What neither Minter nor her mother seemed to know was that Taylor was a semicloseted gay man who had formed a passionate relationship with a male colleague. Indeed, his lack of erotic interest in the opposite sex was one of the things that endeared him to another screen beauty, his close friend Mabel Normand. An enormously popular comedienne—who, like so many other Hollywood actresses, had spent years contending with the crude advances of the men who controlled the motion picture business—Normand cherished her platonic relationship with the courtly Taylor.

While the lovestruck Minter dreamed of marrying Taylor and the big-hearted Normand wanted nothing more than his friendship, another lovely young woman was hoping for something else from him. Margaret Gibson (known to her friends as Gibby) had been an up-and-coming starlet when her career was derailed by an arrest for prostitution at a Chinatown brothel, where she went to work at the urging of a lowlife boyfriend. Determined to revive her career, she decided to reach out to all the contacts she had. One of these, someone she had worked with years earlier when they were both starting out in show business, was her old pal William Taylor.

* * *

On the morning of Wednesday, February 1, 1922, Henry Peavey—Taylor's valet—showed up for work at his usual time, a few minutes before 7:30 a.m. Unlocking the front door, he was stunned to discover his employer dead on the floor—faceup, impeccably dressed, arms at his side, a crust of dried blood around his mouth.

Roused by Peavey's frantic shouts, neighbors hurried into the director's home, hopelessly compromising the crime scene. A studio troubleshooter was quickly dispatched

*Mary Miles Minter trading card.*

with orders to confiscate or destroy anything potentially scandalous: alcohol, drugs, love letters. By the time detectives arrived almost an hour later, Taylor's home had been so thoroughly ransacked that all forensic evidence had been obliterated.

The first physician summoned by neighbors did such a cursory job that he gave the cause of death as "gastric hemorrhage." It wasn't until a deputy coroner finally showed up at around nine o'clock—an hour-and-a-half after Peavey discovered the body—that the truth was discovered: Taylor had been shot to death at point-blank range, the .38-caliber soft-nosed bullet entering his "left side, six-and-a-half inches below his armpit, before traveling upward through the . . . ribs, penetrating his left lung, passing out of his chest, and finally lodging in his neck."

The crime turned into a media circus, with stories flying of Taylor's supposed affairs with Minter and Normand and his reputed connection to the Los Angeles drug trade. The tabloids blazoned their pages with lurid rumors of his membership in a secret "cult" of gay men who engaged in "wild night parties known as 'orgies.'" Reporters digging into his checkered past uncovered facts— particularly his abandonment of his wife and young daughter—that cast his character in an unflattering light.

Newspaper speculation over possible perpetrators ran rampant. In the course of the investigation, more than three dozen suspects were identified by the press, among them "a disgruntled studio employee," "an old enemy from the Klondike Gold Rush," "the brother of a girl who had died by suicide after Taylor deserted her," and "a lunatic movie fan."

The likeliest candidates were thought to be people with close ties to the slain director. Some believed that Mabel Normand was at least indirectly responsible. Once addicted to cocaine, the beloved comic actress had managed to kick the habit with the support of Taylor, who was so intent on keeping her away from drugs that he had provided federal agents with the names of her suppliers. According to one theory, Taylor's death was an act of retaliation by vengeful Hollywood drug traffickers. Others felt sure that he was shot to death either by Mary Miles Minter—enraged by his refusal to marry her—or by her pathologically controlling mother, Charlotte Shelby, who saw Taylor as a threat to the power she exerted over her little cash cow.

Henry Peavey himself was suspected, as was his predecessor, Edward Sands, a Midwestern sociopath with a long arrest record who served as Taylor's butler and chef before wrecking his employer's car, forging checks, and absconding with thousands of dollars in cash and a closetful of Taylor's expensive suits. And then there was Margaret "Gibby" Gibson, whose appeals for help from Taylor had gone unanswered and who gasped out a confession to the murder as she lay dying in 1964. Though few find the claim credible, one historian has proposed that a blackmailer boyfriend of Gibby's went to the director's home with an armed accomplice and that Taylor was shot while resisting the shakedown.

In the end, however, none of the various hypotheses has been proven beyond a reasonable doubt. Like other celebrated cases—the Black Dahlia murder (see page 156) and the Zodiac killings (see page 203)—this one may remain unsolved forever.

*The dashing William Desmond Taylor, victim of one of Hollywood's most sensational murder mysteries.*

# #33 NATHAN LEOPOLD'S EYEGLASSES

## The Chicago "Thrill Killers" Case

**(1924)**

*Jazz Age "thrill killers" Leopold and Loeb believed they had committed the perfect crime. A simple slip-up, however, led to their swift arrest.*

I n May 1924, a pair of self-professed Nietzschean supermen, Nathan Leopold and Richard Loeb, the pampered sons of two prominent Chicago families, set out to prove their intellectual superiority by committing the "perfect crime." On the twenty-first of that month, they abducted and killed Loeb's fourteen-year-old cousin, Bobby Franks, stuffed his body into a drainpipe in a remote marshy area twenty miles south of Chicago, then contacted the boy's parents and demanded a ten-thousand-dollar ransom for his safe return. Even as Franks's father set out for the bank to withdraw the money the following morning, the boy's nude corpse—his head battered, his face and genitals mutilated with acid—was discovered by some passing workmen. They also found something else in the grass nearby: a pair of horn-rimmed eyeglasses.

Despite the supposed brilliance of their plan, the two college-age "thrill killers" were arrested within two weeks, the police having traced the eyeglasses to Leopold, who had let them slip from the breast pocket of his jacket as the pair hurried from the crime scene.

The sheer senselessness of the murder, the youth and social prominence of the perpetrators, as well as rumors of their "perverted" sexual relationship—all these factors combined to make the Leopold and Loeb case a tabloid sensation. When legendary attorney Clarence Darrow agreed to take on the defense, the public got ready to enjoy what was immediately advertised as the "Trial of the Century."

Knowing that any jury would surely convict his clients and sentence them to hang,

*Nathan Leopold (left) and Richard Loeb, at their trial in 1924.*

Darrow had them enter a plea of guilty. As a result, the "Trial of the Century" was not a trial at all, but a sentencing hearing, in which the "Great Defender" sought to convince the judge that, owing to mitigating psychological factors, his clients should be spared the death penalty. Darrow's closing plea, which lasted twelve hours, reduced even hardened reporters to tears and is still regarded as one of the greatest pieces of oratory in American legal history. In the end, Leopold and Loeb were each sentenced to life, plus ninety-nine years.

In 1936, Richard Loeb was slashed to death in a shower by a former cellmate. After more than thirty years in prison, Nathan Leopold was paroled in 1958. Hounded by the press, he moved to Puerto Rico, where he married, worked as an X-ray technician, taught mathematics, and wrote a book on ornithology before dying of a heart condition in 1971 at age sixty-six.

# #34 THE REVEREND EDWARD HALL'S CALLING CARD

## The Hall–Mills Murder Trial

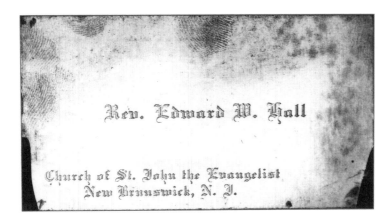

**(1926)**

*With its irresistible mix of prurient ingredients—
a respected, married man of the cloth murdered
alongside his choir girl mistress during one of their
secret outdoor trysts—the Hall–Mills case became
a tabloid sensation.*

One of the Jazz Age's most sensational murder cases began in September 1922 when a young couple came upon a pair of corpses lying side by side beneath a crabapple tree on a Somerset County, New Jersey, lover's lane. The victims turned out to be a married Episcopal priest, the Reverend Edward Wheeler Hall, and his mistress, Mrs. Eleanor Mills, a singer in his choir and the wife of the church's sexton. Autopsies revealed that both had been shot in the head at point-blank range with a .32-caliber pistol. In addition, Mills's throat had been cut so deeply that her jugular vein, windpipe, esophagus, and neck muscles were completely severed.

With its steamy mix of lust, murder, and scandal, the case became an instant tabloid sensation. Hordes of curiosity-seekers descended on the site where the bodies were discovered, stripping every leaf, branch, and bit of bark from the crabapple tree and carrying them off as ghoulish souvenirs. Despite one detective's confident prediction that the crime would be solved in a matter of days, the investigation dragged on for weeks. Two months after the murders, the killer's identity remained unknown, though the likeliest candidates were the pastor's wronged wife and her two brothers, one of whom was reputed to be a crack shot. A grand jury was finally convened in November but failed to issue an indictment. The case seemed to be closed.

Four years later, however, the *New York Daily Mirror* dredged up some new evidence and plastered its front pages with headlines trumpeting the ostensibly shocking revelations about the long-forgotten double murder.

The paper's strident calls for action forced the governor of New Jersey to reopen the case. Finally, on January 28, 1926, Mrs. Frances Stevens Hall, along with her brothers, Willie and Henry, was arrested for the murder of her husband, Edward, and his inamorata, Eleanor Mills. The trial, which began on November 3, 1926, featured such melodramatic moments as the public reading of the Reverend Hall's steamy love letters and the appearance of a purported eyewitness, a farmwife who was dying of cancer and delivered her testimony from an iron hospital bed facing the jury box.

For three solid weeks, the trial kept the country in thrall. In the end, Frances Hall and her brothers were acquitted—and promptly sued the *Mirror* for three million dollars.

*The tree beneath which the bodies of the two illicit lovers were found attracted hordes of morbid souvenir hunters.*

# #35 78 RPM RECORD, "LITTLE MARION PARKER"

## William Edward Hickman, "The Fox"

**(1927)**
*The kidnapping-murder of little Marion Parker was a crime of unspeakable ghastliness, commemorated in a recorded murder ballad written and performed by the country singer-composer Rev. Andrew W. Jenkins (aka Blind Andy).*

Born in Arkansas in 1908 into a family with a long history of mental disorders, William Edward Hickman manifested signs of instability from an early age. Under the influence of his fanatical grandfather, he developed a fierce determination to become a clergyman, even while indulging in what one childhood acquaintance recalled as his "mania for capturing and torturing stray dogs and cats."

An academic star during his first years of high school, he underwent a transformation as a senior, turning from a popular, straight-A student into a paranoid loner with no interest in his classes. Not long after graduation, he made the acquaintance of a fourteen-year-old reprobate named Welby Hunt. Before long, the two embarked on a series of armed robberies.

After a shootout at a Los Angeles pharmacy left a druggist mortally wounded, Hickman decided to lie low, finding work as a messenger at a bank in downtown LA, but that didn't last long. Arrested in June 1927 after forging some checks, he was tried in juvenile court and—largely because the bogus checks were for such paltry sums—let off with probation.

He spent the following months on an aimless, multicity odyssey, financing the trip by knocking over a succession of small shops along the way. The increasingly delusional Hickman felt infused with a renewed sense of religious vocation and resolved to enroll in a seminary. Tuition, however, cost far more than he was able to realize from his penny-ante robberies. To fulfill his holy mission, he came up with a diabolical plan.

Perry M. Parker was chief bank cashier at Hickman's former workplace. During his employment there, Hickman had learned that Parker had a substantial savings account. He also knew that Parker was the doting father of a twelve-year-old daughter named Marion, a student at a nearby junior high school.

Shortly after noon on Thursday, December 15, 1927, Hickman—whose malevolent nature was concealed behind a clean-cut, college-boy persona—appeared at the attendance office of the school and introduced himself to the secretary as a coworker of Mr. Perry Parker. The banker, he explained, had been "gravely injured in a traffic accident" and wanted his daughter by his hospital bedside.

Though it was not her habit to turn a student over to a stranger, the young man was so obviously trustworthy and the situation so urgent that the secretary summoned Marion from her homeroom. Repeating his story to the little girl, Hickman then led her outside to a car he had stolen the previous month and spirited her away.

Over the next two torturous days, Perry Parker received a series of ransom notes—variously signed "Death," "Fate," and "The Fox"—demanding $1,500 for the safe return of Marion. With the approval of the police, he agreed to meet the kidnapper at a remote location and exchange the cash for his daughter.

A few minutes after Perry arrived at the designated spot—a shadowy residential neighborhood with little traffic and no pedestrians in sight—another car, its headlights off, pulled up alongside him. The driver wore a handkerchief over his lower face. Beside him sat a huddled figure, tightly swaddled in a blanket.

When Perry asked to see his child, he was told that she was asleep. Passing the package of cash across to the masked driver, he waited, as instructed, while the other car edged forward about two hundred feet before coming to a halt. Suddenly, the passenger door flew open and his daughter was shoved into the street. An instant later, the kidnapper roared away into the night.

Leaping from his car, Perry rushed to the inert bundle lying in the gutter and scooped it in his arms. Wrapped in the blanket was Marion's limbless and disemboweled torso, her face hideously rouged and her eyes sewn open to make it appear as if she were alive.

The following day, a man walking in a nearby park came upon several newspaper-wrapped bundles containing Marion's severed arms and legs. Later that afternoon, her viscera were found in another neatly wrapped package in the tall grass of the park.

More than eight thousand local, state, and federal lawmen—assisted by untold numbers of outraged citizens—threw themselves into what quickly became the largest manhunt in California history. Hickman, however, was long gone. After ditching his stolen automobile, he had carjacked another vehicle and headed north. On the afternoon of Thursday, December 22, a week after the abduction, his vehicle was spotted by sharp-eyed police officers in Pendleton, Oregon, and pulled over after a high-speed chase. Taken into custody, Hickman reportedly wondered aloud if he "would be as famous as Leopold and Loeb."

Extradited to California, Hickman made a full confession, describing how well he had treated the cooperative little girl, taking her once to the movies and, when she complained about feeling "cooped up," driving her into the countryside. Though Marion was aware that, in his letters to her father, Hickman had threatened to kill her, he reassured her that he "didn't mean it" and promised "that even [if] her father didn't pay me the money," he "would let her go back unharmed."

Even he was surprised when, according to his statement, he was suddenly "gripped" by an overwhelming urge to kill her. Grabbing a dishtowel from the kitchen, he returned to Marion, who was tied to a chair, then "gently placed the towel about her neck and

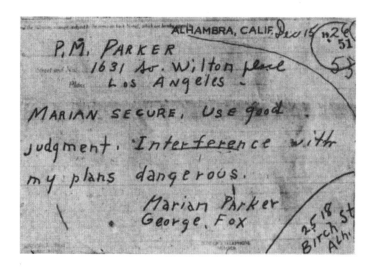

*Ransom letter from Edward Hickman.*

explained that it might rest her head." Before she "had time to doubt or even say anything," Hickman "pulled the towel about her throat and applied all [his] strength to the move. She made no audible noise except for the struggle and heaving of her body during the period of strangulation, which continued for about two minutes."

His exertions having left him somewhat sweaty and disheveled, Hickman washed his face, combed his hair, and straightened his clothing. He then left the building and proceeded to the nearest drugstore, where he purchased rouge, lipstick, and face powder, explaining to the salesgirl that he was purchasing the cosmetics for his sister.

Back in the apartment, he set about dismembering the child's corpse for easy disposal, applying the techniques he had learned back in Kansas City while working in a poultry house.

Stripping the body, he carried it into the bathroom and laid it face down in the tub, head over the drain. He then slit the girl's throat with a butcher knife, turned on the water, and returned to the kitchen for a snack of sardines and crackers while the blood drained from the carcass.

Returning to the bathroom, he stripped down to his undershorts and went to work on the body with a set of "improvised surgical instruments"—the butcher knife, a pocket knife, a kitchen fork, an ice pick, and a package of razors. He began by effecting (in the words of Hickman's defense lawyer Richard Cantillon) "a disjunction from the body of the arms at the elbows and the legs at the knees. Then he cut an opening in the abdomen, removing the viscera. After carrying the upper portion of torso into the living room and placing it upright on the davenport, he wrapped the severed limbs in newspapers, thoroughly scrubbed the bathroom floor, washed out the tub, and took a warm bath."

Once he was dressed, he "picked up the cosmetics and with the ineptitude of an amateur beautician, applied the rouge, lipstick, and face powder to the dead face. He slipped her school dress over the head and torso, carefully pinning it so it would remain in place and cover the wound on the throat." As a final touch, he sewed open her eyelids with two fine strands of picture wire, "brushed and fixed Marion's hair in a ponytail, held in place with her hair ribbon, tied in a neat bow." "The entire effect," Cantillon observed, "was quite lifelike."

At the close of Hickman's widely publicized thirteen-day trial, the jury took less than forty-five minutes to find him guilty of first-degree murder. His hanging, on October 19, 1928, was a grisly affair. As he plunged through the trap, his head struck the side of the gallows. Instead of dying cleanly with a snapped neck, he dangled there, violently convulsing as he slowly strangled to death.

# #36 TOM HOWARD'S ANKLE CAMERA

## The "Double Indemnity Murder"

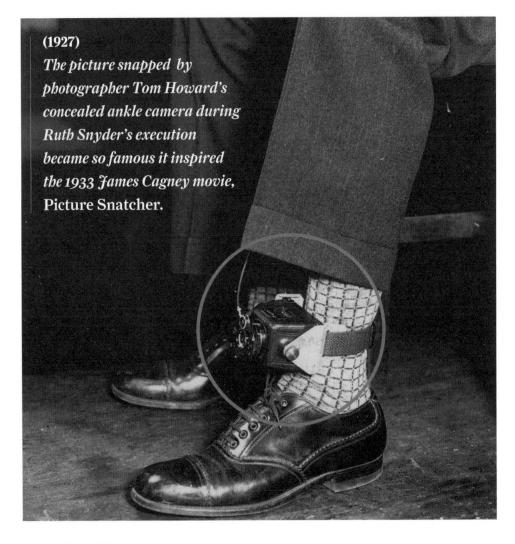

**(1927)**

*The picture snapped by photographer Tom Howard's concealed ankle camera during Ruth Snyder's execution became so famous it inspired the 1933 James Cagney movie,* Picture Snatcher.

As the inspiration for James M. Cain's 1943 novel of the same name, the 1927 slaying of Albert Snyder has come to be known as the "Double Indemnity Murder." At its center was the victim's wife, Ruth, a bored Queens housewife who had embarked on a torrid affair with a married, mousy corset salesman, Judd Gray. At Ruth's instigation, the two plotted to murder Albert, her surly, stick-in-the-mud husband, and collect on his life insurance policy, which included a "double indemnity" clause, providing nearly $50,000 in the event that he met a violent end.

On the night of March 20, 1927, the pair put their plan into action. Armed with a heavy iron sash weight, Gray crept into the Snyders' bedroom and brought the bludgeon down on the sleeping man's head. The blow was so feeble that it only caused Albert to sit up with a roar and grab his assailant's necktie. When Gray screamed for help, Ruth grabbed the sash weight from Gray's hand and smashed in her husband's skull. For good measure, the assassins garroted him with a wire and stuffed chloroform-soaked rags up his nostrils. They then ransacked the house to make it look as if Albert had been killed during a break-in. Though convinced that they had pulled off the perfect crime, the bumbling pair had done such a sloppy job of covering their tracks that they were in custody within twenty-four hours.

The Snyder–Gray case was an immediate sensation, and Ruth instantly became the most detested woman of her time—the Whore of Babylon in the guise of a Queens housewife.

Shortly after 11:00 p.m. on Thursday, January 12, 1928, Ruth went to the electric chair, followed eight minutes later by Judd Gray. Seated among the spectators was Tom Howard. Though posing as a reporter, Howard was actually a photographer hired by the *New York Daily News*. Secretly strapped to his left ankle was a miniature camera. When the first jolt hit Ruth, he released the shutter with a cable that ran up his pants leg to his pocket. The resulting shot—a blurry black-and-white photograph of Ruth at the instant of her execution—occupied the entire front page of the next day's *Daily News* and would go down in newspaper history as the most infamous tabloid picture of all time.

*Ruth Snyder at the instant of her electrocution—perhaps the most infamous front-page photograph in tabloid history.*

# #37 A CRATE OF PYROTOL

## The Bath School Disaster

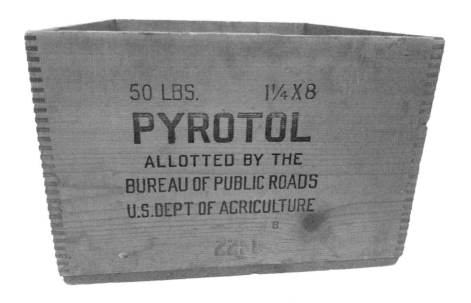

50 LBS.        1¼X8

PYROTOL

ALLOTTED BY THE
BUREAU OF PUBLIC ROADS
U.S.DEPT OF AGRICULTURE

**(1927)**

*When World War I ended, the US government sold its surplus gunpowder to farmers in a low-grade explosive form called Pyrotol. In the hands of a Midwestern madman, it became a weapon of unimaginable destruction.*

In the minds of many, the horrific school killings that have plagued the US in recent years began with the outrage committed in 1999 by a pair of teenage sociopaths, Dylan Klebold and Eric Harris, at their high school in Columbine, Colorado (see page 257). Seventy years earlier, however, the nation was stunned by a school massacre that claimed more victims than any other such atrocity in US history: the Bath School Disaster.

In the closing months of 1926, Andrew Kehoe—a respected farmer in the community of Bath, Michigan—spiraled into paranoid madness, blaming his fellow townspeople for the problems that had plunged him into near bankruptcy. Over his bitter opposition, they had voted to build a new Consolidated School, to be paid for by an increase in property taxes, an expense that had exacerbated his financial difficulties. Overcome with a toxic brew of emotions—resentment, humiliation, self-pity—he devised a plan to take revenge on the people he held responsible for all that had gone wrong with his life.

Over a period of several weeks, he snuck into the school building at night and rigged its basement with hundreds of pounds of Pyrotol, an explosive made from surplus World War I gunpowder and sold to farmers to aid them in clearing their fields of boulders and tree stumps. He then attached a crude timer and set it to go off on the last day of school, May 18, 1927.

At a few minutes before nine o'clock that morning, the bomb exploded. If it weren't for a malfunction in the wiring, the entire school would have been destroyed and most of the 250 students in attendance that day—virtually every child in the community—would have died. As it was, the blast leveled one wing of the building, killing thirty-eight children and two of their teachers.

Andrew Kehoe's personal Armageddon, however, was not over. Having loaded his Ford pickup with old tools, nails, nuts, bolts, assorted scraps of metal, and a few sticks of dynamite, he drove down to the school and detonated the vehicle, blowing himself and several first responders to shreds. He had also bludgeoned his wife to death; destroyed his farmhouse and outbuildings with firebombs; hobbled his horses by wrapping wire around their ankles, leaving them to burn to death; cut down the beautiful old shade trees surrounding his house; and severed his grapevines.

Wired to a fence at the edge of the farm, investigators found a small wooden sign with the stenciled words: "Criminals are made, not born."

*Officials display hundreds of recovered sticks of Pyrotol that, had they detonated as planned, would have completely destroyed the Bath Consolidated School, killing virtually every child in the town of Bath, Michigan.*

# #38 ALBERT FISH PELVIC X-RAY

## "The Werewolf of Wisteria"

**(1928)**

*"Unique in the history of medical science," as one psychiatrist put it, this X-ray of Albert Fish's pelvic region offered shocking proof of the serial killer's monstrously perverted nature.*

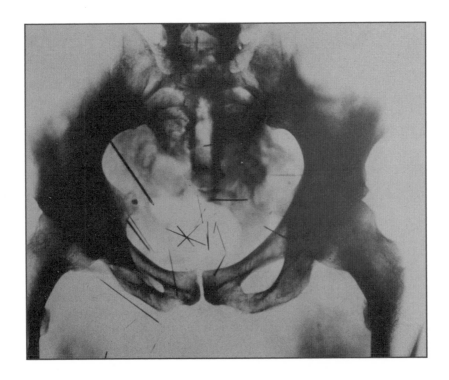

Eighteen-year-old Edward Budd was an able-bodied youth, the eldest son of a working-class family occupying a cramped apartment on Manhattan's West Side. In late May 1928, hoping to escape the city for the summer, he placed a classified in a newspaper: "Young man, 18, wishes position in country."

Several days later, a neatly dressed old man showed up at the Budds' apartment. Introducing himself as Frank Howard, the grandfatherly looking gentleman explained that he was hiring help for his farm on Long Island. Mr. Howard seemed satisfied with what he saw and made Edward a decent offer—fifteen dollars a week, plus room and board. He arranged to return in a few days to pick up the youth and drive him to the farm.

On Sunday, June 3, the old man returned. Edward was out on an errand. Mrs. Budd invited her son's new employer to have lunch with the family while they awaited the young man's return. Shortly afterward, the youngest member of the family—a glowing little girl named Grace—wandered into the room. She instantly caught the old man's eye. He called her over and sat her on his knee. She reminded him, he said, of his own ten-year-old granddaughter.

Suddenly, he made a surprising announcement. He had come by, not to fetch Edward, but to say that their departure for the farm would have to be delayed for a few hours. His niece, who lived in upper Manhattan, was having a birthday party that afternoon and he felt obliged to attend. He would return that evening, after the party, and pick up Edward then.

All at once, an idea seemed to strike him. Perhaps Grace would like to come along with him? It was going to be quite a party—with lots of children and games and ice cream. Mrs. Budd felt uncertain about letting her

*Grace Budd, whose disappearance set off one of the most intensive manhunts in New York City history.*

child go off with a virtual stranger. Still, Mr. Howard came across as so utterly harmless that her qualms seemed foolish. Grace was gotten up in her prettiest outfit.

Then Frank Howard—whose name was really Albert Fish and whose kindly demeanor concealed a mind of unimaginable depravity—took the child by the hand and led her away from home. Her family never saw her again.

Fish was born into a household characterized by poverty and psychosis. When he was five, his widowed mother placed him in a public orphanage, where Fish had a teacher whose preferred form of discipline was to strip her young charges naked and beat their bare bodies while the other boys and girls watched. What Fish learned, as he later put it, was "to enjoy everything that hurt." His preferred victims throughout his long life were children.

His criminal career began in earnest when, at age seventeen, he became a house-painter. Donning painter's overalls over his nude body, he would lure children into the basement of whatever building he was working on, strip off his clothes, and assault them. For decades he roamed the country, perpetrating scores of pedophiliac rapes.

Gradually, his depraved desires grew stronger. He became possessed, as he put it, with a lust for blood. No one knows the precise number of his victims, but it seems certain that, in addition to the hundreds of children he molested, he slew at least fifteen. Some were subjected to hideous cruelties before death.

According to psychiatrists who later examined Fish, he routinely indulged in "every known sexual perversion and some perversions never heard of before." Among these were flagellation, coprophagia (eating feces), undinism (a preoccupation with urine), and self-mutilation. Sometime in his late fifties, his fantasies turned to the only unspeakable act he had yet to experience: cannibalism.

Grace Budd's disappearance set off a massive manhunt. Over the following months, hopes were raised and dashed with dismaying regularity as investigators pursued one dead-end lead after another. Gradually, the trail grew ice cold. Six years after abducting the little girl, however, Albert Fish's demons got the best of him.

Among his myriad perversions, Fish was a habitual sender of obscene letters. In November 1934, he was gripped with a compulsion to write Grace Budd's mother. Fish began by recounting a story he had heard from an acquaintance, who claimed that during a terrible famine in China, "all children under 12 were sold to the Butchers to be cut up and sold for food in order to keep the others from starving. . . . He told me so often how

good [it] was," wrote the deranged old man, "I made up my mind to taste it."

The moment he had first set eyes on Grace, Fish wrote, he resolved "to eat her." Taking her to "an empty house in Westchester," he "choked her to death then cut her in small pieces so I could take my meat to my rooms, cook and eat it."

Though the letter was unsigned, Fish had enclosed it in an envelope he had found in his Manhattan boardinghouse. Embossed on the flap was the insignia of a New York City chauffeurs' association. Despite Fish's efforts to scratch it out, parts of the insignia remained legible. By dint of old-fashioned sleuthing, one heroic detective managed to trace the stationery to the boardinghouse. A trap was laid, and Fish was captured. As

*Albert Fish, considered by many to be the most heinous serial killer in the annals of US crime.*

he had in his vile letter, he freely confessed to leading Grace out of the city to a house in Westchester he had previously picked out for his diabolical purpose. Leaving her in the front yard to pick wildflowers, he climbed to an upstairs bedroom and—after carefully laying out the saw, butcher knife, and cleaver he had brought with him—stripped completely naked. He then called out the window, telling Grace to come upstairs. When she reached the landing, he stepped into the hallway.

At the sight of the naked old man, Grace began to scream. As she turned and made for the stairs, Fish pounced. Digging his fingers into her throat, he wrestled her to the floor, then knelt on her chest and choked her to death, climaxing twice as she expired. Afterward, he cut off her head, dismembered her body, and disposed of the pieces in various spots around the property—all except for a few pounds of her flesh, which he wrapped in newspaper and carried back to the city. There, in his boardinghouse room, he cooked her flesh "in various ways with carrots and onions and strips of bacon and ate of them over a period of nine days."

While awaiting trial, Fish revealed that one of his favorite forms of masochistic pleasure was to shove sewing needles up behind his testicles, so deeply that they remained permanently embedded inside his body. To check the truth of this incredible story, Fish's pelvic region was X-rayed at a local hospital. The X-rays clearly showed twenty-seven sharp, thin objects, unmistakably needles, lodged around the rectum and bladder, just below the tip of the spine, and in his groin. Their location made it clear that they had not been swallowed but inserted into the old man's body from below, through the perineum.

Fish was found guilty and sentenced to death. On January 16, 1936, he was led to the electric chair. Rumors later spread that, when the switch was pulled, the needles in his body caused a burst of blue sparks to explode from his groin.

# #39 AL CAPONE'S RAP SHEET

## "The St. Valentine's Day Massacre"

**(1929)**

*Al Capone's rise from street thug to underworld czar and media celebrity is a quintessentially American story. When the whole country was mesmerized by the tommy-gun carnage of Chicago's gangland killers, "Scarface Al" was the greatest gangster of them all.*

L ike other legendary badmen of the American past—Jesse James, Billy the Kid, Butch Cassidy and the Sundance Kid—Al Capone has become a fixture of our national mythology. In his bloody rise, violent reign, and sordid fall there is a quintessentially American fable.

"Scarface Al" got his famous nickname from the Chicago tabloids. He got the scars when he was eighteen and working as a bouncer in Brooklyn. When Capone lavished some ill-advised flattery on the sister of a neighborhood punk named Frank Gallucio, Galluch (as everyone called him) whipped out a pocketknife and carved three savage cuts into Capone's cheek. Capone recognized talent when he saw it and later hired Galluch as his personal bodyguard at $100 a week.

Summoned to Chicago by his mentor, Johnny "The Fox" Torrio—whose double life of devoted family man and ruthless racketeer he would emulate—Capone quickly rose from fearsome enforcer to trusted partner in Torrio's booming bootlegging operation. When Torrio retired after an assassination attempt, Capone inherited his empire of speakeasies, brothels, and gambling dens.

Setting himself up in a $1,500-a-day suite in the Metropole Hotel, Capone basked in his notoriety, portraying himself as a civic-minded businessmen, a patron of the arts, and a benevolent employer of the city's immigrant poor. He hobnobbed with movie stars and visiting dignitaries and supplied the tabloids with a steady stream of colorful copy and memorable quotes. ("Public service is my motto. Ninety percent of the people of Cook County drink and gamble and my offense has been to furnish them with those amusements.") The St. Valentine's Day Massacre—orchestrated by Capone, who made sure he was vacationing at his Florida estate when the slaughter took place—only cemented his reputation as ruler of the US underworld.

That shooting took place on February 14, 1929. At around 10:30 a.m., four of Capone's hitmen—two dressed as police officers—stormed into a Lincoln Park garage, lined seven men against a wall, and gunned them down with Thompson submachine guns. All but one of the victims—an optometrist who got a thrill from consorting with gangsters—were members of the North Side Gang headed by Capone's main rival in the bootlegging business, George "Bugs" Moran. Moran himself, the primary target, escaped assassination, arriving late at the garage after sleeping in that morning.

By the time of the Wall Street crash eight months later, Capone's estimated yearly income from his varied criminal enterprises was $100,000,000. Tax free. His flouting of the tax laws proved to be his undoing. Convicted of tax evasion in October 1931, he was sentenced to eleven years in prison. Sent to Alcatraz, he began to show signs of syphilitic dementia. By the time he was paroled in November 1939, his mind was gone. He lived quietly at his Palm Island, Florida, estate for his remaining years, dying in January 1947 at the age of forty-eight—a doddering, prematurely old man who bore no resemblance to the flamboyant, larger-than-life crime lord who continues to exert a powerful hold on the American imagination.

# #40 BONNIE AND CLYDE DEATH CAR

## Bonnie and Clyde

**(1930–1934)**

*Sold to a carnival operator, the stolen 1934 Ford Fordor Deluxe sedan in which Bonnie and Clyde met their violent end became a popular amusement park attraction.*

In contrast to the glamorous title characters of the groundbreaking 1967 movie, the real-life Bonnie and Clyde were a pair of sociopathic lowlifes. Born and raised in hardscrabble circumstances, twenty-one-year-old Clyde Barrow had a long string of petty crimes behind him when, in 1930, he hooked up with Bonnie Parker, a sharp-featured nineteen-year-old stuck in a dead-end existence and desperate for adventure.

Following a stint of hard labor on a notoriously brutal prison farm, Clyde reunited with Bonnie and, along with a shifting gang of reprobates, embarked on a multistate crime spree, holding up filling stations, luncheonettes, drugstores, and other small businesses, along with the occasional town bank. Unlike his Hollywood avatar—who is shown committing a single murder in the heat of a getaway—the real Clyde was a cold-blooded killer, ultimately responsible for the murder of nine lawmen and three civilians. The gang saw casualties of its own, most dramatically in July 1933, when—while holed up in some tourist cabins outside of Platte City, Missouri—Clyde's brother Buck suffered fatal wounds during a blazing gun battle with police.

By then, the increasingly brazen activities of the Barrow Gang had made them front-page news throughout the central US. Their notoriety also owed much to the publicity-hungry Bonnie, who eagerly supplied newspapers with photographs of the outlaw couple posing with guns and cigars. She also sent examples of her doggerel poetry; her most famous poem, "Trail's End" aka "The Story of Bonnie and Clyde," contains sixteen verses that include the lines:

**If a policeman is killed down in Dallas
and they have no clues for a guide,
if they can't find the fiend,
they just wipe the slate clean
and hang it on Bonnie and Clyde.**

The final verse of the poem is:

**Some day they will go down together
and they will bury them side by side,
to few it means grief,
to the law it is relief,
but it is death to Bonnie and Clyde.**

Though big-time gangsters like John Dillinger derided them as penny-ante crooks—a view shared by J. Edgar Hoover—the reckless, shoot-'em-up exploits of the rampaging couple captured the public imagination. Hell-bent on wiping them out, authorities hired Frank Hamer, a forty-nine-year-old former Texas Ranger and implacable manhunter. After three and a half months on their trail, Hamer got word that his quarry was hiding out in Bienville Parish, Louisiana, and a trap was set for the fugitive couple. On May 23, 1934, Hamer and a posse of six other lawmen set up an ambush along a rural road regularly traveled by the pair. When Clyde's car—a stolen 1934 Ford sedan—came into view, the posse opened fire, massacring the outlaws with a barrage of more than 150 shots.

# #41 "THE CRIME AT QUIET DELL" SHEET MUSIC

## The Bluebeard of Quiet Dell

**(1931)**

*Like other murder ballads, "The Crime at Quiet Dell" offered morbid titillation under the guise of moral edification.*

Born in the Netherlands in 1892, Herman Drenth immigrated to New York in 1910. Over the next dozen years, he changed his name to Harry Powers and led a rootless life, eventually settling in Clarksburg, West Virginia, where, in 1927, he married a forty-one-year-old divorcée and made his living as a door-to-door vacuum cleaner salesman and used furniture dealer. He also began conducting a sinister secret life that would earn the pudgy, middle-aged psychopath a lasting reputation as one of the nation's most notorious "Bluebeard" killers.

Using the pseudonym "Cornelius O. Pierson," he began corresponding with women who had signed up with various matrimonial bureaus: mail-order "lonely hearts clubs" that provided love-starved singles with lists of prospective mates. In his letters, he described himself as a successful civil engineer with a net worth of $150,000 (more than two million in today's dollars) and "a beautiful ten-room house, completely furnished."

Exactly how many widows and spinsters were lured into Powers's clutches is unknown. He himself ultimately suggested that he had slain as many as fifty. There is no doubt, however, about the last five people he killed.

In 1931, he made contact with a fifty-year-old Danish-born widow named Asta Buick Eicher, mother of three children: fourteen-year-old Greta, twelve-year-old Harry, and nine-year-old Annabelle. After an exchange of increasingly ardent letters, she invited him to visit her home in suburban Chicago. Despite a glaring disparity in the way he had described himself (tall, handsome, with wavy dark hair and bright blue eyes) and his actual appearance ("squat, pig-eyed, and paunchy," in the words of one contemporary), she seems to have been quite taken with him, gushing to

neighbors that "romance had again entered her life."

That June, Mrs. Eicher and her children disappeared from their home. Alerted by concerned neighbors, police searched the premises and uncovered two dozen love letters from Cornelius O. Pierson who, upon closer investigation, turned out to be Harry Powers of Clarksburg, West Virginia. Confronted with the correspondence, Powers made contradictory statements about his knowledge of the Eicher family's whereabouts, heightening the lawmen's suspicions. It wasn't long before they learned that Powers and his wife owned a small plot of land in a place called Quiet Dell, a bucolic little village nestled in the hills just a few miles outside Clarksburg.

Proceeding to the property, detectives found a large, shed-like structure. Breaking open the padlocked door, they made a horrifying discovery. Beneath a trapdoor in its concrete floor lay a foul-smelling cellar that Powers had turned into a makeshift prison, consisting of four cramped, sound-proofed cells, each fitted with a heavy wooden door and furnished with a filthy mattress. Though articles of bloody clothing were strewn about, the Eichers were nowhere to be seen.

Their corpses—stuffed in burlap sacks and buried in a shallow drainage ditch that ran from the rear of the garage to a nearby creek—were found the following day, along with the remains of a fifth victim. She was quickly identified as fifty-one-year-old Dorothy Lemke of Northborough, Massachusetts, who had not been seen since the previous month, when she withdrew $1,555 from her bank and went off with her mail-order fiancé, Cornelius O. Pierson.

Powers was subjected to a particularly brutal third degree. He was beaten with a ballpeen hammer, his left arm was broken, and hot boiled eggs were pressed under his armpits. Eventually, he confessed to everything. Locked in their cages, the three Eicher children had been starved and forced to watch their mother being hanged from a ceiling beam. When the boy, Harry, tried to struggle free to save his mother, his skull was beaten in with a hammer. An autopsy revealed that he had also been castrated. His sisters were strangled to death, as was Dorothy Lemke.

Though diagnosed as a homicidal psychopath "possessed of an exaggerated lust to kill which dominates his entire personality," Powers—who clearly knew right from wrong—was deemed legally sane. To accommodate the hordes of spectators who flocked to Clarksburg for his trial, the proceedings were held in the city's 1,200-seat opera house. On December 11, after five days of testimony, the jury needed less than two hours to find him guilty. He went to the gallows at Moundsville three months later, on March 18, 1932.

Like other high-profile homicides of the era, the atrocities of "The Bluebeard of Quiet Dell" generated a murder ballad. Written by songwriters A. H. Grow and Leighton D. Davies and published in 1931, the ballad was, according to a note appended to the lyrics, "not written to appeal to the morbid fancies" of listeners. Rather, its goal was to serve as a warning. The last verse includes the lines:

> **To all the ladies fair,**
> **Do not confide in strangers . . .**
> **Lest you be lured unto your doom**
> **Like those at Quiet Dell.**

*Powers would become the inspiration for one of the most terrifying villains in Hollywood history: the psychopathic preacher Harry Powell played by Robert Mitchum in the 1955 thriller,* Night of the Hunter.

# #42 WINNIE RUTH JUDD'S BAGGAGE

## "The Trunk Murders"

**(1931)**

*Exactly how and why Winnie Ruth Judd's two victims ended up dead and stuffed inside trunks would remain a mystery for more than seventy years until her shocking confession came to light.*

orn in Indiana in 1905, Winnie Ruth McKinnell displayed vengeful behavior from an early age. At sixteen, to get back at a boyfriend who had jilted her, she staged her own abduction and had him arrested for kidnap and rape.

The following year, she met and fell in love with William C. Judd, a morphine-addicted physician twenty-two years her senior. Soon after their marriage, they moved to Mexico, where he worked as a medic for an American mining company. After having two miscarriages and contracting a mild case of tuberculosis, Ruth (as everyone called her) returned by herself to the States, where she settled in Phoenix, Arizona.

It wasn't long before the strikingly pretty Ruth found herself engaged in an adulterous affair with one of the city's wealthiest businessmen, a married forty-four-year-old playboy, known to his many friends as "Happy Jack" Halloran. She also befriended another recent arrival to the city, an X-ray technician named Annie LeRoi, a stunning, twice-divorced, thirty-two-year-old who had relocated to Phoenix with her twenty-four-year-old companion (and reputed lover), Hedvig "Sammy" Samuelson. Before long, Ruth had become roommates with the two women, sharing a bungalow that served as a party place for Halloran and his circle of philandering buddies. Within a few months, Ruth moved out, though she remained on good terms with the pair. At around 9:30 p.m. on Friday, October 16, 1931, Ruth showed up at the duplex to spend a quiet evening with her friends. No one ever saw Annie LeRoi or Sammy Samuelson alive again.

Two days later, after informing her landlord that she was taking the night train to Los Angeles to visit her husband, Ruth enlisted his aid to transport a pair of unusually heavy trunks to the Union Depot. Despite a bandaged right hand—burned, she claimed, while ironing—she herself carried a battered suitcase, a hatbox, and a small valise. By the time the train reached its destination early the following day, the two trunks—the larger weighing over two hundred pounds, the smaller around ninety—were oozing blood and emanating a repulsive smell.

When Ruth showed up at the baggage claim to retrieve the trunks, the supervising agent demanded that she open them. Explaining that her husband had the keys, she left, promising to return shortly. When she failed to reappear, the agent summoned a policeman who broke open the trunks. Crammed inside the larger one was the decomposing corpse of Annie LeRoi. Sammy Samuelson's body, neatly cut into three sections, was stuffed into the smaller trunk.

Four days would pass before Ruth surrendered herself in response to an emotional appeal issued by her husband. She claimed that, while visiting she became embroiled in a violent argument with Sammy Samuelson, who "got hold of a gun and shot me in the left hand. Mrs. LeRoi grabbed an ironing board and started to strike me over the head with it. In the struggle, I got hold of the gun, and Sammy got shot. Mrs. LeRoi was still coming at me with the ironing board, and I had to shoot her." Returning to her apartment, she had found Jack Halloran waiting for her. It was Halloran, she claimed, who had returned with her to the crime scene and packed the bodies into the trunks while she mopped up the blood.

The findings of the medical examiner, who determined that both victims had been shot in the head at close range, cast serious doubts on this story. For decades, the events of that fatal night would be shrouded in mystery. The truth emerged in 2014, when a confession, handwritten by Ruth to her attorney in 1933, unexpectedly came to light.

In it, she revealed that she had been lashed into a rage by the incessant "taunts" of Annie LeRoi, who had humiliated her by flirting openly with Halloran in her presence. On the night of Friday, October 16, she went to LeRoi's house, armed with a .25-caliber handgun. Both her former roommates had retired for the night. Sneaking in through the unlocked front door, she "sat down on the couch in the semidark living room and soon fell asleep clutching the gun."

Awakening in the early morning, she could hear Sammy in the bathroom. Determined to carry out her mission, she tiptoed past the bathroom, stepped into Annie's bedroom, and shot her in the head. As she turned to hurry away, Sammy burst from the bathroom, saw the gun, and snatched it away. Ruth tried to grab it back. As they grappled, Sammy fired, shooting Ruth in the left hand. "We fell to the floor," Ruth recounted, "struggled, and I finally got the gun and in my wild state I shot her in the head."

After dragging Sammy's body into the bathroom and cleaning the blood from the hallway, Ruth went out to the garage, dragged a large steamer trunk into the house, and wrestled LeRoi's corpse into it. She then went to the office, put in a full day's work, and made a brief stop at her own apartment to feed her cat before returning to the bungalow. When she attempted to stuff Sammy's body into the trunk, however, she found that it "was too heavy and her body was stiff." Fetching two kitchen knives, she cut up the body "into portions I could lift." Eventually, she managed to cram most of Sammy's corpse into a smaller trunk, though not all of it would fit, so she packed a piece of lower torso into a suitcase.

Following a three-week trial that began in mid-January 1932, Ruth was convicted of first-degree murder and sentenced to be hanged. Less than a week before her scheduled execution, however, Arizona authorities—responding to an outpouring of support from political leaders, clergymen, and ordinary citizens who believed she was mentally ill—agreed to a sanity hearing, at the climax of which Ruth was judged insane and committed to the Arizona State Asylum for the Insane.

After multiple escapes from the asylum across two decades, she absconded a final time in October 1963. Ending up in the San Francisco Bay area, she assumed a new identity—Marian Lane—and found employment as a live-in housekeeper in a mansion owned by an elderly woman. She remained at large for almost seven years before the law caught up with her. Extradited to Arizona, she was judged sane by medical examiners and consigned to the state penitentiary, where she remained until late 1971. Upon her release, she returned to California where, under her identity as Marian Lane, "Infamous 1930's 'Trunk Murderess'" (as the *New York Times* called her in its obituary), she lived quietly until her death in October 1998 at the age of ninety-three.

# #43 RACIST ANTI-HAWAIIAN CARTOON

## The Massie Affair

**(1931–1932)**

*The flagrantly racist coverage of the Massie case created an uproar in Hawai'i—and led to the murder of an innocent, falsely accused man.*

Known as the Hawaiian counterpart of the infamous Scottsboro case—in which nine Black teenaged boys were falsely accused of raping two white women on a train in Alabama in March 1931—the so-called Massie Affair began in September of that same year. On the evening of Saturday, September 12, Thalia Massie—a heavy-drinking, high-living twenty-year-old with a reputation for brazen behavior around men—visited a popular Waikiki nightclub with her husband, Tommie, a young naval officer assigned to a submarine squadron in Pearl Harbor. Left alone while Tommie hung out with his buddies, Thalia, bored and angry, drifted upstairs, where she managed to get into a nasty altercation with a drunken naval lieutenant who called her an insulting name. Shortly afterward—sometime around midnight—Thalia, by then in a highly inebriated state, left the nightspot on her own and proceeded by foot toward the nearby beach.

A few minutes before 1:00 a.m., two couples driving to a restaurant for a late-night snack were flagged down by a frantic young woman, her face badly bruised. Giving her name as Thalia Massie, she told them that she had been attacked by "five or six Hawaiian boys" who had pulled up behind her as she was walking home, dragged her into their car, punched her in the mouth, then drove her to "a clump of trees" and dumped her out before speeding away. She assured them that she had not been sexually assaulted and asked to be driven home.

Not long after she was dropped off, Tommie called home to check on Thalia's whereabouts. "Come home," she cried. "Something awful has happened." By the time he arrived a few minutes later, Thalia's story had changed. Sobbing, she now claimed that she had not only been "kidnapped and beaten

by a gang of Hawaiians" but dragged into some bushes and "violently raped six or seven times."

Tommie immediately phoned the police. Questioned by detectives, Thalia repeated the story of her rape. Beyond identifying her assailants as "Hawaiian," however, she could provide few details. In the dark of the moonless night, she had not been able to make out the faces of the men. When asked about the car, she replied that she believed it was a black "old-model" Ford with a ripped cloth top.

By the time Thalia finished her story, police already had their suspects in mind. About ninety minutes earlier, at 12:45 a.m., a married couple named Peeples had nearly gotten into a collision with a carload of young men. Both vehicles screeched to a halt, angry words flew, and one of the young men—a prizefighter named Joe Kahahawai—burst from his car shouting threats at the couple. A scuffle ensued between Kahahawai and Mrs. Peeples, a tall, solidly built Hawaiian woman. Before their fight could escalate, the two were separated and the cars sped off in different directions, though not before Mrs. Peeples wrote down the license plate number of the other vehicle. She then ordered her husband to drive to police headquarters, where she reported the assault.

Assuming that Thalia's assailants and the rowdies who had tussled with the Peeples were one and the same, the police quickly tracked down the owner of the car, a Japanese woman named Haruyo Ida. Miss Ida, they learned, had loaned the car to her brother Horace, who had driven it to a luau with four of his buddies: Joe Kahahawai, Benny Ahakuelo, David Takai, and Henry Chang. Under interrogation, Horace and the others admitted that they were the ones who had engaged in the tiff with Mrs. Peeples but adamantly denied any involvement in the attack on Thalia Massie.

The five suspects had an array of facts in their favor: airtight alibis as to their where-abouts at the time of the attack and a parade of corroborating witnesses; Thalia's insis-tence that all the assailants were Hawaiian, whereas Ida and Takai were Japanese; her description of their car as a black Model T with a tear in its top, whereas the Ida's vehi-cle was a new, light-tan Model A, its cloth roof perfectly intact. Several physicians who examined Thalia, moreover, found no evi-dence that she had been raped.

None of these factors, however, kept the local tabloids from denouncing the five sus-pects as a "gang of fiends" who had kidnapped and repeatedly ravished a young "white woman of refinement and culture." The press demanded swift punishment for the five "dark-skinned brutes."

They were brought to trial in November 1931. The prosecution did its best to portray the defendants as a vicious gang of "lust-sodden beasts" who had horribly violated the inno-cent victim. With no corroborating evidence beyond Thalia's highly dubious testimony, however, the case against the five young men was easily dismantled by the defense. After deliberating for more than ninety-seven hours, the mixed-race jury declared them-selves deadlocked and the defendants were released pending retrial.

The outcome raised racial tensions on the islands to a fever pitch. Among the non-white population, there was little doubt that Ida and the others were being framed for a rape they didn't commit—indeed, that might not have happened at all. Most white people, on the other hand, were infuriated by the jury's failure to arrive at a verdict against the five "depraved mongrels." Lashed into a frenzy by

*The domineering and unabashedly racist Grace Fortescue, with her three fellow defendants in the notorious "Massie Affair," managed to get away with murder, thanks in part to the efforts of legendary defense attorney Clarence Darrow.*

the racist press, a group of sailors abducted Horace Ida at gunpoint, drove him to a remote area, and subjected him to a savage assault with fists, belts, and gun butts.

Worse was still to come. Determined to vindicate her daughter's good name, Thalia's domineering mother, Grace Fortescue, decided to take matters into her own hands. Convinced that the only way to ensure a conviction was to wrest a confession from one of the accused, she enlisted Tommie and two other navy men in a plot to abduct Joe Kahahawai. On January 8, 1932, he was lured into a car and driven to Fortescue's home, where—after threatening to kill him unless he confessed—one of the sailors shot him dead with a bullet in the chest.

After wrapping the bloody corpse in a bedsheet and loading it onto the back seat of their automobile, Fortescue, Tommie, and Edward Lord headed toward Hanauma Bay, intending to dump the body off a promontory called Koko Head into the surging waters below. En route, however, they were apprehended by police who had been alerted by Kahahawai's cousin Eddie, a witness to the abduction.

The Massie case, until then a local affair, exploded onto the front pages of newspapers around the country. Far from displaying remorse, Fortescue expressed unalloyed pride in having avenged her daughter's shame. Though Fortescue herself couldn't afford his services, her high-society friends chipped in to retain the greatest defense attorney of the day, Clarence Darrow. A lifelong champion of progressive causes, the seventy-four-year-old legend was in desperate financial straits. Much to the dismay of his admirers, the man who had only recently been involved in the defense of the Scottsboro Boys now agreed to represent four racist vigilantes.

During the April 1932 trial, Darrow argued that Joe Kahahawai's murder was justified under the "unwritten law"—the belief that a husband has the right to kill a man who has assaulted his wife. The jury was not convinced. Fortescue and her three codefendants were found guilty of manslaughter, a verdict that carried a mandatory ten-year sentence.

Justice would not be served. Bowing to political pressure from the mainland, Territorial Governor Lawrence Judd commuted the sentences from ten years to one hour, which the four defendants spent in his office—drinking champagne, by some accounts. Four days later, they boarded an ocean liner for San Francisco, where they were greeted like Hollywood celebrities.

# #44 HAUPTMANN'S LADDER

## The Lindbergh Baby Kidnapping

**(1932)**

*The fate of alleged Lindbergh baby kidnapper Bruno Richard Hauptmann was sealed when an expert "wood technologist" testified that the homemade ladder used in the crime was partially constructed from a floor plank in Hauptmann's attic.*

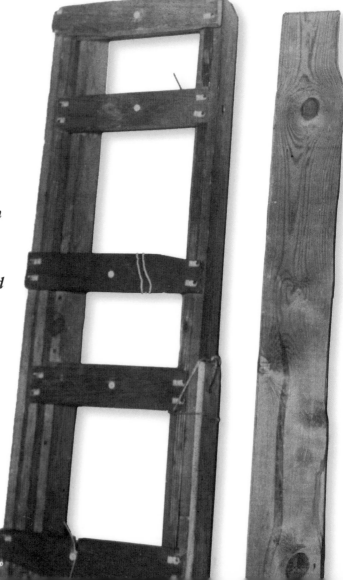

On the evening of Saturday, February 27, 1932, the twenty-month-old son of Charles Lindbergh—whose epic 1927 transatlantic flight had turned him into the world's most famous human being—was stolen from his crib in the family's East Amwell, New Jersey, home. Police searching the property found the crude homemade ladder used by the kidnapper to climb to the baby's second-story bedroom window and carry him away. The baby's corpse, his tiny skull fractured, would later be uncovered in a thicket a few miles away.

Two years passed before a suspect was arrested: a German-born carpenter, Bruno Richard Hauptmann. In the attic of his Bronx home, investigators found that a portion of pine board was missing from the flooring. Summoned by the police, wood expert Arthur Koehler easily determined that one of the side rails of the kidnap ladder was a perfect match for the missing piece. Police also found $14,000 hidden in Hauptmann's garage, with serial numbers that matched those of the ransom money Lindbergh paid. On a closet wall, they discovered the penciled phone number of Dr. John Condon, an ex-schoolteacher who had served as an intermediary between Lindbergh and the kidnapper.

To the jury that convicted Hauptmann, the evidence against him was overwhelming. In addition to the wood from his attic floor that had been used to construct the kidnap ladder and the cache of ransom money found in his garage, eyewitnesses testified that they had seen him prowling around the Lindbergh estate in the days before the kidnapping.

Experts determined that the handwriting on the ransom note bore unmistakable similarities to Hauptmann's. Misspellings in the note—"ouer" instead of "our," for example—were also characteristic of the German-born Hauptmann's writing. What's more he had quit his job as a carpenter immediately after the ransom was paid and gone on a shopping spree, purchasing a fancy radio, expensive clothing, and new furniture.

An investigation into his background revealed that he had spent five years in a German prison for robbery and had once used a homemade ladder to burglarize a home.

Over the decades, however, questions have been raised about Hauptmann's guilt. More than a dozen books have been written, arguing that the evidence against him was rigged, tampered with, or wholly fabricated, and proposing that other individuals were responsible for the baby's death, including the far-fetched conjecture that Lindbergh himself (according to one) killed his own son because the child was afflicted with various deformities. It seems likely that the Lindbergh baby kidnapping will remain, as the title of one book puts it, a "case that never dies."

Koehler's testimony at Hauptmann's trial in early 1935 was key to the defendant's conviction and execution—the final nail in the coffin of the man found guilty of what one commentator called "the most revolting crime of the century." He was electrocuted on April 3, 1936.

# #45 POSTCARD OF "OLD SPARKY," THE OHIO ELECTRIC CHAIR

## "The Blonde Borgia"

**(1933–1937)**
*Serial killer Anna Marie Hahn earned a dubious distinction in Ohio criminal history: The first woman ever to die in the state's electric chair.*

Death Chamber, Ohio Penitentiary, Columbus, O.

In the summer of 1936, George Heis, a sixty-three-year-old bachelor living in Cincinnati, Ohio, fell under the seductive spell of a vivacious blonde woman half his age. Claiming to be a divorcée (though in fact she was married), she visited him frequently at his home over the following months, often in the nurse's uniform she had taken to wearing (though she had no training as a nurse). Following the old saw that the way to a man's heart is through his stomach, she indulged him with the German delicacies she had learned to cook as a girl growing up in Bavaria, as well as with other more intimate pleasures. As his infatuation grew, he began to talk of marriage and willingly loaned her the money she began to request with increasing frequency, a sum that eventually amounted to $2,000 (roughly equivalent to $40,000 today).

About four months into their relationship, Heis asked that the money be repaid, and an odd thing happened. "Every time she prepared food for him in the fall of 1936," writes one historian, "he became ill with diarrhea and agonizing stomach pains." When he began to have trouble walking, he confided to an acquaintance that he feared his paramour might be poisoning him. Not long after, during one of her visits, she brought him a mug of beer. As it sat on the table, some houseflies landed on the rim, sampled some of the brew, and immediately fell dead. Heis ordered his lover out of his house and told her never to return.

Though he had lost a significant amount of money, Heis was a lucky man—the only one to survive the fatal ministrations of the serial killer who would come to be called the "Blonde Borgia": Anna Marie Hahn.

Born Anna Marie Filser in Bavaria in 1906, and the youngest of twelve children, she was a handful from an early age. Impregnated at nineteen—reportedly by a married physician—

she was shipped off to America by her scandalized parents and settled in Cincinnati, where she resided with distant relatives before striking out on her own. She met and married a mousy telegraph operator, Philip Hahn, whose wages were not large enough to bankroll his new wife's gambling habit.

It wasn't long before she hit on the deadly scam that would earn her both a sizable income and everlasting notoriety. Despite her utter lack of professional qualifications, she offered her services as a practical nurse to elderly widowers and bachelors in the German community. Between 1933 and 1937, she wormed her way into the affections of a string of old men, at least five of whom suffered agonizing deaths from poisoning after signing over their assets to her.

She was finally caught when her last victim died horribly in a Colorado hotel room while on what he supposed was his honeymoon with his sweetheart. After a postmortem revealed lethal amounts of arsenic in his stomach, Cincinnati authorities exhumed the bodies of two other men who had died in her care and found that they, too, had been poisoned.

After a four-week trial in the fall of 1937, the Blonde Borgia was convicted of first-degree murder. Since no woman had ever been sent to the electric chair in Ohio, Judge Charles Steele Bell felt certain that Hahn would escape the death penalty. But the jury returned a guilty verdict "with no recommendation of mercy," meaning that Bell had no choice but to impose the ultimate punishment.

While awaiting her date with "Old Sparky," Hahn composed a lengthy, self-pitying confession in which, while admitting to the murder of four of her elderly male clients, she denied responsibility for the other ten poisonings she was suspected of. She was executed on December 7, 1938.

# #46 JOHN DILLINGER'S WOODEN GUN

## The Crown Point Escape

**(1934)**

*Already a legendary figure, John Dillinger burnished his daredevil reputation with one of the most audacious escapes in the annals of US crime using a fake gun like this one.*

Of all the large-than-life gangsters that dominated the headlines in the 1930s—"Pretty Boy" Floyd, "Machine Gun" Kelly, "Mad Dog" Coll, "Baby Face" Nelson—the most celebrated was the dashing John Dillinger. He was born in Indianapolis in 1903. Biographical accounts of his early years differ, some describing him as a high-spirited teen with a taste for reckless but essentially harmless pranks, others as a hard-bitten punk who ran with a street gang that committed at least one brutal rape of an underage girl. Whatever the case, it is certain that in 1923, he barely escaped arrest after stealing a car and, the following year, committed an armed robbery that put him behind bars for nearly a decade.

Within weeks of his parole in 1933, he embarked on the yearlong bank-robbing spree that would turn him into a Depression-era legend. Nicknamed "Jackrabbit" for his swashbuckling way of vaulting over counters, he was viewed by millions of hard-hit Americans as a latter-day Robin Hood, a bandit who preyed only on the rich. To the FBI, on the other hand, he was Public Enemy Number One.

However, Dillinger was not the remorseless killer that J. Edgar Hoover made him out to be. During a getaway in early 1934, he and a policeman named O'Malley exchanged a fusillade of gun shots. Though hit four times in the chest, Dillinger was saved by a bulletproof vest he had stolen during an audacious raid on an Indiana police station. O'Malley took eight rounds from Dillinger's submachine gun and died on the spot. It was the first and only time Dillinger killed a man.

Not long afterward, while holed up in Tucson, Arizona, Dillinger was tracked down and arrested by local police. Extradited to Indiana, he was locked up in a supposedly "escape-proof" jail, where he used his spare time to fashion a fake handgun, whittling a section of washboard into the rough form of a pistol, then blackening it with shoe polish. On March 3, 1934, he pulled off the most daring escapade in his legendary career. Brandishing the wooden gun, he forced his jailers to open his cell, grabbed two machine guns, then locked up the guards and fled in the sheriff's car.

Though now pursued by a special FBI task force, Dillinger resumed his lawless spree, robbing banks throughout the Midwest over the next few months. His brief, storied career came to a suitably spectacular end. In July 1934, Dillinger and his latest girlfriend, a waitress named Polly Hamilton, moved into the Chicago apartment of an acquaintance, Anna Sage, a Romanian-born brothel owner. Eager to cash in on the reward for Dillinger's capture—and hoping to avoid deportation by cooperating with the Feds—Sage contacted the authorities and informed them that she, Hamilton, and Dillinger would be attending the movies the following evening, Sunday, July 22. At 10:30 p.m. that night, as the trio left the Biograph Theater, FBI agents drew their revolvers and closed in. Grabbing a gun from his pocket, Dillinger ran for an alley but was cut down in a hail of bullets and died at the scene.

# #47 DEATH MASK OF "MAD BUTCHER" VICTIM

## "The Cleveland Torso Killer"

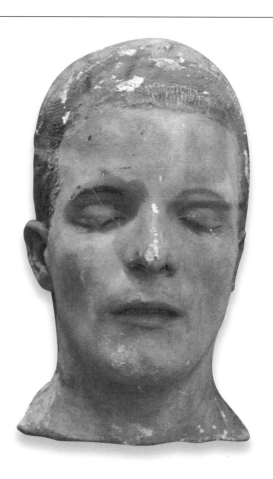

**(1935–1938)**

*Despite the involvement of legendary lawman Eliot Ness, the serial sex-butcher preying on Cleveland vagrants remains unidentified.*

A few years after he and his team of "Untouchables" helped bring down Al Capone's gangland empire, Eliot Ness became involved in one of the most notorious unsolved murder cases in American history.

In the years of the Great Depression, Kingsbury Run—a weed-choked, garbage-strewn ravine on the east side of Cleveland—was the site of a sprawling shantytown inhabited by transients and the city's dispossessed. On September 23, 1935, two boys were roaming the area when they stumbled upon a headless and castrated male corpse, naked except for a pair of black socks. When the police arrived, they discovered a second body nearby, butchered in the same way. Postmortem examinations suggested that the men had been decapitated—and probably emasculated—while still alive. While the older of the two was never identified, fingerprints showed that the younger victim was twenty-eight-year-old Edward Andrassy, a "snotty punk" (as one cop described him) with a long rap sheet of petty arrests. After hearing rumors that he had stabbed an Italian man while shooting craps in an alley, police surmised that Andrassy and his companion had fallen victim to an Italian gang out for vengeance.

They were obliged to reassess a few months later when, on January 26, 1936, the dismembered remains of a forty-one-year-old sex worker were found in an alley, stuffed inside a bushel basket. The following June, two boys cutting through Kingsbury Run on their way to go fishing stumbled upon a man's decapitated head rolled up in a pair of pants. The next morning, the body to which it belonged was found a quarter mile away by a pair of railroad workers. The badly decomposed head and matching body of another male victim were discovered the next month, on July 22. In early September, a vagrant waiting to hop one of freight trains that ran through Kingsbury Run spotted the bisected halves of a human torso floating in a stagnant pond. The missing body parts—which included the head, arms, and genitals—were never found.

With the city in an uproar over the atrocities, Eliot Ness—who had left Chicago the previous year to become Cleveland's Safety Director—found himself under enormous pressure to track down the maniac, alternately dubbed the "Cleveland Torso Killer" and the "Mad Butcher of Kingsbury Run." His efforts, however, along with those of a dozen full-time detectives, were fruitless. Between February 1937 and August 1938, the hacked-up remains of six more anonymous victims—four female and two male—turned up, bringing the official total to twelve.

Various theories have been put forth as to the identity of the "Mad Butcher." Ness himself believed that he was an alcoholic physician named Frank Sweeney, who had honed his dismemberment skills while performing amputations as a medic during World War I, failed two polygraph tests while under interrogation by Ness, and was ultimately committed to a veteran's hospital. Some are of the opinion that the killer absconded from Cleveland and made his way to California where he claimed at least one more victim: Elizabeth Short, the "Black Dahlia."

# #48 HAND-CARVED WOODEN BOX MADE BY ROBERT IRWIN

## "The Mad Sculptor"

**(1937)**

*During his incarcerations in various mental institutions, Robert Irwin would earn cash by selling small portrait busts and other objects to staff members. One was this wooden box, decorated with bas-relief carvings of a nude Ronnie Gedeon, who would gain posthumous notoriety as a victim of the "Mad Sculptor."*

Robert Irwin was born in 1907 to fanatically devout parents. His earliest memories were of being dragged to frenzied tent meetings where members of the church spoke in tongues and underwent hysterical healings. He was only three when his father deserted the family, plunging them into a state of permanent hardship. To support her brood—Bob, his two brothers, and a little girl who would die at age two of whooping cough—Mrs. Irwin worked at assorted jobs, from scrubwoman to sweatshop seamstress, rarely earning more than three dollars a day. Toys being an unaffordable luxury, Bob's only plaything was the bathroom soap. Molding it into various shapes, he discovered a gift for sculpting.

At eighteen, unemployed and a burden on his mother, he had himself voluntarily admitted to a juvenile home in the hopes of learning a trade. He befriended a sympathetic attendant there who encouraged his artistic pursuits by providing him with modeling clay.

Fifteen months later, he embarked on a wandering life, working briefly in an art studio in Hollywood and studying with the eminent sculptor Lorado Taft in Chicago before ending up in New York City in 1930 at the age of twenty-three. There he found temporary employment as a clerk in an art supply shop, as an assistant to the master sculptor Alexander Ettl, and as a taxidermist's helper.

In early 1931, troubled with increasingly violent fantasies, he had himself committed to the psychiatric ward of Kings County Hospital in Brooklyn, explaining to the supervising physician that he was afraid he "would kill somebody so I would be hung." After a three-week incarceration, he was sent to a convalescent home in White Plains where he remained until the spring of 1932. He returned to Manhattan and found a job as a dishwasher. In October 1932, he rented a spare room in the Upper East Side flat of a family named Gedeon.

Four members of the family inhabited the fourth-floor walk-up: the fiftyish father, Joseph Gedeon, a Hungarian émigré who ran a little upholstery shop; his wife, Mary; an older daughter named Ethel, a "placid brunette with impeccable morals"; and a younger, party-girl daughter, Veronica. A stunning eighteen-year-old, Ronnie, as she was known, worked as an "artist's model," posing nude for the members of a seedy amateur camera club. She also modeled regularly for pulp detective magazines.

Bob Irwin had been living in their overcrowded flat for only a couple of days when—"in order to bottle up his sexual energies for higher purposes" (as he later explained)—he locked himself in the bathroom, took a brand-new razor blade to his penis and tried to slice it off.

Even after his admission to the Bellevue psychiatric ward, Irwin was intent on having his penis amputated, begging several of the surgical interns to perform the operation. He would remain at Bellevue for five months before committing himself voluntarily to the Rockland State Hospital for the insane. Irwin remained there until May 1934, when he returned to New York City and found work at various odd jobs. He moved back in with the Gedeons. Within days, he had become fixated on the older daughter, the sweet-natured and virtuous Ethel.

At first, she responded warmly to Irwin's overtures. Eventually, however, she grew weary of him. Dejected by her growing indifference—and by his failure to find fulfilling work—Irwin had himself recommitted to Rockland.

Upon his discharge in September 1936 as "improved," Bob applied for admission to the

Theological School of St. Lawrence in Canton, New York. He remained there for six months. By the spring of 1937, however, his behavior had become sufficiently erratic that he was expelled from the school. Taking a bus to New York City, he showed up at the Gedeons' flat on the morning of Good Friday, only to learn that there was no vacancy, the spare room having been rented to an Englishman named Frank Byrnes. Later that day, Bob found a furnished room a few blocks away.

Embroiled in increasingly bitter arguments with his wife, Mary, over their younger daughter's untrammeled behavior, Joseph Gedeon had moved out of the family flat earlier that year, taking up residence in a room behind his upholstery store. In a conciliatory gesture, Mary had invited him for Easter dinner. They were to be joined by their older daughter, Ethel, now married and living with her husband in the suburbs.

It was Joseph who discovered the massacre. Arriving at noon, he entered the unlocked flat and found Ronnie's nude and lifeless body sprawled on her mattress. Mary's corpse was stuffed beneath the bed. Their boarder, Frank Byrnes, lay dead in the next room, killed in his sleep by multiple stab wounds to the head. Autopsies conducted later that day by the city's chief medical examiner established that both women had been manually strangled, while Byrnes's face and skull had been punctured fifteen times with a pointed implement, evidently an ice pick.

Suspicion initially fell on Joseph, who admitted that he despised his wife and "had nothing but contempt for his daughter Ronnie." Hauled to the station house, he was grilled for thirty-three hours straight, while the tabloids rushed to announce that the cops had found their killer. But detectives were focusing on a different lead. In their search of the murder scene, detectives had found a sculpted bar of Castile soap on the bedroom floor, evidently carved by the killer as he patiently waited for his final victim to come

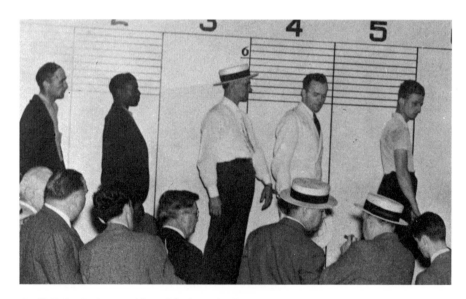

*A spiffy Robert Irwin, second from right, in a police lineup.*

home. Questioning Ethel about the family's boarders, the investigators heard the name of the young sculptor Bobby Irwin. Their suspicions were heightened by several references to Irwin in Ronnie's diary. "I think he is out of his head," she had written in one entry. "I am afraid of B.," she confided in another. Tracking his path back to Canton, detectives discovered Irwin's own diary, left in the rooming house where he had lived while at the theological school. One entry left little doubt that Irwin was the culprit: "God, how I adore Ethel. Perfection. That's what she is. Absolute perfection. . . . If only Ronnie and her mother hadn't interfered. It has made a shipwreck out of me. . . . How I hate Ronnie and her mother for what they have done to me."

America's most wanted criminal would remain at large for three months. On June 26, 1937, a phone call came into the newsroom of the *Chicago Herald and Examiner*. Identifying himself as Robert Irwin, the caller offered to surrender himself to the paper for a suitable price. A deal was struck. After signing a contract for five thousand dollars, Irwin was spirited off to a hotel where, for the next twenty-four hours, he was kept incommunicado while he dictated a lengthy confession to the city editor, John Dienhart, who then arranged for Irwin's surrender.

Irwin admitted that he first considered suicide when he returned to Manhattan, but instead "I made up my mind to kill Ethel and go to the chair for it." He then headed for the Gedeons' apartment, arriving around 9:00 p.m. When Mary, who was out, finally arrived home, Irwin sat with her in the kitchen, announcing that he intended to stay until he saw Ethel. After repeatedly informing him that Ethel was married and no longer living there, Mary angrily demanded that he leave. Flying into a rage, Irwin leapt at her, strangled her to death, and shoved her corpse under a bed. He then waited for Ronnie, who returned from a date at around 3:00 a.m. When she emerged from the bathroom, Irwin "grabbed her by the throat," dragged her onto the bed, and strangled her.

Though both murders occurred only a few feet from the second bedroom, Frank Byrnes, the boarder, never stirred, being almost completely deaf. In a frenzy of bloodlust, Irwin dispatched the sleeping Englishman with his ice pick, then calmly left the apartment.

Convicted on three counts of second-degree murder, Irwin was sentenced to life in Sing Sing, where he was examined by prison psychiatrists who promptly ruled that he was insane. On December 10, 1938, he was transferred to Dannemora State Hospital. He remained institutionalized for the rest of his life, dying of cancer in 1975 in the Matteawan State Hospital for the Criminally Insane.

# #49 SHOES BELONGING TO MADELINE EVERETT, MELBA MARIE EVERETT & JEANETTE STEPHENS

## The "Babes of Inglewood" Murders

**(1937)**

*After perpetrating one of the most appalling sex crimes in US history, Albert Dyer carefully lined up his little victims' shoes because he "wanted whoever found them to think the children were orderly to the last."*

In the spring and summer months of 1937, the nation seemed to be plagued with an epidemic of sex crimes against children. Between March and April of that year, three little girls between the ages of four and nine were the victims of savage rape-murders in New York City. A few months later—during the "Summer of Perverts," as one journalist dubbed it—a crime of singular atrocity took place on the opposite coast.

It happened in Centinela Park, a forty-acre urban oasis in the city of Inglewood, about twelve miles southwest of Los Angles. On the morning of Saturday, June 26, three girls—the Everett sisters, Melba Marie and Madeline, seven and nine respectively, and their best friend and next-door neighbor, eight-year-old Jeanette Stephens—arrived for a picnic. A few hours later, a witness saw them going off with a "dark-haired, unshaven man in his late twenties, wearing a tan work shirt and dungaree trousers."

When the girls failed to return home that evening, their frantic parents notified the police. By the following day, more than five hundred searchers were scouring the countryside for the missing children. On Monday afternoon the bodies were found in a gully thick with undergrowth.

All three lay facedown, strangled with lengths of cord still tightly wound around their necks. They were half naked, their skirts having been pushed above their waists. It was clear to investigators that they had been raped. Oddly, their shoes were lined up in a precise, almost ritualistic fashion not far from their bodies.

Dozens of "known degenerates" were brought in for questioning. Stymied in their search, investigators called on a man who had worked as a consulting psychiatrist for the LAPD, Dr. J. Paul de River. After viewing the ravaged corpses of the victims and examining the crime scene, de River submitted a report that is now considered one of the earliest examples of criminal profiling. The killer, he surmised, was a sadistic pedophile in his twenties "who might have been arrested before for annoying children." In all probability, he was a "very meticulous" person who, having "expressed [his] sadism," was "now remorseful." The crime itself was committed, "not on sudden impulse but as a deliberately planned affair." It was de River's opinion that the slayer "had obtained the confidence of these little girls. I believe they knew the man and trusted him."

A few days later, after his increasingly erratic behavior drew renewed attention from the police, Albert Dyer was arrested. Brought to Los Angeles for a relentless grilling, he finally broke down and spilled out a confession that, on several key points, confirmed de River's speculations.

Despite a seemingly satisfactory sex life with his wife of two years, Dyer had become increasingly obsessed with the thought of sex with little girls. After scouting out a remote ravine in the parkland, he lured his victims to the spot by promising to show them how to trap rabbits. He had then set upon them, strangling, raping, and sodomizing each in turn. Afterward, he "arranged their shoes neatly, because he wanted whoever found them to think the children had been orderly to the last."

Examined by psychiatrists for both the prosecution and defense, Dyer was deemed "a low-grade moron and sadistic degenerate" but legally sane. Tried in August 1937, he was found guilty of three counts of first-degree murder. In September 1938, he was hanged in San Quentin.

# #50 LEONARDA CIANCIULLI'S MUGSHOT

## "The Soap-Maker of Correggio"

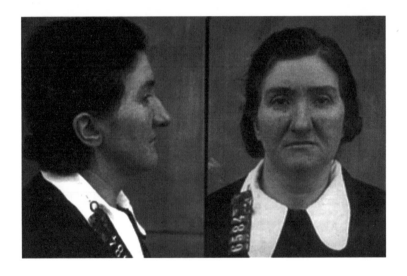

**(1939–1940)**

*Murderabilia from Leonarda Cianciulli*
*is extremely rare, but her legend has*
*inspired artists for going on a century.*

The cannibal witch who boils her victims in a cauldron is one of the most nightmarish figures in folklore. During a nine-month span between 1939 and 1940, that nightmare came to life in the Italian village of Correggio.

Leonarda Cianciulli was a forty-six-year-old shop owner who had moved to Correggio with her husband, Raffaele, nine years earlier. Unstable from an early age (she attempted suicide several times in her twenties and once, in an ecstatic frenzy, pulled out several of her own teeth as an offering to the Madonna), Cianciulli had endured a series of tragedies during her marriage. Of her seventeen pregnancies, three had ended with miscarriages. Ten others had produced children who died before reaching their maturity. To the intensely superstitious Cianciulli, their fates were the grim fulfillment of a prophecy she had received from a palm reader in her youth: that she would marry young and have many children, but all of them would perish early.

Of her four surviving offspring, her favorite was her conscription-age son, Giuseppe. Knowing that he would be in harm's way when Italy, allied with Germany, entered the war in 1939, she became convinced that the only way to protect his life was to sacrifice three people in his stead.

To supplement her shopkeeping income, Cianciulli did some fortune-telling on the side. One of her clients was a middle-aged spinster named Faustina Setti. Convinced by Cianciulli that a husband awaited her in the town of Pola, Setti packed up her possessions and bid farewell to her family, neighbors, and friends. On the day of her planned departure, she went to say goodbye to Cianciulli. As she confessed in a memoir, Cianciulli drugged Setti with an "elixir," then struck her with an axe, nearly decapitating her. After cutting up and disposing of the body, she combined the coagulated blood with flour, sugar, chocolate, milk, and eggs and baked the ingredients into "crunchy tea cakes" that she served to visitors.

Victim number two was a fifty-five-year-old widow, Francesca Soavi, who, left penniless upon the death of her husband, had sought Cianciulli's counsel. Cianciulli proclaimed that Soavi could find employment at a girls' school in Piacenza. On September 5, 1940, having made all the arrangements for her move, she paid a farewell visit to Cianciulli who, after treating her to some spiked wine, dispatched her with her axe and rendered her into teacakes.

That same month, Cianciulli conducted her third and final sacrifice. The victim was a fifty-five-year-old former opera singer, Virginia Cacioppo, who had fallen on hard times. Cianciulli employed her otherworldly powers to secure her a secretarial job in Florence. On the last day of September, Cacioppo went to say goodbye to her fortune-telling friend and, as Cianciulli wrote, "ended up in the pot, like the other [two . . .]"

Cacioppo's sudden disappearance aroused the suspicions of her sister-in-law, who had last seen the missing woman entering Cianciulli's house. She alerted the police who, paying a visit to the murderess, found ample evidence of her crimes, including articles of her victims' clothing and the kitchen equipment she had used to cut them up and cook them.

She was sentenced to thirty years in prison and an additional three in a women's criminal asylum, where she died of cerebral apoplexy at age seventy-seven in October 1970.

# #51 GEORGE METESKY PIPE BOMB

## The "Mad Bomber"

**(1940–1956)**
*A disgruntled former employee of a public utilities company kept New Yorkers on edge for years, until a pioneering piece of criminal profiling brought his reign of terror to an end.*

Between 1940 and 1956 (with a temporary "truce" during the war years, declared as an act of personal "patriotism"), an unknown bomber planted at least thirty pipe bombs around Manhattan: in public buildings, movie theaters, railway stations, and the facilities of the Con Edison utilities company. Some of these devices failed to detonate, though more than twenty went off, severely injuring more than a dozen people. The bombs were accompanied by anonymous notes, composed of cut-and-pasted letters from various publications, in which the writer—who identified himself only by the initials "F. P."—ranted at and swore vengeance on Con Ed.

After years of fruitless search for the "Mad Bomber" (as the tabloids dubbed him), investigators decided to consult Dr. James A. Brussel, Assistant Commissioner of Mental Hygiene for the State of New York. After reviewing all the evidence, Brussel suggested that police focus their search on a paranoid, middle-aged Roman Catholic bachelor of medium build and Eastern European descent who lived with a brother or sister in a Connecticut city, hated his father, and bore a grudge against Con Ed. He was also likely to be meticulous in his personal habits.

"When you find him," the report famously concluded, "chances are he'll be wearing a double-breasted suit. Buttoned."

Not long afterward, thanks partly to Brussel's profile, police tracked down the perpetrator, a disgruntled former Con Ed employee named George Metesky who had suffered an on-the-job injury in 1931 that left him disabled and whose claims for workers' compensation had been denied. Just as Brussel had predicted, Metesky—whose cryptic signature "F. P." stood for "Fair Play"—was a fifty-four-year-old bachelor of Lithuanian stock who lived with two older sisters in Waterbury, Connecticut. He was a regular churchgoer, had not gotten along with his father, and experienced acute paranoia. Before being led away by the police, he changed into a carefully pressed pin-striped, double-breasted suit, which he made sure to button before leaving the house.

Brussel's contribution to the solution of the "Mad Bomber" case is widely acknowledged as a pioneering feat of criminal profiling, a stunning piece of psychological detective work that led to the creation of the FBI's celebrated Behavioral Science Unit and gave birth to a new pop culture archetype: the heroic, brilliantly analytical "Mind Hunter."

# #52 SUITCASES BELONGING TO MARCEL PETIOT'S VICTIMS

## "Le Docteur Satan"

**(1944)**

*Dozens of people desperate to escape Nazi-occupied France turned for help to self-professed Resistance member Dr. Marcel Petiot, unaware that they were placing their lives in the hands of a remorseless serial murderer.*

As a child, Marcel Petiot was distinguished by both his exceptional intelligence and unstable behavior. A sadist who enjoyed poking out the eyes of baby birds with a needle, he was repeatedly expelled from school for reasons ranging from mail theft to firing a pistol in his classroom. During the Great War, he did time at the front until a foot wound, possibly self-inflicted, sent him to an army hospital, where he began manifesting symptoms of what one doctor described as extreme "mental disequilibrium." He was in and out of mental asylums and psychiatric clinics for the remainder of the war.

Discharged in 1919, he decided to pursue a medical career, earning his degree two years later. He spent the next decade in the town of Villeneuve-sur-Yonne, where—even while operating a flourishing medical practice and making a successful run for mayor—he engaged in various criminal activities, ranging from petty theft to embezzlement to suspected murder. The same pattern recurred after he and his wife moved to Paris in 1931.

The full extent of his depravity, however, did not become known until the tail end of World War II. On March 11, 1944, firemen arrived at a townhouse owned by Petiot to investigate complaints of a foul-smelling smoke pouring from the chimney. Breaking into the unoccupied building, they descended into the basement where they were stunned to see a charred human hand protruding from a roaring coal stove. Looking around, they were assaulted by an even more horrific sight: a pile of arms, legs, skulls, rib cages, jawbones, and chunks of rotting flesh. Further investigation turned up a pit filled with quicklime and at least ten decomposed bodies in the garage.

Summoned to the scene, Petiot declared that he was a member of the Resistance and that the remains were those of Nazi occupiers and French collaborators. This explanation, however, failed to account for subsequent discoveries made by the police: nearly fifty suitcases packed with men's and women's clothing, shoes, and toiletry items. The truth, when it emerged, would make Petiot known to his countrymen as *le Docteur Satan*— "Dr. Satan."

Under the pretense of operating an "escape agency," Petiot had offered his services to people desperate to flee Nazi persecution, promising to smuggle them to safety for a hefty fee. When his "clients"—most of them wealthy Jews—showed up at his house bearing their most precious possessions, they received an injection, purportedly an immunization shot. In reality it was strychnine. Once the lethal injection had taken effect, Petiot would dismember their corpses and dispose of them in his basement crematorium. At least twenty-seven victims, and perhaps as many as sixty-three, met their ends in what one historian calls Petiot's "private death camp."

Arrested in October 1944 after eight months on the lam, Petiot was put on trial in March 1946. Throughout the proceedings, he continued to maintain that he was a hero of the Resistance who deserved a medal for eliminating dozens of traitors and Gestapo spies. The jury disagreed. He was found guilty, sentenced to the guillotine, and beheaded on May 6, 1946.

# #53 JOHN GEORGE HAIGH'S RUBBER GLOVES

## "The Acid Bath Murderer"

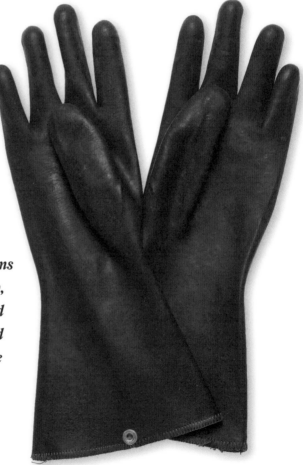

**(1944–1949)**

*Other serial murderers have claimed more victims than John George Haigh, but his diabolical method of corpse disposal earned him a special place in the annals of infamy.*

The tabloid nicknames of serial killers often derive from their signature murder methods: the Boston Strangler, the Axeman of New Orleans, the .44-Caliber Killer (as Son of Sam was initially called). In some cases, however—like the "Trunk Murderess," Winnie Ruth Judd—the names have to do with their favorite means of corpse disposal. Such was the case with the British psycho-killer, John George Haigh, aka the "Acid Bath Murderer."

Born in 1909, Haigh was raised in Yorkshire, England, by strict parents who were members of a fundamentalist sect known as the Plymouth Brethren. They regarded the modern world as a sinkhole of sin and did their best to keep their little boy isolated from all corrupting influences, including sports, socializing with peers, listening to the radio, and reading anything but the Bible. Paradoxically—or predictably—Haigh grew up to be an inveterate hedonist, with an unquenchable appetite for fast cars, fine food, and expensive clothing.

Unable to satisfy his taste for the finer things with his salary from legitimate jobs, he embarked on a second career as a small-time swindler. Arrested for fraud in October 1934, he did the first of several stints in prison. Upon his release in 1936, he eventually moved to London, where he befriended a young man named William McSwan, who offered him a job as chauffeur. The industrious Haigh quickly worked his way up to the position of manager. But he was soon back to his felonious ways.

It was during this stretch that Haigh dreamed up the scheme that would earn him lasting notoriety. Poring over some law books in the prison library, he acquired the notion that a murder could not be legally proved without a dead body, a misconception based on his flawed understanding of the term *corpus delicti* (which does not refer to a corpse, but to the body of evidence that shows a crime has been committed). He also read newspaper accounts of a French murderer, Georges-Alexandre Sarret, who dissolved the bodies of his victims in sulfuric acid.

By 1943, Haigh was back in London, where he set up a basement "workshop" equipped with a forty-gallon oil drum and several ten-gallon carboys of sulfuric acid. His first victim was his old pal, William McSwan, who was lured to Haigh's nightmarish cellar, bludgeoned to death, then reduced to fetid sludge and poured down the drain. Next to go were McSwan's parents. Employing his skills as a forger, Haigh managed to gain power of attorney over the McSwans' properties and

*The protective gear worn by Haigh.*

*Police remove the oil drum in which Haigh's victims were dissolved.*

was soon in possession of a considerable fortune, which he promptly squandered at the dog track.

Haigh then turned his psychopathic sights on a wealthy couple, Dr. Archibald Henderson and his wife, Rosalie. After dispatching and liquefying them in his basement, he once again forged documents that gave him access to his victims' estate.

In early 1949, he encountered his next victim, a wealthy, sixty-nine-year-old widow named Henrietta Helen Olivia Roberts Durand-Deacon. But when her disappearance was reported to the authorities, Haigh found himself under scrutiny. After intensive grilling by police—who had not only turned up Haigh's criminal record but learned that he had pawned some of Durand-Deacon's jewelry—the audacious con man made a startling confession: "Durand-Deacon no longer exists. I have destroyed her with acid," he declared. "How can you prove murder if there is no body?" In a later confession, he admitted to doing away with the Hendersons, the McSwans, and three other never-to-be-identified victims.

Haigh's smug belief that he had left no physical evidence of his atrocities was quickly shattered when investigators discovered a fetid pile of sludge in his backyard containing twenty-eight pounds of human fat, three human gallstones, eighteen fragments of human bone, portions of a human foot, and Durand-Deacon's undissolved dentures. The jury at his July 1949 trial needed just seventeen minutes to come back with a verdict of guilty. He was hanged the following month.

# #54 WILLIAM HEIRENS'S LIPSTICKED MESSAGE

## "The Lipstick Killer"

**(1945)**

*The famous cry for help that William Heirens scrawled at one of his crime scenes proved tragically prophetic when, one month later, he perpetrated an unspeakable crime.*

At around 1:00 p.m. on June 5, 1945, the nude body of a forty-three-year-old Chicago woman, Mrs. Josephine Ross, was discovered by her teenaged daughter, who had come home for lunch. Sprawled on a tumbled bed, Ross had been stabbed repeatedly in the face and neck, and her jugular vein had been severed. A red evening gown, secured with a nylon stocking, was wrapped around her head. Though the bedsheets were drenched in blood, there was none on her body. Bloody water in the half-filled bathtub indicated that her killer had washed the corpse clean.

Gruesome as it was, the slaying of Ross generated little press coverage. The situation was very different with another, strikingly similar murder that occurred six months later. On December 10, a maid at a residential hotel on Chicago's north side was horrified to discover the half-naked corpse of thirty-year-old stenographer Frances Brown draped with her head over the bathtub, her pajama top wrapped around her neck. When police removed the garment, they discovered a ten-inch bread knife shoved through the victim's throat. She had also been shot in the head and right arm. As in the Ross case, the killer had carefully washed the body.

Authorities quickly concluded that the Brown and Ross murders were the handiwork of the same perpetrator. What made the later crime so sensational, however, was the bizarre message left at the crime scene. Inscribed in red lipstick on the living room wall were the words:

**For heavens
Sake catch me
Before I kill more
I cannot control myself**

The "Lipstick Killer," as the tabloids dubbed him, committed his third, last, and most horrific crime a month later. Just after midnight on January 7, 1946, six-year-old Suzanne Degnan, daughter of a Chicago executive, was abducted from her first-floor apartment bedroom. A crudely misspelled ransom note demanding $20,000 in exchange for the child's safe return was left at the crime scene. It was a hollow offer. At around 7:00 p.m. that same day, police found Suzanne's severed head floating in a sewer catch basin not far from the Degnans' home. Other body parts were recovered from various sewers in the following hours.

Panic seized the city. A thousand temporary police officers were added to the force, assisting in the biggest manhunt in the city's history. Though the killer had spattered his ransom note with oil to obscure any fingerprints, the FBI experts managed to retrieve the clear print of a left pinkie finger. Six months later, on the evening of June 26, 1946, police received a call about a prowler in an apartment on Chicago's north side. Quickly arriving at the scene, Detective Tiffin P. Constant cornered the suspect. The young man aimed his gun at Constant, but his weapon was jammed. He hurled it at Constant's head, then flung himself onto the detective. As the two men grappled, an off-duty officer, Abner T. Cunningham—just returned from the beach and still in his swimming trunks—ran up, grabbed three flowerpots, and battered the suspect into unconsciousness.

Taken to Bridewell Hospital, the young man—"a husky six-footer," as the papers described him—was identified as William Heirens, a seventeen-year-old University of Chicago student who had a lengthy criminal record. He had been convicted of nearly two dozen burglaries before the age of fourteen and spent time in several homes for wayward boys. Searching his dorm room, police found two suitcases crammed with stolen goods: jewelry, watches, war bonds, and more, along with several handguns. What at first appeared to be a relatively minor burglary case became a nationwide sensation when police matched the fingerprint of Heirens's left little finger to the print recovered from the Degnan ransom note.

Strapped to his hospital bed, Heirens was subjected to a three-day interrogation that—according to certain accounts—included genital torture, vicious pummelings, and relentless grilling under a blazing spotlight. On the fourth day, he was injected with sodium pentothal. Under the effects of this "truth serum," he claimed that the crimes had been committed by an evil alter ego named George, who had also written the infamous lipstick message on Frances Brown's living room wall.

After learning that Heirens had first invented this alter ego after repeated viewings of his favorite movie, the 1941 version of *Dr. Jekyll and Mr. Hyde,* examining psychiatrists concluded that George was not a symptom of psychosis but a device that enabled Heirens to live with the conflict between his criminal compulsions and his "otherwise exemplary" behavior. He could maintain a sense of his own goodness while blaming his iniquitous actions on the make-believe George. Heirens, in short, was not legally insane.

To avoid the electric chair, Heirens confessed to all three slayings. Soon after being sentenced to three consecutive life terms, he recanted his confession and maintained his innocence for the rest of his life. Many supporters agreed that he was railroaded, pointing to another suspect—a drifter named Richard Russell Thomas with a long record of brutal crimes—as the likelier culprit. A model prisoner, Heirens became the first convict in Illinois to earn a degree from a four-year college. When he died in March 2012 at age eighty-three—more than sixty-five of those years spent behind bars—he was the fourth-longest-serving prisoner in US history.

# #55 H. C. WESTERMANN PRINT

## Nannie Doss, "The Giggling Granny"

**(1945–1955)**

*Few homicidal maniacs have projected a more jolly demeanor than Nannie Doss, who couldn't contain her girlish giggling as she confessed to an appalling string of murders.*

**D**ubbed the "Giggling Granny" because of her habit of chortling in amusement while discussing her crimes, Nannie Doss was born Nancy Hazle to a hardscrabble Alabama farm family in 1905. Her father was a harsh, demanding taskmaster. Forbidden from enjoying a social life, Nannie sought refuge in her mother's true romance magazines.

At the age of sixteen, while working at a linen factory, she met a young man named Charley Bragg and they soon married. Their troubled seven-year union produced four children, two of whom died mysteriously. The couple divorced in 1928, with Bragg being the only one of Nannie's five husbands to come out of their marriage alive.

A year later, she wed again, this time to Frank Harrelson, a handsome, hard-drinking factory hand she met through a "lonely hearts" ad. They remained married for sixteen years, during which time (as she later confessed) Nannie killed her newborn granddaughter with a hatpin to the brain and asphyxiated her two-year-old grandson after taking out a $500 life insurance policy on him. Her marriage to the womanizing Harrelson ended in September 1945 when she spiked his corn liquor with rat poison.

Two years later, she responded again to a "lonely hearts" ad, this one placed by another tomcatting alcoholic, Arlie Lanning. Two days after meeting in person, the couple tied the knot. Nannie played the role of devoted, churchgoing housewife. Her charade lasted three years, at which point she dispatched him with a poisoned bowl of stewed prunes.

When her house burned down shortly after Lanning's funeral, Nannie collected the insurance money and moved in with her mother-in-law, who died in her sleep not long after. Nannie then went to care for her sister, Dovie, who was bedridden with cancer and who, like the elderly Mrs. Lanning, died shortly after Nannie came to live with her.

The next to go was husband number four, a skirt-chasing ex-salesman named Richard Morton. She quickly grew tired of his compulsive philandering and did away with him three months after their wedding. During that time, Nannie also murdered her recently widowed mother, who had come to live with her.

One month after Morton was buried, the matronly forty-eight-year-old Nannie married her fifth husband, Samuel Doss. A Nazarene minister who frowned on his new wife's addiction to true romance magazines and TV soap operas, he kept such a tight grip on the household finances that Nannie left him and went back to Alabama. Only after he put her name on his bank account and made her the beneficiary of two life insurance policies did she consent to return. Shortly thereafter, she fed him a big slice of arsenic-laced prune cake that sent him to the hospital but failed to kill him. She finished off the job with a thermos of poisoned coffee as soon as he got back home.

His sudden death raised the suspicions of his doctor, who ordered an autopsy that revealed enough arsenic in Samuel's stomach to kill eighteen men.

Under arrest, Nannie cheerfully confessed to the murders of her four husbands, though she indignantly denied that she had killed them for profit. Her motive, she claimed, was love. "I was searching for the perfect mate, the real romance of life," she told interrogators. Of course, that didn't explain why she had also done away with two children, two grandchildren, her sister, her mother, and her mother-in-law.

Convicted of the murder of Samuel Doss at her 1955 trial, she was spared the electric chair because of her sex and sentenced to life imprisonment. She died of leukemia in June 1965.

# #56 CUT-AND-PASTE MESSAGE

## The Black Dahlia Murder

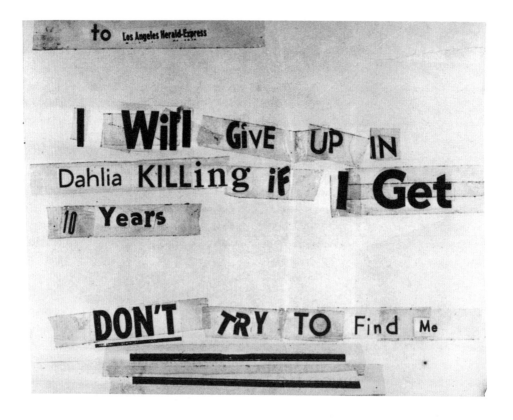

**(1947)**

*Elizabeth Short aspired to be a movie star. Her ghastly end turned her into something more: a legendary figure who continues to exert a powerful grip on American culture.*

A dark-haired, blue-eyed beauty originally from a suburb of Boston, twenty-two-year-old Elizabeth Short came to Los Angeles with dreams of becoming a movie star. She ended up as America's most legendary murder victim.

She achieved that dubious distinction on January 15, 1947, when her bisected corpse was found in a vacant lot in a residential neighborhood of the city. The torso, expertly severed at the waist, was completely drained of blood. Her lovely face wore a grotesque Joker's grin, the corners of her mouth having been slit nearly up to the ears. In the days before her identity was established, the tabloids—evidently inspired by the recent film noir hit, *The Blue Dahlia*—tagged her with the glamorous nickname that would ensure her immortality: the "Black Dahlia."

Nine days after the discovery of her body, a package was sent to the *Los Angeles Examiner* with a crude note made from cut-and-pasted newspaper letters. "Here Is Dahlia's Belongings," it read. Inside were Elizabeth Short's birth certificate, her Social Security card, several photographs of servicemen she had dated, claims checks for suitcases she had left at a Greyhound bus depot, and—seemingly most significant of all—a small address book containing the names and phone numbers of more than seventy-five men. Everything had been soaked in gasoline to eliminate fingerprints.

All the men in the address book were tracked down and questioned. Hundreds of suspects, among them every known sex offender in Los Angeles County, were picked up, interrogated, and released. As in all highly publicized cases, the police were inundated with false leads and fake confessions from a wide assortment of cranks. The killer, however, remained maddeningly elusive.

Over the years, various theories have been put forth. Bestselling books, proffering definitive solutions to the case, have appeared at regular intervals. In the end, though, the Black Dahlia murder remains what it has been since the morning a young Los Angeles housewife, out for a walk with her three-year-old daughter, stumbled upon the two halves of Elizabeth Short's naked body: the most famous unsolved American homicide of the twentieth century.

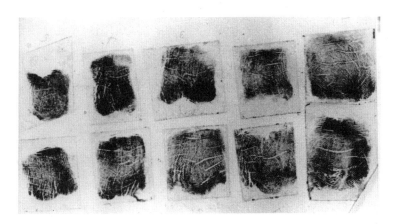

*Fingerprints lifted from the body of murdered actress Elizabeth Short.*

# #57 HOWARD UNRUH'S WEAPON COLLECTION

## The Camden Massacre

**(1949)**

*While we think of mass shootings as a uniquely contemporary phenomenon, the homicidal rampage of Howard Unruh in September 1949 has led to his epithet as "The Father of Mass Murder."*

Mass shootings feel like a uniquely twenty-first-century phenomenon, but there are incidences of earlier gun-wielding rampage killers. In fact, the man who is called the "Father of Mass Murder" was a twenty-eight-year-old World War II veteran named Howard Unruh, whose shooting spree on the morning of September 6, 1949, in Camden, New Jersey, was at the time the worst massacre of its kind on record.

Born in Camden in 1921, Unruh was a socially isolated child whose favorite activities were studying the Bible and building elaborate train sets. His parents separated when he was nine. As he matured into adolescence, he found himself increasingly tormented by both his incestuous longings for his mother and his burgeoning attraction to men. Enlisting in the army in 1942, he discovered an aptitude for marksmanship, earning the military rating of sharpshooter. He saw action in Italy, France, Belgium, and Germany, making meticulous diary entries about every enemy soldier he killed. Honorably discharged in 1945 with the rank of private first class, he returned to the three-room apartment he shared with his mother.

Over the next few years, Unruh descended into an empty, aimless, dead-end existence. He had no job, no friends, no prospects for the future. He tried college but dropped out. A closeted gay man in an intensely homophobic era, he led a secret life, traveling to Philadelphia several times a week for sex with anonymous pickups. Otherwise, he spent much of his time playing with his toy trains or practicing pistol-shooting in a makeshift target range in his basement.

He became increasingly convinced that his neighbors were talking behind his back, viewing him with contempt as a parasitic "mama's boy," and whispering that he was "queer." As Unruh's paranoia grew, he began once again to keep a diary. This time he filled it with lists of grievances against his neighbors. Besides each of their names he made cryptic notations: "Ret. W. T. S." or "D. N. D. R." The abbreviations stood for "Retaliate When Time Suitable" and "Do Not Delay Retaliation."

On Monday night, September 5, 1949, Unruh drove to Philadelphia for one of his furtive trysts at a Market Street movie house. He was delayed by traffic and by the time he arrived, the man he hoped to meet was gone. Howard sat through three showings of the double feature before heading home in a state of dejection. When he returned home around 3:00 a.m., he discovered that his newly installed backyard gate was badly damaged. Unruh assumed that neighbors had destroyed it out of spite (though, in fact, it had been vandalized by some local boys).

The following morning, after finishing the breakfast prepared by his mother, Unruh got his 9mm Luger pistol and, with an extra loaded clip and thirty-three loose cartridges in his pocket, hit the streets. His first stop was the neighborhood shoe repair shop, where, without a word, he killed the cobbler with two shots in the face and head. He headed next door to the barbershop, stepped up to the chair where the owner was trimming a six-year-old boy's hair, and shot them both dead. Over the next ten minutes, he calmly made his way through the neighborhood, shooting victims as he went, both specific targets of his paranoid hatred and random passersby. When he ran out of ammunition, thirteen people lay dead or dying and another three were badly wounded.

Returning to his apartment, Unruh flopped down on his bed. Moments later, about sixty heavily armed officers surrounded the

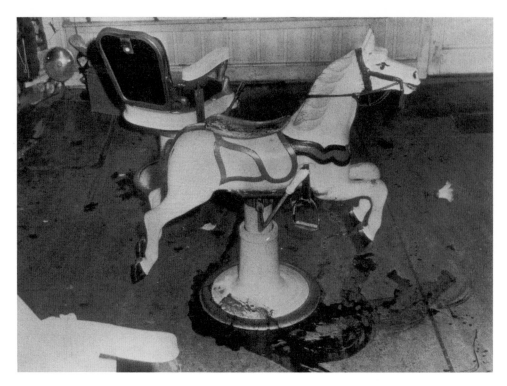

*The child's barbershop chair where six-year-old Orris Smith was having his hair cut when Howard Unruh gunned him down.*

house. A ferocious gun battle ensued. It wasn't until police lobbed a tear gas canister through his window that Unruh surrendered. As he was being handcuffed, one officer asked: "What's the matter with you? You a psycho?"

"I'm no psycho," came the indignant reply. "I've got a good mind."

The state disagreed. Though Unruh insisted that he knew the difference between right and wrong and expected to go to the chair, he persisted in seeing himself as the true victim and expressed only a single regret—that he hadn't shot more of his neighbors. "I'd have killed thousands if I'd had bullets enough," he said. After two months of psychiatric examination, he was diagnosed as a paranoid schizophrenic and committed to the maximum-security wing of the state hospital for the criminally insane. He remained confined for the rest of his long life, dying in October 2009 at the age of eighty-eight.

# #58 FLOOR PLAN OF 10 RILLINGTON PLACE

## "The Ripper of Rillington Place"

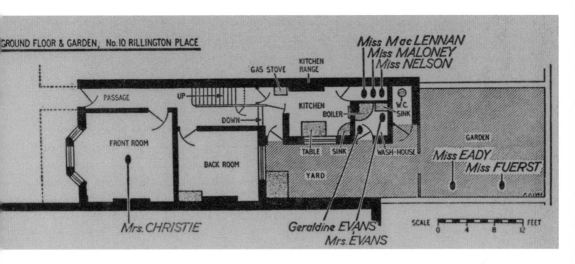

GROUND FLOOR & GARDEN; No.10 RILLINGTON PLACE

Miss Mac LENNAN
Miss MALONEY
Miss NELSON

GAS STOVE

KITCHEN RANGE

PASSAGE

UP

KITCHEN

W.C.

SINK

DOWN

BOILER

GARDEN

FRONT ROOM

BACK ROOM

TABLE  SINK

WASH-HOUSE

Miss EADY

Miss FUERST

YARD

Mrs. CHRISTIE

Geraldine EVANS
Mrs. EVANS

SCALE

0  4  8  12  FEET

**(1949–1953)**

*When a new tenant moved into a vacated flat in a run-down section of London, he made a horrific discovery that sent shockwaves through the world.*

ometime in March 1953, Beresford Brown and his family, immigrants from the West Indies, rented a few cramped rooms on the top floor of 10 Rillington Place, a run-down, three-story house in the then-seedy Notting Hill neighborhood of London. Not long afterward, a more spacious flat became available on the ground floor when its tenant abruptly departed. Partly because his own kitchen was barely usable, Beresford decided to move into the newly vacated rooms.

On the twenty-fourth of the month, he began clearing out some of the debris left by its former inhabitant. Looking for a place to install a wooden shelf for his radio, he decided to mount it on a wall in the kitchen. When he tapped the spot where he intended to screw in the brackets, however, it sounded strangely hollow. He peeled back a strip of the wallpaper and saw that it was covering a wooden door. He shone his flashlight through a large crack in the door, illuminating a little alcove behind it—the pantry. In it, seated on a pile of rubble, was a partially clothed female body. Two large, blanket-wrapped bundles lay beside her.

Police were soon on the scene. The seated corpse—held upright by her bra straps, which were attached to a hook in the wall behind her—was soon identified as a twenty-six-year-old homeless woman named Hectorina MacLennan. An autopsy revealed that she had been gassed, strangled, and raped. The bundles were the corpses of two sex workers, Rita Nelson and Kathleen Maloney, who had been killed and sexually assaulted in the same way. A search of the premises turned up a fourth woman's body beneath the floorboards of the parlor and the remains of two other female corpses in the tiny garden behind the house.

There seemed little doubt that the perpetrator of these atrocities was the tenant who had taken flight a few days earlier. A description of the fugitive was immediately broadcast by the police:

**Aged 55, height 5 ft. 9 in., slim build, dark hair thin on top, clean shaven. Sallow complexion, long nose, wearing horn-rimmed spectacles, dentures, top and bottom, walks with military bearing. Wearing a dark blue herringbone suit, brown leather shoes, fawn belted raincoat, and brown trilby hat.**

His name was John Reginald Halliday Christie.

\*\*\*

There is little in Christie's background that accounts for his future psychopathology. Born in 1899, he grew up in comfortable circumstances with a doting mother and a strict father—hardly unique in that era. Endowed with an impressive IQ, Christie distinguished himself as a student, though his shyness and diffidence made him a target for teasing—again, the kind of humiliation suffered by countless socially awkward schoolboys.

Shortly after serving—and being gassed—in the Great War, he met and married a twenty-two-year-old typist, Ethel Simpson. Their troubled, largely sexless union would come to a temporary halt when they separated four years later. It was during this time that Christie's criminal tendencies manifested themselves. While employed at a variety of jobs, he was arrested and did time for a series of petty larcenies. His first crime of violence occurred in 1928 when—now living apart from Ethel in London and cohabiting with a woman named Maud Cole—he assaulted her with a cricket bat and was sentenced to six months with hard labor for causing her "grievous bodily harm." Savage as this incident was, it paled before the horrors to come.

A psychological peculiarity shared by many serial killers is their attraction to police work. So it is not surprising that in 1939—now reunited with Ethel and living at 10 Rillington Place—Christie became a special constable. He would serve on the force for four years—the longest he had ever held a job. He was still in uniform when he killed his first victim.

Her name was Ruth Fuerst. A twenty-one-year-old factory worker who supplemented her meager wages with part-time prostitution, she visited Christie at home in August 1943 while Ethel was away visiting relatives. "While I was having intercourse with her," Christie later explained, "I strangled her with a piece of rope. There was a struggle. But she died quickly. She looked more beautiful in death than life."

With his wife due to return, he stashed Fuerst's corpse under the floorboards of the front room before burying it in his rear garden. Christie would recall the "strange, peaceful thrill" he experienced as he "embarked in the career I had chosen for myself—the career of murder."

Not long afterward, having left the constabulary and gone to work in a factory making electrical equipment, he befriended a coworker named Muriel Eady, a thirtyish woman who had bronchitis. Convincing her that he had a cure for the condition, he lured to his house in October 1943 and showed her what he claimed was his "patented inhaler," guaranteed to relieve her chronic congestion. The contraption consisted of a glass jar containing perfumed water and sealed with a metal lid. Two rubber pipes ran through the

*Sir Richard Attenborough perfectly captured Christie's ineffable creepiness in the 1971 film* 10 Rillington Place.

lid into the jar. One was attached to a crude nose- and mouthpiece. The other, unbeknownst to her, was connected to the gas main. After a few deep breaths of the fumes, she slipped into semiconsciousness. Christie raped her, strangled her with one of her nylon stockings, then buried her in the garden beside Ruth Fuerst's corpse. "Once again," he recalled, "I experienced that quiet peaceful thrill. I had no regrets."

Christie's homicidal drives lay dormant for the next several years. Then, during the Easter weekend of 1948, the Evanses arrived at 10 Rillington Place. A pathological liar and petty thief with a hair-trigger temper, twenty-four-year-old Timothy Evans earned a pittance as a van driver, much of which he squandered in the local pub. He had been married for a year to nineteen-year-old Beryl Thorley, who gave birth to a daughter, Geraldine, a few months after they moved into the squalid top-floor rooms. The couple were constantly at each other's throats. During one especially violent argument—so Beryl reported to her mother—Timothy tried to strangle her.

When Beryl found herself pregnant again in the fall of 1949, she resolved to get an abortion. She confided in Christie, who persuaded her that he had acquired some medical expertise during his years as a police officer and volunteered to perform an abortion. Much controversy exists over exactly what happened next. What is known is that Beryl and her daughter, Geraldine, ended up strangled to death and stashed below the sink in the backyard washhouse. Though the mother and child were almost surely killed by Christie, Timothy Evans was eventually tried and executed for murder.

Three years passed before Christie's bloodlust reasserted itself. This time, the victim was his wife, Ethel, who he strangled in her sleep on December 14, 1952, and stashed beneath the floorboards of the parlor. In mid-January 1953, he brought a twenty-six-year-old sex worker, Kathleen Maloney, to 10 Rillington Place, gassed, raped, and strangled her, then stowed her body in his pantry. In the following weeks Rita Nelson and Hectorina MacLennan met the same fate. On March 20, Christie—having sold his furniture, pawned his wife's wedding ring, and withdrawn her savings from her bank account—absconded from Rillington Place. Four days later, Beresford Brown made his appalling discovery.

Christie was arrested without incident on March 31, when—after running out of money and wandering the streets for several days—he was spotted on an embankment of the Thames by a sharp-eyed police officer and taken into custody.

Examined by psychiatrists, Christie was deemed "not normal" but sane. He eventually confessed to his murders, though he insisted that the victims were to blame—in effect, that they were "asking for it." Tried over four days in June 1953 for the murder of Beryl Evans, he was convicted, condemned, and hanged less than a month later. In October 1966, Timothy Evans received a posthumous royal pardon.

# #59 EXTRACTED TEETH SAMPLE FROM SHEPPARD MURDER TRIAL

## The Sam Sheppard Murder Case

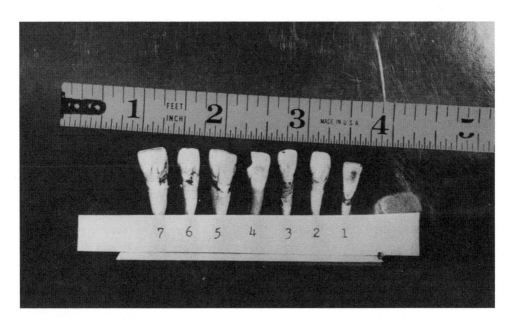

**(1955)**

*The brutal murder of Dr. Sam Sheppard's wife Marilyn led to one of the most sensational criminal cases of the twentieth century, one that continues to generate controversy.*

T he inspiration for the hit 1960s TV show *The Fugitive* and its blockbuster 1993 film adaptation, the case of Dr. Sam Sheppard had its start in the early morning hours of July 4, 1954. A popular osteopathic physician who resided in an upper-class Cleveland suburb with his high-school-sweetheart wife, Marilyn, and their seven-year-old son, Chip, Sheppard had fallen asleep on the living room couch after a long day at the hospital and an evening with friends. Sometime in the middle of the night—according to his own account—he was awakened by the cries of his wife, who was moaning and calling his name. Drowsily, he made his way upstairs and, entering the bedroom, saw a "white form" looming over his wife's pajama-clad body. He "started to wrestle" with the figure but was struck on the head and lost consciousness.

When he came to, he was lying on the floor beside his wife's bed. Marilyn had been so savagely beaten that, even at a glance, he could tell that "she was gone." Dashing into his son's room, Sheppard found the boy fast asleep. He heard a noise from below and bolted downstairs. The back door was open and he could make out "a form progressing rapidly toward the lake." It appeared to be a middle-aged man about six feet, three inches tall, with dark "bushy hair" and a white shirt.

Sheppard chased the fleeing figure down the steps to the beach below and threw himself at the man. After a brief, violent struggle, the thirty-year-old physician—a 170-pound six-footer who had been captain of his high school football team—felt "a choking sensation" and lost consciousness. Coming to at daybreak, he staggered back to the house and phoned for help.

Though newspapers initially speculated that the murder had been committed by either a jewel thief or a junkie, suspicion quickly alighted on Sheppard himself. Investigators found it hard to believe that the athletic six-footer had been knocked out twice by the mysterious assailant, or that seven-year-old Chip, whose bedroom adjoined his parents', had somehow slept through his mother's savage murder and his father's supposed struggle with the "bushy-haired intruder." Though he stoutly denied his guilt, Sheppard's case wasn't helped by his apparent reluctance to cooperate with the police. He refused to take a lie detector test and immediately retained a well-known criminal defense attorney. Public opinion, already shifting from sympathy to outrage, turned even more fiercely against him when a young woman came forward and confessed that she and Dr. Sheppard had been conducting a torrid affair. With Cleveland newspapers openly accusing Sheppard of the murder and demanding his arrest, he was taken into custody on July 29, 1954.

During Sheppard's trial, which began in October, defense witness Dr. Paul Kirk asserted that Marilyn had bitten her attacker on the hand, an argument he supported by displaying a set of human teeth in a simulated jawbone. Since Sheppard had no bite wounds on his hands, he could not be the culprit. Despite this and other testimony on Sheppard's behalf, the outcome of his trial was a foregone conclusion.

On December 21, after six weeks of testimony the jury brought in a verdict of guilty in the second degree and Sheppard was sentenced to life in the Ohio Penitentiary. Nine years later, however—thanks to his family's unremitting efforts to prove his innocence—he was released from prison after a district judge ruled that his constitutional rights had been violated by the irresponsible behavior of the press. Two years later, on June 6, 1966, the

US Supreme Court upheld the ruling, agreeing that the initial proceedings had been an egregious case of "trial by newspapers."

That November, the state of Ohio put Sheppard on trial again. This time, he was represented by one of the most colorful and effective defense lawyers of the age, F. Lee Bailey. Just as important was the enormous popularity of the top-rated prime-time TV drama *The Fugitive*. The American public's

*After winning his freedom, accused wife-murderer Sheppard turned himself into a professional wrestler nicknamed "Killer."*

deep sympathy for the program's hero, Dr. Richard Kimble, inevitably spilled onto his real-life inspiration, Dr. Sam Sheppard. On November 16, 1966, the jury brought in a not guilty verdict.

In contrast to his television counterpart, Sheppard's life did not have a Hollywood ending. Readmitted to the practice of medicine, he was sued for malpractice after the death of one of his patients. He took to alcohol and drugs. In 1968, the woman he had married in prison divorced him, claiming that he had stolen money from her, threatened her life, and thrown bottles at her. He became a professional wrestler in a pre-WWE era when a disreputable, freak-show air hung about the so-called sport. In April 1970, he was found dead of liver failure. He was only forty-six years old.

In subsequent years, Sheppard's adult son pursued his own campaign to prove his father's innocence. Newly analyzed evidence pointed to another possible suspect: the Sheppards' window washer, a man named Richard Eberling, who had been convicted and imprisoned for bludgeoning an old woman to death and who fit the general description of the "bushy-haired" intruder. Eberling—who died in prison in August 1998—went to his grave denying that he committed the murder.

# #60 THE CRUCIFIX OF ED GEIN'S MOTHER

## "The Butcher of Plainfield"

**(1957)**

*Raised by a fanatical mother who instilled in him a pathological hatred of women, Ed Gein committed crimes so appalling that they have inspired some of the most terrifying movies ever made.*

L ate in the afternoon of November 16, 1957—the opening day of deer-hunting season, when the town of Plainfield, Wisconsin, was largely depleted of its male population—fifty-eight-year-old Bernice Worden disappeared from the hardware store she operated with her son. Suspicion immediately lighted upon Edward Gein, a middle-aged recluse who resided in a ramshackle farmhouse a few miles outside town and who had been hanging around the store in recent days, paying unwanted attention to the widowed Mrs. Worden. Unbeknownst to his neighbors, Gein had been in the grip of a deepening psychosis since the 1945 death of his mother, Augusta, a fanatical and paranoid woman who railed incessantly against the sinfulness of her own sex.

Breaking into Gein's summer kitchen that evening, police found Worden's gutted and beheaded corpse dangling by its heels from a rafter like a butchered farm animal. Inside the house itself, they discovered an unspeakable collection of human artifacts: chairs upholstered with skin, soup bowls fashioned from skulls, a shoebox full of female genitalia, faces stuffed with newspapers and hung on the walls, and a "mammary vest" flayed from the torso of a woman. Gein later confessed that, on various occasions, he arrayed himself in this and other human-skin garments and pretended that he was his mother.

Though Gein confessed to the murders of Worden and a local tavern keeper named Mary Hogan, he was not a serial murderer but a necrophile. The bulk of his "trophies" were taken from the corpses of middle-aged and elderly women whose graves he had plundered over a seven-year period following his mother's death. The discovery of these atrocities sent shockwaves throughout America. *Time* magazine covered the case in lip-smacking detail, while *Life* published a lavishly illustrated nine-page feature, headlined "House of Horror Stuns the Nation."

Diagnosed as schizophrenic, Gein was committed to Central State Hospital for the Criminally Insane in Waupon, Wisconsin. After a pro forma trial in 1968, he was returned to the mental hospital and remained institutionalized for the rest of his life. A model inmate, he died of cancer at Mendota Mental Health Institute in 1984 and was buried beside his mother in Plainfield.

By the time of his death, Gein had become an undying part of American popular culture. In 1959, horror writer Robert Bloch used the sensational case as the basis for his novel, *Psycho*, which was transformed the following year into Alfred Hitchcock's cinematic masterpiece. Tobe Hooper's midnight-movie classic *The Texas Chain Saw Massacre* was directly inspired by the Plainfield horrors, and "Buffalo Bill," the skinsuit-wearing serial killer of Thomas Harris's *The Silence of the Lambs* was partly modeled on Gein.

# #61 1950s ROLLEIFLEX CAMERA

## "The Glamour Girl Slayer"

**(1957–1958)**

*Henry Glatman used his Rolleiflex camera to lure unwary models into his clutches. The photographs that resulted—saved in a toolbox as sick souvenirs—were chilling evidence of his sexual depravity.*

As one criminologist observed, the very name Harvey Glatman sounds like that of the nebbish "who sat next to you in eighth-grade biology class." He looked the part, too, with Dumbo ears and oversized eyeglasses. Behind that nerdy veneer, however, lurked one of the more twisted minds in the annals of American serial murder.

Born in the Bronx in 1927 to immigrant Jewish parents, Glatman was a prodigy of perversion, indulging in bizarre erotic practices at an early age. He was four when he began stimulating himself by tying one end of a length of twine around his penis, sticking the other end in a tightly closed dresser drawer, then leaning backward so that the taut string tugged his member. By the time Harvey was eleven, he was into the perilous activity

known as autoerotic asphyxiation: putting his head in a noose, throwing the rope over a rafter, and choking himself while he masturbated with his free hand.

As he got older, Glatman's behavior grew worse. He began breaking into homes while in high school in Denver, where he had moved with his parents. He came away from one of these forays with a stolen gun. Soon he had progressed from thievery to sexual assault. Sneaking into the houses of attractive young women, he would tie them up at gunpoint and fondle them while he masturbated. In June 1945, the seventeen-year-old Glatman abducted a woman and molested her before driving her home. She informed the police, and the teenager was soon behind bars in Colorado State Prison.

Paroled after eight months, Glatman continued his assaults, eventually ending up in Sing Sing where he was diagnosed as a "psychopathic personality—schizophrenic type" with "sexually perverted impulses as the basis for his criminality."

In early 1957, Glatman moved to Los Angeles, where his psychopathic cravings burst into deadly bloom. He began to frequent seedy camera clubs where sex-starved creeps could shoot "art pictures" of naked young models. Many of these women were aspiring starlets, eking out a living any way they could. Glatman, using the pseudonym Johnny Glenn, approached a baby-faced nineteen-year-old named Judy Dull. He explained that he worked as a freelance photographer for a true detective magazine and asked if she would be interested in posing for him. The pay was $20 an hour. Dull agreed.

Taking her to his apartment, Glatman explained that she would have to be bound and gagged and look convincingly frightened, as though she were about to be raped. Trussed up

*Nineteen-year-old model Judy Dull thought she was posing for a true detective magazine when she was bound, gagged, and photographed before being raped and strangled.*

and placed in an armchair, the young woman threw herself into her part—assuming a terrified expression and twisting in her seat—while Glatman snapped away with his Rolleiflex camera. All at once, the game turned terribly real. Pulling out a gun, he undid her bonds and forced her to strip, promising that he "wouldn't hurt her if she did as she was told." Then he raped her repeatedly. After he was finished, he drove Dull out to the desert, strangled her with a length of cord, took some photographs of her corpse, and left her there for the buzzards and coyotes.

Seven months later, in March 1958, Glatman—this time passing himself off as a plumber named George Williams—arranged a date with thirty-year-old divorcée, Shirley Ann Bridgeford. After driving her to a remote spot off the highway, he produced his .32-caliber Browning automatic and raped her twice in the back seat. He then drove her out into the desert, forced her to lie facedown on a blanket, hog-tied her, took a half-dozen photos, and garroted her to death.

Twenty-four-year-old Rose Mercado was the third woman to die at Glatman's hands. In July 1958, shortly after placing a classified ad in the *Los Angeles Times* seeking work as a model, she was visited by a funny-looking photographer who gave his name as Frank Wilson. After checking out her portfolio and agreeing on a price, "Wilson" left, saying he'd be in touch soon. The following night, he snuck into her apartment, raped her at gunpoint, then drove her to the desert, where—like his two previous victims—she was bound, photographed, strangled, and left for carrion.

A few months later, a state patrolman cruising the Santa Ana Freeway happened upon a man and a woman struggling beside a car parked on the shoulder. Stopping to investigate, the officer found Glatman grappling with twenty-eight-year-old model Lorraine Vigil, who had managed to wrestle the killer's gun away from him as he was attempting to abduct her.

In custody, Glatman—aka the "Glamour Girl Slayer," as the tabloids dubbed him—confessed to everything. Searching his apartment, police discovered a toolbox containing his horrifying photo collection. Condemned to die in San Quentin's gas chamber, Glatman was philosophical about his fate. "It's better this way," he remarked, a sentiment few people would have argued with. His execution took place on the morning of September 18, 1959.

# #62 MOVIE POSTER FOR TERRENCE MALICK'S *BADLANDS*

## The Starkweather–Fugate Spree Killings

**(1958)**

*The bloody saga of Charlie Starkweather and Caril Ann Fugate inspired a number of movies, most notably Terrence Malick's acclaimed 1973 directorial debut,* Badlands.

Though he thought of himself as a romantic young rebel in the mold of his idol, James Dean, Charlie "Little Red" Starkweather was seen by others as nothing but a swaggering punk. Growing up in Lincoln, Nebraska, he was mercilessly teased for his sawed-off size, bowlegs, and speech impediment. At the age of nineteen he progressed from troubled youth to psycho-killer when, in late November 1957, he knocked over a gas station on the outskirts of town, abducted the twenty-one-year-old attendant, drove him out to the countryside, and shot him in the head with a hunting rifle.

Seven weeks later, rifle in hand, he showed up at the home of his sweetheart, fourteen-year-old Caril Ann Fugate, who hadn't yet come back from school. When her mother and stepfather let him know that they didn't want him hanging around their daughter anymore, Starkweather shot them dead. He then murdered their two-and-a-half-year-old daughter—Fugate's half-sister—by beating in her skull with the rifle butt. He stuck the baby's corpse in a cardboard box and stashed Fugate's mom and stepdad in an outhouse and a chicken coop, respectively.

Fugate, who shared a good deal of her boyfriend's sociopathic disposition, was not overly upset by the carnage. Tacking a note to the front door—"Stay a Way Every Body is Sick with the Flu"—she and Starkweather stayed shut up in the house for the next six days, watching TV, pigging out on junk food, and having sex.

With the food running low and Fugate's relatives growing suspicious, the teen lovers took off in Starkweather's souped-up jalopy. Stopping at a local farmhouse, they shot both the seventy-year-old owner and his dog, then, after driving Starkweather's car into a ditch, hitched a ride with two high school sweethearts. Starkweather put a bullet in the back of the boy's head, attempted to rape the girl, and shot her dead.

Heading back to Lincoln, they invaded the home of a wealthy businessman, C. Lauer Ward. Ward's wife, Clara, and their housemaid were forced into a bedroom, bound, gagged, then stabbed to death. Ward himself was shot when he returned from work later that day.

Escaping in Ward's high-end automobile, the killer couple headed for Wyoming. By then, a hundred-man posse, along with the Nebraska National Guard, were hunting for them. After trying, and failing, to switch cars, the couple ended up in a high-speed chase with police. They ultimately surrendered after Starkweather was grazed by a police bullet fired through the fugitives' windshield.

In custody, Starkweather readily, even proudly, admitted to all eleven murders. At first, he went along with Fugate's claim that she had been his captive and had no part in the slaughter. But when she offered to testify against him, he changed his tune, accusing her of being an active accomplice in the killing spree. Convicted of first-degree murder, Starkweather was sent to the electric chair. Fugate was likewise convicted but received a sentence of life imprisonment and won parole after seventeen years behind bars.

# #63 KNIFE USED BY CHERYL CRANE

## The Killing of Johnny Stompanato

**(1958)**

*One of Hollywood's most sensational scandals, the 1958 stabbing of movie goddess Lana Turner's gangster lover Johnny Stompanato remains shrouded in mystery.*

One of the reigning sex symbols of Hollywood's Golden Age, Lana Turner led a private life tailor-made for the tabloids. In the intervals between her eight marriages to seven different husbands, she had a revolving door of boyfriends. Among them was a small-time hood named Johnny Stompanato.

A smooth-talking, darkly handsome ex-marine, Stompanato moved to Hollywood a few years following his discharge. After serving as a lackey for the West Coast crime boss Mickey Cohen, he struck out on his own, supporting himself as "a gigolo-type character" (in the words of one police official) who lived off the earnings of the beautiful, older movie stars he was skilled at seducing. Evidence also suggests that he occasionally resorted to blackmail. Targeting a rich married woman, he would secretly photograph their trysts, then threaten to turn the pictures over to her husband unless she coughed up "big money."

In 1957, he set his sights on Lana Turner, thirty-eight at the time and recently divorced from her fourth husband, the actor Lex Barker. Using the alias "John Steele," he began wooing her with the well-practiced skills of a professional Lothario. By the time Turner discovered his true identity, they were involved in a tumultuous affair. Though Turner had qualms about publicly dating a gangster, she found it hard to resist Stompanato's bad-boy appeal. "Call it forbidden fruit or whatever," she later wrote in a memoir, "but this attraction was very deep—maybe something sick in me—and my dangerous captivation went far beyond lovemaking."

For his part, Stompanato—enjoying the perks of being a movie star's kept man—grew increasingly possessive. When she began trying to distance herself from him, he became abusive, reportedly manhandling her so violently during one film shoot that the production had to shut down while she recovered.

On March 26, 1958, Turner—who had been nominated for an Oscar for her role in *Peyton Place*—attended the ceremony without Stompanato, taking her fourteen-year-old daughter, Cheryl, as her date. When she returned home, Stompanato flew into a rage, accusing her of being ashamed to be seen with him. "You'll never leave me home again!" he shouted, slapping her so hard that she was knocked to the floor, then yanking her up and pummeling her with his fists.

Just over a week later, on Friday, April 4, Turner—who had decided to end the affair—became embroiled in another, even more violent altercation with her lover, who threatened

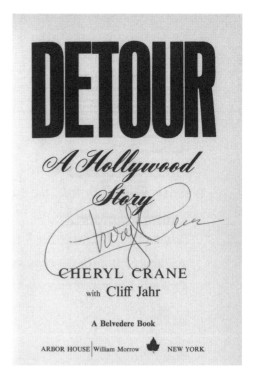

*Autographed title page of Cheryl Crane's memoir, containing her version of the stabbing.*

to disfigure her, to "destroy [her] face" so that she would never be able to "make [her] living" again. Overhearing the vicious fight, Cheryl grabbed a knife with an eight-inch blade from the kitchen, ran up to her mother's bedroom, and pounded on the door until it opened. "Mother stood there, her hand on the knob," Cheryl later recounted. "He was coming at her from behind, his arm raised to strike. I took a step forward and lifted the weapon. He ran on the blade. It went in. . . . He looked straight at me, unblinking. 'My God, Cheryl, what have you done?'"

Whether the stabbing was accidental, as Cheryl claimed, or deliberate remains a mystery. What is certain is that Stompanato collapsed on the floor, bleeding heavily and "making dreadful sounds from his throat." He was dead within five minutes.

Arrested and charged with murder, Cheryl was represented by legendary defense attorney Jerry Giesler, the go-to lawyer for Hollywood stars who ran afoul of the law. Putting Turner on the stand at the coroner's inquest, Geisler walked her through an hour-long recitation of the incident. Thanks in large part to her highly emotional testimony—the greatest performance of her career, as some cynics dubbed it—the jury reached a unanimous verdict of justifiable homicide and exonerated Cheryl of any wrongdoing. Years later, having turned her life around after a troubled youth that included two suicide attempts, she would publish an autobiography in which she asserted that she had been sexually molested by both Lex Barker and Johnny Stompanato.

# #64 SOCIAL WORKER'S REPORT ON SALVADOR AGRON

## "The Capeman" Murders

**(1959)**

*At a time when the US was gripped with panic over juvenile delinquency, the "Capeman" crimes committed by teenager Salvador Agron confirmed every adult's worst nightmare.*

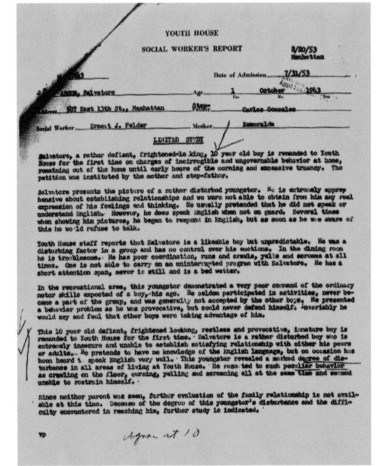

Though the teenage punks of the 1950s—with their black leather jackets, duck's ass haircuts, and switchblades—might seem quaint compared to the gun-wielding gangs of today, they were viewed as a grave social menace in their day. In 1959, New York City was the site of a sensational crime that made these fears seem justified.

Born in the small Puerto Rican town of Mayagüez in 1943, Salvador Agron spent eight years of his childhood at a Roman Catholic asylum for the poor, a place that he would always remember as "a house of madness." Agron underwent various tortures at the hands of the nuns in the asylum. A bed-wetter, he was forced to stand in the yard in front of the other children with the urine-soaked mattress on his head, spanked unmercifully, and, on one occasion, thrown onto an anthill. When he emerged from the place at age ten, he had the equivalent of only one year's schooling and was unable to read or write.

In 1952, Agron came to New York City to live with his mother, now with her second husband, an abusive Pentecostal minister. By age thirteen Agron had become a junior member of a gang, the Chaplains, whose primary activities were hanging out on street corners and engaging in knife-, chain-, and zip-gun-wielding rumbles with rivals from neighboring turfs.

A few years later he joined a Puerto Rican street gang, the Vampires, and moved into a seven-dollar-a-week apartment in Harlem with another member, Tony Hernandez. In keeping with the gang's name, Hernandez occasionally sported a black cloak lined with red satin—a close approximation of the cape worn by Bela Lugosi's Count Dracula, one of the classic movie monsters then appearing regularly on TV "creature feature" programs.

Around midnight on Sunday, August 30, 1959, after getting word that one of their gang members had been beaten up by a white gang called the Nordics, Agron borrowed the cape, armed himself with a Mexican dagger with a seven-inch blade, and headed out with Hernandez, who was carrying an umbrella with a sharpened point. After rendezvousing with several other Vampires, they proceeded to the Nordics' usual hangout, an unlighted concrete playground in the West Side tenement neighborhood known as Hell's Kitchen.

A group of neighborhood teens were sitting on the benches, shooting the breeze, when Agron and his cohorts showed up. Among them were Anthony Krzesinski and Robert Young, both sixteen, and their eighteen-year-old friend, Ewald Reimer, none of whom belonged to the Nordics or any other gang. Sensing trouble, Krzesinski and his pals headed for the exit but were blocked by one of the Vampires. All at once, a melee broke out, in the course of which Agron stabbed all three of the teenagers. Only Reimer survived.

Two nights later, Agron and Hernandez—soon to be known in the tabloids as the "Capeman" and the "Umbrella Man"—were spotted by patrolmen and arrested. Following a thirteen-week trial in the summer of 1960, Agron was found guilty of first-degree murder and sentenced to the electric chair in Sing Sing—the youngest person in New York State's history to get the death penalty.

One week before his scheduled execution in May 1962, New York governor Nelson Rockefeller commuted the sentence to life in prison. Over the next twenty years, Agron became a born-again Christian. He was paroled in November 1979 and went to live with his mother in the Bronx. He died of natural causes on April 22, 1986, just a few days shy of his forty-third birthday.

# #65 DICK HICKOCK'S SHOTGUN

## The Clutter Family Massacre

**(1959)**

*The senseless massacre of a wholesome Kansas farm family went from local news story to nationwide sensation when it became the subject of Truman Capote's true crime classic* **In Cold Blood.**

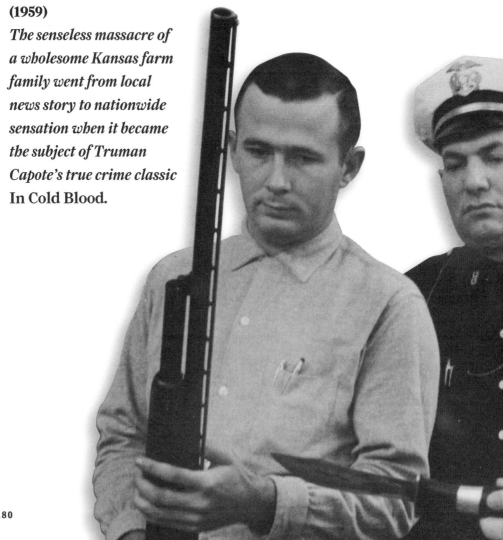

A self-made man who rose from humble beginnings to become the owner of a thousand-acre farm in Holcomb, Kansas, Herbert Clutter was a civic leader, devout Methodist, and caring neighbor who was widely respected throughout the region.

He was devoted to his wife of twenty-five years, Bonnie, an emotionally fragile homemaker who had chronic depression. They had four children; in 1959, only the two youngest remained at home—Nancy and Kenyon, sixteen and fifteen respectively, both popular, straight-A students.

In stark contrast to this almost stereotypically upright all-American family were the two lowlife ex-cons who would annihilate them. The son of poor farmworker parents, Richard Eugene Hickock had transformed from a bright and popular high school student-athlete into a smooth-talking, sociopathic crook, partly the result of a devastating car accident that left him with serious head injuries and a lopsided face. Arrested for passing bad checks, he landed in the Kansas State Penitentiary, where he met and befriended Perry Smith, his eventual accomplice.

The son of itinerant rodeo performers who split up in his early childhood, the half-Cherokee Smith seemed never to have known a stable moment in his life. Consigned to a Catholic orphanage following the death of his alcoholic mother, he was regularly beaten by the nuns for his chronic bed-wetting. Later reunited with his bootlegger father, he lived a knockabout existence. After a stint in the military—during which he was repeatedly tossed in the stockade for beating up fellow soldiers—he eventually found himself in the Kansas State Penitentiary on a charge of breaking and entering.

The seed of the crime that would earn the pair everlasting infamy was inadvertently planted by another prisoner: Hickock's former cellmate, Floyd Wells, who had once worked as a farmhand for Herb Clutter. Reminiscing, Wells described Clutter as a wealthy man who kept a safe crammed with at least $10,000 in cash in his at-home office.

Following his parole in August 1959, Hickock wrote to Smith, who had been released two months earlier, urging Smith to "go partners with him" on the Clutter robbery. On the night of November 14, equipped with rubber gloves, duct tape, a roll of stout cord, a flashlight, and Hickock's hunting knife and shotgun, they drove across Kansas to Holcomb, arriving at the darkened Clutter house around midnight. Entering through an unlocked door, they searched in vain for the safe described by Floyd Wells. Frustrated, they roused Herb Clutter demanding to know where he kept his money, only to learn that Clutter never kept much cash around the house and had never owned a safe.

The two reprobates then rounded up Bonnie and the kids and stuck them, bound and gagged, in different parts of the house—mother and daughter in their respective bedrooms, Kenyon in the basement along with his hog-tied father. Then, in a fit of violence he could never explain, Perry Smith took Hickock's hunting knife and slit Herb Clutter's throat. As the dying man struggled with his bonds, Smith finished him off with a shotgun blast to the head. Kenyon was next, shot point-blank in the face. Nancy and her mother followed. Then the two murderers fled into the night with their loot—forty dollars, a cheap portable radio, and a pair of binoculars—before embarking on an aimless

*The Clutter family in their caskets.*

odyssey that took them to Mexico, Miami, Las Vegas, and ultimately back to Kansas.

By then, Floyd Wells had heard reports of the Clutter massacre on the radio. Motivated partly by a proffered reward and partly by his warm memories of his former employer, he informed authorities about his conversations with Hickock. Just before New Year's Day, 1960, Hickock and Smith were arrested. Smith offered a chilling description of the act that set the massacre in motion: "I thought [Mr. Clutter] was a very nice man. Soft-spoken. I thought so right up to the minute I cut his throat." Their trial in March 1960 lasted less than a week and climaxed with

their inevitable conviction. Sentenced to be hanged, the two remained on death row for five years before going to the gallows.

Horrific as it was, the slaying of the four-member Clutter family was barely noted outside the Midwest. The *New York Times*, for example, devoted just three hundred words to the tragedy in an article buried on page 39. As fate would have it, that item caught the eye of writer Truman Capote. Taking the Clutter killings as his subject, Capote eventually produced his 1966 bestseller *In Cold Blood*, a phenomenal success that elevated the previously disreputable genre of true crime into the realm of serious literature.

# #66 "STRANGLER IN THE NIGHT" 45 RPM SINGLE

## The Boston Strangler

**(1962–1964)**
*Serial murder is no laughing matter, but as this record shows, there has long been an audience for macabre novelty items related to infamous crimes.*

"... These are my thoughts, feelings and emotions."

Albert H DeSalvo

STRANGLER IN THE NIGHT Productions, Inc.
Cambridge, Massachusetts

Born in 1931, Albert DeSalvo experienced a nightmarish childhood. His father brought home sex workers and fornicated with them in front of his children, then beat his wife savagely when she complained. One of DeSalvo's most vivid early memories was watching his father knock out all his mother's teeth, then break her fingers one by one by bending them back until they snapped. DeSalvo himself was regularly brutalized by the old man who, on one occasion, clubbed him with a lead pipe when the boy, told to perform an errand, didn't move fast enough.

Unsurprisingly, the young DeSalvo developed an early taste for sadism. One of his favorite childhood pastimes was placing a starving cat in a wooden crate with a puppy and watching the cat scratch the dog's eyes out. He was twelve when he had his first run-in with the law after beating up a newsboy and robbing him of a few dollars. Not long afterward, he was sent to a reform school for breaking into a house and stealing some jewelry.

Following his release from reform school for stealing a car in 1944, he enlisted in the army and was sent overseas, where he married a German girl. In January 1955, less than a year after a return to the States, he was indicted on a charge of carnal abuse after molesting a nine-year-old girl. DeSalvo walked free when her mother decided not to press charges. He received an honorable discharge and settled with his wife and child in Malden, Massachusetts, supporting them with various blue-collar jobs and the proceeds from occasional burglaries.

To satisfy his demonic sex drive, he began posing as a door-to-door scout for a modeling agency. If an attractive woman fell for his line and invited him into her apartment, he would produce a tape measure and proceed to check out her assets—a ploy that allowed him to indulge his taste for crude sexual fondling. Dubbed the "Measuring Man," he was arrested after pulling this scam on a dozen or so victims. Diagnosed as a sociopathic personality, he was charged with assault and battery and sentenced to two years behind bars, winning parole for good behavior after just eleven months.

Not long after his release, DeSalvo progressed from molestation to rape, talking his way into the homes of countless women throughout New England while posing as a handyman in green work clothes. Now known as the "Green Man," he assaulted as many as three hundred women throughout New England between 1962 and 1964. Thirteen of them—single women residing in Boston—also met savage deaths.

The initial murder victims were all older women, ranging in age from fifty-five to eighty-five. Each had willingly let her killer into her apartment, taken in by his story that he was a repairman sent by the landlord. Besides raping and strangling the women, he desecrated their corpses, sometimes shoving bottles or other objects into their vaginas. In most cases, he left a grotesque "signature," knotting his makeshift garrote (often a nylon stocking) into an ornamental bow beneath the dead woman's chin. This series of outrages earned DeSalvo his third and final nickname: the "Boston Strangler."

Toward the end of 1962, his MO changed. He began preying on much younger women, most in their twenties. And his murders became even more bizarre. In one instance, he left his victim propped against the headboard of her bed, a pink bow tied around her neck, a broomstick handle jutting from her vagina, and a "Happy New Year's" card resting against her left foot.

In October 1964, DeSalvo was arrested not for the Boston Strangler murders but for one of the Green Man rapes. During a stint in a state mental hospital, however, he began boasting of his homicidal career to a fellow inmate. Only then did authorities discover that they had unwittingly nabbed the infamous serial killer.

DeSalvo, however, was never punished for the atrocities perpetrated by the Boston Strangler. Thanks to deal struck by his hot-shot lawyer, F. Lee Bailey, he was sentenced to life for the Green Man rapes and committed to the Bridgewater State Hospital, an institution for the criminally insane. Following an escape and swift recapture, he was transferred to the Walpole maximum-security prison where, in November 1973, he was stabbed to death by a fellow inmate.

His criminal exploits lived on for a time in song. Looking to make a few bucks from the Boston Strangler horrors, Astor Records, a small label headquartered in Cambridge, Massachusetts, reportedly paid Albert DeSalvo fifty dollars for the rights to release a song under his name. Supposedly spoken by DeSalvo himself, the resulting 1967 novelty record (whose crudely punning title is a play on Frank Sinatra's 1966 hit single, "Strangers in the Night") was actually composed and narrated by Boston journalist Dick Levitan, with musical accompaniment provided by a local garage band, The Bugs.

DeSalvo's story also remained fresh because, from the time of his confession, doubts about his guilt were raised both by his own family members and relatives of his victims. Some believed that the real culprit was the man to whom DeSalvo supposedly confessed in prison, George Nassar. A psychopathic killer with a Hannibal Lecter–level IQ, Nassar—according to this scenario—fed details of the crimes to DeSalvo who happily confessed to the Boston Strangler murders to slake his desperate hunger for notoriety.

# #67 MARCUS HARVEY'S CONTROVERSIAL PORTRAIT OF MYRA HINDLEY

## "The Moors Murderers"

**(1963–1965)**

*Created out of a mosaic of children's handprints, this painting of one of the most detested murderers in British history created an uproar when it was first put on display.*

A textbook psychopath who put his superior intelligence to malevolent use, Ian Brady was born in January 1938, the illegitimate son of an impoverished waitress who found it best to have him raised by a middle-class foster family. As a child growing up in Glasgow, he reputedly manifested one of the classic symptoms of incipient homicidal mania, deriving pleasure from torturing small animals. Though his formal education ended when he dropped out of school at fifteen, he was an avid reader whose favorite books included works by Nietzsche, Machiavelli, and the Marquis de Sade, along with Hitler's *Mein Kampf*.

In 1961, while working as a stock clerk, Brady met eighteen-year-old Myra Hindley, the daughter of an alcoholic ex-soldier who had subjected her to a brutal upbringing. Their courtship included date nights at X-rated movies and romantic afternoons reading accounts of Nazi atrocities to each other. Hindley posed for pornographic photos, at least one of which showed the whip marks on her buttocks inflicted by her lover. Modeling herself on the notorious Irma Grese—a female SS guard at Auschwitz and Ravensbrück concentration camps—she dyed her mousy hair blonde and took to dressing in "Aryan" regalia.

By this point, the pair had forged the kind of toxic relationship that the French call a *folie à deux*—a pernicious bond between two people who bring out the worst in each other, egging each other on to engage in criminal acts that neither would commit on their own.

On July 12, 1963, sixteen-year-old Pauline Reade, a neighbor of Hindley's mother, disappeared on her way to a neighborhood dance and was never seen alive again. Precisely what outrages were visited upon her remains unclear since her killers offered conflicting accounts of the atrocity. What is certain is that she was waylaid by the pair, sexually assaulted, and slaughtered with two vicious slashes to the throat that nearly decapitated her. Her corpse was then buried in the moor outside Manchester.

Three more children died at the couple's hands between November 1963 and December 1964: two twelve-year-old boys, John Kilbride and Keith Bennett—both abducted, raped by Brady, garroted with shoelaces, and buried in the moor—and a ten-year-old girl, Lesley Ann Downey, whose murder was, in many ways, the most appalling of all. Snatched from a local fair, she was brought back to Hindley's house where she was stripped, gagged, and forced to pose for pornographic pictures. Then—while Brady tape-recorded her piteous screams for mercy—she was strangled to death. She, too, ended up in the moor, where her remains, along with those of John Kilbride, were eventually uncovered. (Pauline Reade's would be located nearly twenty-five years later on information provided by Hindley; Keith Bennett's have never been found.)

In October 1965, the bisexual Brady picked up a gay seventeen-year-old named Edward Evans, brought him back to Hindley's house, and split his skull open with a hatchet in full view of a witness, Hindley's brother-in-law, Dave Smith. Sickened by the crime, Smith notified the police. Promptly arrested, the "Moors Murderers" were tried in the spring of 1966. When the prosecution played the recording of Lesley Ann Downey's torture, people throughout the courtroom—not only jury members and spectators but hardened police officers—openly wept. Only Brady and Hindley appeared unmoved.

Convicted of multiple murders, the pair were sentenced to life in prison. Both died in captivity, Hindley at age sixty in November 2002 and Brady at seventy-nine in 2017.

# #68 NEWS STORY WIRE FEED

## The Slaying of Kitty Genovese

**(1964)**

*The horror of Kitty Genovese's brutal murder was amplified by a news report claiming that more than three dozen of her neighbors witnessed the savage attack and did nothing to intervene.*

ADVANCE FOR SUNDAY AMS,
JAN. 29, WITH STORY SLUGGED:
GENOVESE.
(NY92-Jan. 27)LEGACY OF
KITTY GENOVESE--In life,
Kitty Genovese drew little
public notice. In death,
she gained fame tragically
when 38 witnesses did nothing
as a killer stalked and stabbed
her in a quiet Queens, New York
community 2o years ago. (AP
Laserphoto)(slg62330mbr/NY
Daily News)1984
(EDS: An undated photo)

Of the 636 homicides committed in New York City in 1964, arguably the ghastliest—and unquestionably the one with the greatest impact on our nation—was the slaying of Catherine "Kitty" Genovese. A Brooklyn-born twenty-eight-year-old bartender, Genovese lived with her girlfriend in a quiet, middle-class neighborhood in Queens. Returning from work in the early morning hours of March 13, she parked in the lot of the nearby Long Island Rail Road station and stepped out of her car, unaware that she was being stalked by a homicidal psychopath.

His name was Winston Moseley. A soft-spoken, highly intelligent twenty-nine-year-old, Moseley lived with his wife and two young sons in a modest home in Queens and spent his workdays punching data cards at a business-machine company in Yonkers. He was also a serial sex-killer with a taste for necrophiliac rape. At around 1:30 a.m. on that fateful Friday, after tucking his boys into bed and watching TV for a few hours, he armed himself with a serrated hunting knife, got into his car, and went on the prowl.

Spotting Genovese as she drove home from work, he tailed her to the LIRR lot, then came up behind her as she walked toward her building. Realizing that someone was following her, she began to run, but Moseley easily caught up with her and stabbed her twice in the back. When a neighbor, hearing her screams, threw open a window and shouted, "Leave that girl alone!" Moseley hurried back to his car. He waited until he was sure he was safe, then returned to the building. By then, Genovese had made it into the vestibule, where she had collapsed at the foot of the staircase. Moseley stabbed her a dozen more times, raped her, then left her to die. From beginning to end, the attack lasted thirty minutes.

Horrific as it was, the murder received scant attention in the press until, two weeks later, the *New York Times* published a page-one story headlined "37 Who Saw Murder Didn't Call the Police." As the *Times* itself later conceded, "The article grossly exaggerated the number of witnesses and what they had perceived. None saw the attack in its entirety. Only a few had glimpsed parts of it, or recognized the cries for help. Many thought they had heard lovers or drunks quarreling. . . . And afterward, two people did call the police. A 70-year-old woman ventured out and cradled the dying victim in her arms until they arrived."

In spite—or rather because—of its inaccuracies, the *Times* article immediately made the murder a cause célèbre, inspiring a host of sociological studies on what came to be known as the "bystander effect" or "Genovese syndrome," and introducing a notorious phrase into the lexicon, originally voiced by a resident of the building: "I didn't want to get involved."

The Genovese case had another even more momentous impact on America. At the time of the murder, the only way to contact the police was by calling the local precinct, either directly (assuming you knew the number) or through the operator. Both were highly inefficient, particularly in the days of slow-dialing rotary telephones. The public outcry over the Kitty Genovese murder led to a major innovation that has saved countless lives: the creation of the 911 emergency call system.

# #69 CHARLES SCHMID'S BOOTS

## "The Pied Piper of Tucson"

**(1964–1965)**

*To enhance his stature among his fawning teen followers, sawed-off psycho-killer Charles Schmid stuffed his boots with rags and crushed beer cans.*

Charles Schmid—born in Tucson, Arizona, in 1942—grew up to be a textbook sociopath, possessed of the classic traits of the breed: a glib tongue, dark charisma, and ruthlessly exploitive streak, all in the service of a malignant narcissism. As a teenager, he set about transforming himself into the figure that would assume larger-than-life proportions among the disaffected teens of his hometown: the swaggering, fast-living outsider called Smitty.

Though a darkly handsome, blue-eyed young man, Schmid began affecting a look that turned him into a grotesque caricature of a 1950s teen heartthrob. He dyed his hair black, coated his face with tan pancake makeup, applied white lipstick, darkened his eyelashes with mascara, and adorned one cheek with a "beauty mark" made of putty and axle grease. In emulation of the androgynous beauty of his idol, the young Elvis Presley, he wore an exaggerated pout and was known to clip a clothespin to his lower lip to make it swell out more seductively. Ashamed of his diminutive stature, he stuffed rags and crushed beer cans into his cowboy boots, adding three inches to his height.

Despite—even because of—his bizarre appearance and preening weirdness, he exerted a seductive pull on the habitués of Speedway Boulevard, the nightly cruising strip for Tucson's restless teens. He became a local legend, a mystery man rumored to have been a drugrunner, pimp, and member of the Hells Angels. A group of wayward girls and unstable young men fell under his increasingly insidious sway. Among his most dedicated followers were a misfit named John Saunders and a high-school dropout, Mary Rae French. Sometime in the spring of 1964, Smitty shared with these two a fantasy that he'd harbored for months and was now determined to act out.

"I want to kill someone," he said. "I want to kill a girl."

Living a few houses from Mary French was a pretty fifteen-year-old high school sophomore named Alleen Rowe. Though her mother, Norma, bore a keen dislike of French and the unsavory characters she hung out with—particularly the "little creep" called Smitty—her daughter laughed off her worries. Mary French might be a little adrift, Alleen declared, but she was basically "a nice girl." As for Smitty, Alleen admitted that he sometimes "made her skin crawl." Still, she assured her mother, he could "be nice when he wants to."

Before leaving for her job as a hospital night-shift nurse on the evening of May 31, 1964, Norma looked in on her daughter who appeared to be sleeping peacefully in her bedroom. The following afternoon, when Alleen failed to return home, Norma telephoned the high school and was alarmed to discover that her daughter had not shown up for classes. She immediately notified the police that Alleen was missing. Though the police tried to assure her that her fears were premature, Norma was convinced that something dreadful had happened to her daughter. She also believed that she knew the person responsible: the "cocky, sawed-off weirdo" named Smitty. At Norma's insistence, police picked up and questioned Smitty. With unblinking coolness, he admitted that, at about eleven o'clock on the night of the thirty-first, he, Mary French, and John Saunders had come by the Rowe home and knocked on Alleen's window. When they got no response, they had left.

Smitty eventually began bragging to friends that he had murdered Alleen and buried her in a remote wash in the desert with the help of French and Saunders. Most people dismissed the story as more of his outrageous posturing. However, one of his sidekicks—Richie Bruns, who had done two stints in prison for burglary before he was eighteen—became convinced that Smitty was telling the truth.

Among the people Smitty told about Alleen Rowe was his new girlfriend, sixteen-year-old Gretchen Fritz. To demonstrate his devotion, Smitty not only told Gretchen about killing Alleen Rowe but drove her out to the burial site. Sometime in the course of their tumultuous yearlong relationship, Gretchen threatened to reveal his guilt to the world unless Smitty married her.

At around 7:30 p.m. on the evening of August 16, 1965, Gretchen and her thirteen-year-old sister, Wendy, left for the local drive-in to see the latest Elvis Presley movie. They never returned.

The following day, the Fritz girls' worried parents contacted the police, who initially assumed that Gretchen and her sister had run away from home. They did some perfunctory checking around and questioned her friends, including Smitty, who professed ignorance of her whereabouts.

Smitty told a different story to Bruns, revealing that he had strangled both girls to death in the living room of his cottage, then put the bodies in the trunk of Gretchen's car and dumped them in the desert. "That makes three," Smitty boasted. "Each time it gets easier."

Fearing that he now might be considered an accomplice, Bruns insisted that Smitty take him out to the desert and show him the bodies. "If they're laying out there," said Bruns, "we better go out there and bury them."

Smitty led Bruns to the decomposed corpses. They spent the next twenty minutes trying to dig a grave, taking turns with the shovel, but the ground was so hard that they made little headway. Finally, they dragged the remains to a more concealed spot beneath a mesquite tree and left.

Just weeks after murdering the Fritz sisters, Smitty, who had just turned twenty-three, fell wildly in love with a fifteen-year-old named Diane Lynch. After a whirlwind courtship, the two were wed with her parents' consent in October.

At the same time, Richie Bruns developed a passionate, if unrequited love, for an ex-girlfriend of Smitty's, eighteen-year-old Kathy Morath. When he turned into a stalker, her father notified the police. Arrested for harassing Morath's family, Bruns was offered probation if he agreed to leave Tucson until he got over his infatuation.

No sooner had he arrived at his grandmother's farm outside Columbus, Ohio, than he became tormented by the thought that Smitty might have evil designs on the now-unprotected Morath. Three nights later, after imbibing a few beers, he telephoned his father, spilling out everything he knew about Smitty, the Fritz sisters, and Alleen Rowe.

Bruns's dad lost no time in informing the police, who immediately notified their counterparts in Tucson. The next day, Bruns was escorted back to Tucson where, early on the morning of November 10, 1965, he led detectives to the now-skeletal remains of the Fritz girls. A few hours later, Smitty was under arrest for the double murder. His accomplices in the slaying of Alleen Rowe—John Saunders and Mary French—were swiftly arrested and returned to Tucson, where they readily confessed.

Smitty's trial for the murder of Gretchen and Wendy Fritz began on February 15, 1966, and lasted twelve days. The star witness was Richie Bruns, who described the trip he

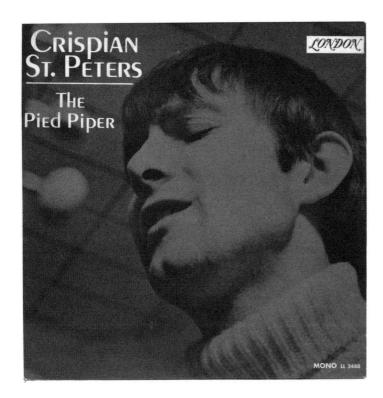

*The cover of the album whose hit title song provided the nickname for the lowlife sociopath Charles Schmid. Little did Crispian St. Peter realize his brief music career would end up associated with such notoriety.*

had made to the desert with Smitty and their clumsy efforts to bury the sisters' bodies. On Tuesday, March 1, after just thirty minutes of deliberation, the jury found Smitty guilty of first-degree murder. He was sentenced to die in the gas chamber. Three months later, after pleading guilty at a second trial to the murder of Alleen Rowe, he agreed to lead authorities to her remains.

Among the Top 40 hits at the time of Smitty's crimes was an infectious ditty by a one-hit wonder named Crispian St. Peters. The song was called "The Pied Piper" and,

inspired by this tune, *Life* magazine writer Don Moser christened Smitty the "Pied Piper of Tucson" in a sixteen-page article on the murders that ran in the March 4, 1966 issue.

On June 29, 1972, the US Supreme Court abolished the death penalty. Spared from the gas chamber, Smitty would meet a more gruesome end. On March 20, 1975, he was found lying in a pool of blood with nearly four dozen shiv wounds to his body and one eye stabbed out. He managed to survive for ten days. He died on March 30 and was buried, unmourned, in the prison cemetery.

# #70 GERTRUDE BANISZEWSKI'S HOUSE

## "The Torture Mom"

**(1965)**

*When Sylvia Likens's parents left her in the care of Gertrude Baniszewski, they could not possibly have known that they were placing her in the hands of a sadistic monster who would subject her to unimaginable horrors.*

Though Indiana has produced its share of horrific homicides, from the butcheries of Belle Gunness (see page 68) to the enormities of serial killer Herb Baumeister (an "upright" family man who buried eleven people in his suburban backyard), the 1966 torture-murder of sixteen-year-old Sylvia Likens is widely regarded as the most unspeakable crime in the history of the state.

In July 1965, Sylvia and her younger sister Jenny, a polio survivor who wore braces on both legs, were turned over to the care of an Indianapolis woman named Gertrude Baniszewski while their carnival-worker parents hit the road for a few months. A hard-bitten, thirty-seven-year-old divorcée with seven children of her own, Baniszewski had a dark reputation in the neighborhood. "I'd as soon have Gertrude Baniszewski babysit my kids as have my hair cut by Jack the Ripper," a neighbor later declared.

When their parents' first weekly payment of twenty dollars failed to arrive on time, Baniszewski flew into a rage, flogging the sisters with a paddle while screaming, "I took care of you bitches for nothing!" Her mistreatment of the young boarders—particularly Sylvia—escalated from there.

Over the next three months, the pretty sixteen-year-old was subjected to tortures that, when they finally came to light, would cause the world to reel in disbelief and horror. She was starved, beaten, burned with cigarettes, forced to eat her own vomit, made to sleep in her own filth, and sexually violated with Coke bottles. Descending into depravities straight out of the annals of the Marquis de Sade, the increasingly crazed Baniszewski invited her own children and some of their friends to participate in the tortures, encouraging one neighborhood boy to use a red-hot needle to carve the words "I am a prostitute and proud of it" onto Sylvia's naked belly. Death, when it finally came to the abused teen on October 26, 1965, was a mercy.

Baniszewski, two of her children, and a pair of neighborhood boys were arrested, tried, and convicted. In 1985, after eighteen years in prison, Baniszewski became eligible for parole. Thousands of letters poured into the parole board, demanding that the "Torture Mother" (as the tabloids dubbed her) be kept behind bars for life. Despite the public outcry, she was released in 1985. Assuming a new identity, she moved to Iowa, where she died of lung cancer five years later.

# #71 RICHARD SPECK'S KNIFE

## The Richard Speck Murders

**(1966)**
*A Chicago forensic scientist displays the knife used in Richard Speck's rampage, a crime that heralded the coming age of American serial and mass murder.*

Hulking, acne-scarred, and sporting a "Born to Raise Hell" tattoo, Richard Speck was a hard-drinking criminal from his early teens. By the time he reached his midtwenties, he had racked up more than forty arrests on charges ranging from forgery to aggravated assault.

In the summer of 1966, on the run from the law for burglarizing a Dallas grocery store, Speck made his way to Chicago where he sought work as a merchant seaman. On July 13, while waiting to be shipped out, he brought a fifty-three-year-old barfly back to his flea-bag hotel room, raped her at knifepoint, and stole the .22-caliber handgun she carried for protection.

At around 11:00 p.m. that same night, a drunken, doped-up Speck broke into a two-story townhouse used by a local hospital as a dorm for its nurses-in-training. He then knocked on the door of a second-story bedroom, which was opened by twenty-three-year-old Corazon Amurao, who found herself face-to-face with a pockmarked stranger brandishing a .22-caliber pistol and a switchblade knife.

Speck led her upstairs, where he found five more student nurses. Herding them into a bedroom, he ordered them to lie on the floor. Using his knife to slice a bedsheet into strips, he proceeded to truss his terrified victims. Over the next hour, three more young women arrived at the townhouse and ended up bound and helpless.

After untying twenty-year-old Pamela Wilkening, he led her into an adjoining bedroom, stabbed her in the breast, and strangled her. Mary Ann Jordan and Suzanne Farris were next. Speck shoved them into another bedroom and savaged them with his knife.

One by one the young women were led into different bedrooms and brutally killed—some had their throats slashed, others were strangled. The last to die was twenty-two-year-old Gloria Davy. Speck took his time with her, raping her twice before sodomizing her with a foreign object and strangling her to death.

Having dispatched every one of the young women—or so he thought—Speck slipped out of the house. During his rampage, however, he had lost count of his victims. Amurao had managed to hide herself under a bunk bed. Waiting until daybreak, she wriggled out from under the bed, climbed onto a window ledge, and began shrieking, "They're all dead! My friends are all dead! Oh, God, I'm the only one alive!"

Though heavily sedated in the wake of the massacre, Amurao provided detectives with a detailed description of the attacker. It wasn't long before investigators knew the name of the man they were hunting. Learning that he had left a survivor and that the police were on his trail, Speck, holed up in a seedy hotel, slashed his wrists with the shards of a smashed wine bottle. He was taken to Cook County Hospital, where a young physician who had been following the case in the papers recognized his distinctive tattoo and notified the police.

Tried in April 1967, he was condemned to the electric chair but was resentenced to eight consecutive terms of 50 to 150 years when the US Supreme Court declared the death penalty unconstitutional in 1972. On December 5, 1991, just shy of his fiftieth birthday, he had a fatal heart attack in the Stateville penitentiary.

# #72 6MM SHELL CASING FIRED BY CHARLES WHITMAN

## The Texas Tower Massacre

**(1966)**

*For years, Charles Whitman's gun rampage was "the deadliest mass shooting by a lone gunman in US history," a record that, tragically, has been surpassed many times since.*

T
hough the origin of the mass school shooting is generally traced to the Columbine massacre of 1999 (see page 257), that atrocity was foreshadowed by a campus crime that shook the nation thirty years earlier: the "Texas Tower" shooting of 1966.

Its perpetrator was twenty-five-year-old Charles Whitman. Born to an upwardly mobile, middle-class couple in Lake Worth, Florida, young Whitman was, to all outward appearances, an almost stereotypical embodiment of the ideal, clean-cut, 1950s, all-American boy. Shortly before his eighteenth birthday—both to spite his hated, abusive father and to get as far away from him as possible—he enlisted in the marines, where he excelled as a marksman. After becoming a commissioned officer, he entered the University of Texas at Austin, where he met and married a pretty education major, Kathleen Leisner.

Over the next four years, Whitman's life began to deteriorate. His scholarship was revoked, he was court-martialed for gambling, and he struggled financially. He also had begun to experience debilitating headaches and to entertain increasingly violent, homicidal fantasies.

*Charles Whitman's arsenal.*

On the evening of July 31, 1966, Whitman drove to the apartment of his divorced mother, where he strangled her into unconsciousness with a five-foot rubber hose, stabbed her in the chest with a hunting knife, then crushed her skull with a heavy object. Returning to his own apartment at around 2:00 a.m., he stabbed his sleeping wife five times in the chest with his hunting knife. He then spent the next seven hours packing his military footlocker with an assortment of weapons and enough provisions to last several days.

Driving to the university campus with his arsenal, he took an elevator to the twenty-seventh floor of the school's landmark tower, where he killed the receptionist, forty-seven-year-old Edna Townsley, with a mortal blow to the back of her skull with a rifle butt. Minutes later, a family of sightseers appeared at the top of the stairs. Whitman blasted them with his sawed-off shotgun, killing two and permanently disabling two others.

Barricading the door leading to the observation deck, Whitman then settled down to his main business, firing down at random targets with his scoped high-powered rifle. By the time the massacre ended more than ninety minutes later, twelve people would be killed and another thirty-one wounded. Shielded by the stone parapet surrounding the observation deck, Whitman was invulnerable to the barrage of gunfire from the more than one hundred lawmen who rushed to the scene. It wasn't until off-duty patrolman Ramiro Martinez, along with two other officers and a courageous university employee, managed to reach the tower that the horror came to an end. McCoy was able to get a bead on Whitman and shoot him between the eyes. But, as events would tragically prove, the modern age of the mass school shooter had just begun.

# MARY BELL MURDER NOTE

## Mary Bell, "The Devil's Spawn"

WE did murder martain brown Fuck of you Bastard

**(1968)**
*Police found this crudely scrawled note shortly after the brutalized corpse of four-year-old Martin Brown was discovered. It was written by the killer: an angelic-looking, eleven-year-old sociopath, the child of a monstrously abusive mother who saw her as "the devil's spawn."*

On the afternoon of Saturday, May 25, 1968, three boys foraging for scrap wood in a derelict house in the north of England came upon the body of four-year-old Martin Brown, faceup on the floor, arms outstretched, blood and saliva trickling from his mouth. An ambulance was summoned and the child was rushed to the hospital, where he was declared dead on arrival.

When a postmortem conducted on Martin's corpse revealed no signs of violence, the authorities declared the death accidental, though its cause remained unknown.

Returned to his family for burial, the little boy's body was laid out in the parlor of his home when, on May 29, his grieving mother responded to a knock on her front door. Two neighborhood girls stood there. One of them, a strikingly pretty eleven-year-old with a heart-shaped face and piercing blue eyes, asked if they could see Martin.

"No, pet," said Mrs. Brown. "Martin is dead."

"Oh, I know he's dead," the girl replied with a grin. "I wanted to see him in his coffin."

The name of the morbid, angelic-looking little girl was Mary Bell.

Bell's mother—a teenage sex worker who specialized in flagellating her masochistic clients—made her maternal feelings clear moments after giving birth. "Get the thing away from me!" she yelled when a nurse came to place the newborn in her arms. In the following years—on those rare occasions when she was present at all—she made several attempts to kill the little girl with drug overdoses and at least one "accidental" shove out of a third-floor window; tried to sell her to a childless woman desperate to adopt; and reportedly pimped her out to her pedophiliac customers.

Three months after Martin Brown's death, on the afternoon July 31, three-year-old Brian Howe went outside to play and never returned. When his worried older sister Pat went looking for her him, she ran into Mary Bell and her thirteen-year-old friend Norma,

*Mary Bell painting,*
And a Child Shall Lead
Them, *by Joe Coleman.*

who eagerly offered to help search for the toddler. Bell led the girl to a stretch of industrial waste ground where local children liked to play and where Howe's corpse was later discovered between two concrete blocks. The little boy had been strangled and sexually mutilated with a broken pair of scissors that lay nearby. The letter "M" had been carved into his naked belly with a razor.

Largely because of the nature of the injuries—particularly the pressure marks on his throat, which appeared to have been made by small fingers—the pathologist who conducted the postmortem surmised that the boy had been killed by another child. Before long, investigators focused their suspicions on Bell and Norma, who had been seen playing with Howe shortly before his disappearance. At Howe's funeral on August 7, Chief Inspector James Dobson kept his eye on Mary Bell. "I watched her as she stood in front of the Howes' house while the coffin was brought out," he later explained. "That was when I knew I couldn't risk another day. She stood there laughing, laughing and rubbing her hands. I thought, 'My God, I've got to bring her in or she'll do another one.'"

Questioned by police, Bell and Norma accused each other of the murder of Brian Howe. After nine days of testimony, Norma—deemed to be a passive girl of "subnormal intelligence" who had fallen under the "evil and compelling influence" of a demonic, "dominating personality"—was acquitted. Bell, who had been labeled a cunning, remorseless psychopath by expert witnesses, was found guilty of manslaughter in the murders of Martin Brown and Brian Howe and sentenced to detention for life.

At first, eleven-year-old Bell was placed in a reform school, where, according to her accusations, she was sexually abused by a housemaster. Later, she was transferred to a prison, and at the age of twenty was moved to a less secure facility from which she promptly escaped, and then was quickly captured again.

Paroled in 1980, she became a wife and mother in 1984. Granted lifelong anonymity by the courts, she eventually settled in a small town under a new name but was driven out by angry residents when they discovered her true identity. A wider furor erupted in 1998 when the public learned she had been paid £50,000 to collaborate with author Gitta Sereny on a bestselling book about the case, *Cries Unheard*. Her subsequent whereabouts and identity remain unknown.

# #74 **CODED MESSAGE**

## The Zodiac Killings

**(1968–1969)**

*The taunting cryptograms sent by the still-unidentified serial killer.*

One of the most notorious unsolved cases in US history, the Zodiac murders began on the night of December 20, 1968. A high school couple, Betty Lou Jensen and David Faraday of Vallejo, California, drove to a remote lovers' lane and didn't notice another car pulling up alongside them. As police later reconstructed the crime, the driver of the second car, armed with a .22-caliber semiautomatic pistol, stepped out and started firing through the rear passenger window of Faraday's 1960 Rambler. Pushing open his door, Faraday was killed with a bullet to back of his head as he tried to escape. Jensen made it out of the car but was chased down and killed with five bullets to her back before she got more than a few yards away.

Six months later, shortly before midnight on July 4, 1969, another couple, twenty-two-year-old Darlene Ferrin and nineteen-year-old Michael Mageau, were sharing the front seat of her Chevy Corvair on a popular lovers' lane just a few miles from the site of the earlier murders. They hadn't been there long when another car stopped about ten feet behind the Corvair. Wielding a powerful flashlight and a 9mm Luger, the driver began blasting away at the trapped pair. He then strolled back to his car, but—hearing moans from Mageau—returned and fired two more rounds into the teenager. Miraculously, Mageau survived. Ferrin was not as lucky.

Forty minutes after the attack, the Vallejo Police Department received an anonymous phone call from a gruff-voiced man, calmly admitting to the crime.

Six weeks later, he sent three separate letters to local newspapers, the *Vallejo Times-Herald*, *San Francisco Examiner*, and *San Francisco Chronicle*. Each contained a cryptogram. Working with his wife, Bettye June,

Donald Harden, a Salinas high school teacher and amateur cryptographer, managed to crack the code. Taken together, the three enciphered passages formed a single, misspelled, wildly deranged message:

**I LIKE KILLING PEOPLE BECAUSE IT IS SO MUCH FUN IT IS MORE FUN THAN KILLING WILD GAME IN THE FORREST BECAUSE MAN IN THE MOST DANGEROUE ANAMAL OF ALL TO KILL SOMETHING GIVES ME THE MOST THRILLING EXPERENCE IT IS EVEN BETTER THAN GETTING YOUR ROCKS OFF WITH A GIRL THE BEST PART OF IT IS THAT WHEN I DIE I WILL BE REBORN IN PARADICE AND ALL THE I HAVE KILLED WILL BECOME MY SLAVES I WILL NOT GIVE YOU MY NAME BECAUSE YOU WILL TRY TO SLOI DOWN OR ATOP MY COLLECTING OF SLAVES FOR MY AFTERLIFE**

The letter was signed with a peculiar symbol that resembled the sight of a rifle scope—a circle intersected by a cross.

"This is the Zodiac speaking," his next letter began, using the pseudonym that immediately entered the mythology of modern-day serial murder.

Two months passed. On September 27, 1969, college students Bryan Hartnell and Cecelia Shepherd were picnicking at a lake near Vallejo when a frightening figure emerged from behind some trees. His face was hidden beneath an oversized black hood, its eyeholes covered with clip-on sunglasses. A bizarre bib, embroidered with the Zodiac's crossed circle device, was draped over his chest. Hanging from his belt was a large wood-sheathed knife—possibly a bayonet. In his hand, he clutched a semiautomatic pistol.

"I just want your money and your car keys," he announced. "Just do what I say and nobody gets hurt."

Extracting pre-cut lengths of plastic cord from his jacket, he hog-tied the couple at gunpoint. Then, as the pair lay facedown on the grass, he holstered his pistol, pulled out his knife, and began plunging the blade into Hartnell's back. When he was done, he turned his attention to the terror-stricken Shepherd. When the frenzied attack was over, he walked to their car and, with a black Magic Marker, inscribed his crossed circle logo on the door, along with the dates and locations of his three Bay Area attacks. An hour later, he put in a call to the police, calmly informing them that he had just committed "a double murder." As it happened, he was wrong. Stabbed ten times, Cecelia Shepherd would die a few days later. Her boyfriend would survive his half-dozen wounds.

Zodiac's last confirmed victim was twenty-nine-year-old Paul Lee Stine, a student at San Francisco State University and part-time taxi driver. On the night of October 11, 1969, two weeks after the attack on Hartnell and Shepherd, Stine was killed with a point-blank shot to the head by a passenger he had driven to Presidio Heights. Before fleeing the scene, the killer cut off a piece of the victim's shirttail, soaked it in the dead man's blood, and carried it away with him.

A few days later, the editor of the *San Francisco Chronicle* received an envelope. Inside was a swatch of Stine's blood-stained shirt and a letter from Zodiac claiming responsibility for Stine's murder. He signed off the note with a bone-chilling scenario: "School children make nice targets, I think I shall wipe out a school bus some morning. Just shoot out the front tire & then pick off the kiddies as they come bouncing out."

Fortunately, he never acted on his threat. Nor—as far as anyone knows—did Zodiac ever kill again. As for his identity, it remains a mystery. An entire cottage industry of books claiming to offer the definitive solution to the case has grown up over the years. Armchair detectives and amateur crytpographers have spent decades attempting to decipher the Zodiac's messages. In December 2020—fifty years after it was mailed to the *San Francisco Chronicle*—a Virginia software developer, assisted by an Australian mathematician and a Belgian computer programmer, cracked the code of the 340 cipher, so called because of the number of symbols it contained. The message—which begins by referring to an incident in which a man claiming to be Zodiac called into a Bay Area television show—reads:

I HOPE YOU ARE HAVING LOTS
OF FUN IN TRYING TO CATCH
ME THAT WASN'T ME ON THE TV
SHOW WHICH BRINGS UP A POINT
ABOUT ME I AM NOT AFRAID OF
THE GAS CHAMBER BECAUSE IT
WILL SEND ME TO PARADICE ALL
THE SOONER BECAUSE I NOW
HAVE ENOUGH SLAVES TO WORK
FOR ME WHERE EVERYONE ELSE
HAS NOTHING WHEN THEY REACH
PARADICE SO THEY ARE AFRAID
OF DEATH I AM NOT AFRAID
BECAUSE I KNOW THAT MY NEW
LIFE IS LIFE WILL BE AN EASY ONE
IN PARADICE DEATH

The decoding of this message was hailed as a cryptographic triumph. Even so, it brought the police no closer to establishing the true identity of the now-legendary Zodiac killer.

# #75 ROCK FROM SPAHN RANCH

## The Charles Manson Murders

**(1969)**

*In May 1969, Hollywood music producer Terry Melcher traveled to the Spahn Movie Ranch to audition aspiring musician Charles Manson who sat on a rock to perform.*

T

hough a fair number of American criminals have achieved lasting notoriety, few, if any, have attained the near-mythical status of Charles Manson.

The product of a spectacularly unstable upbringing, Manson—born No Name Maddox to an unwed sixteen-year-old in 1934—was in trouble with the law by the age of twelve and spent the next twenty years in and out of custody, first in reform schools, then in various prisons for crimes ranging from armed robbery to check forgery to pimping. By the time he came up for parole at the age of thirty-two, he had been locked up so long that even he had doubts about the wisdom of being set free. "Oh no, I can't go outside there," he told prison officials. "I couldn't adjust to that world." Ignoring these protests, the parole board unleashed him on the world anyway.

Manson soon made his way to San Francisco's Haight-Ashbury district, the hotbed of hippiedom in 1967's "Summer of Love." With his con man's charisma and a crackpot "philosophy" concocted from assorted sources, he reinvented himself as a countercultural guru, attracting a band of drug-addled acolytes, many of them emotionally scarred young women, runaways from troubled middle-class homes.

Eventually, Manson and his ragtag commune settled in a dusty ranch outside Los Angeles, once used as a set for Western movies. There, they led a squalid, orgiastic existence while being brainwashed by their wild-eyed messiah. A die-hard racist, Manson had developed a bizarre apocalyptic theory, partly inspired by the song "Helter Skelter" from the Beatles' *White Album*. In his flourishing madness, Manson interpreted the lyrics (which referred to an amusement park kiddie ride) as a prophecy about an impending race war, during which Black people would rise up and exterminate all white people, except for Manson and his "family," who would find refuge in a cave beneath Death Valley before emerging and taking over the world.

To instigate the war, Manson dispatched four of his members—three of them women—on a deranged mission to slay some prominent white people in a way that would implicate Black revolutionaries. On the night of August 9, 1969—in one of the most shocking atrocities of modern times—his demented disciples invaded the home of film director Roman Polanski (who was away on a shoot) and butchered his eight-months-pregnant wife, actress Sharon Tate, along with three of her houseguests and a fourth victim, a friend of a caretaker. Before leaving, they used the victims' blood to scrawl incendiary graffiti on the walls. The following night, Manson himself led a party of his "creepy crawlers" to the home of a couple named LaBianca, who were similarly slaughtered and mutilated.

Quickly caught, Manson was put on trial the summer 1970, where he did his best to turn the proceedings into a circus, appearing in court with an "X" carved into his forehead (which he later reworked into a swastika), lunging at the judge with a pencil, and slugging his own defense lawyer. After nine and a half months of constant courtroom theatrics, he and the three female defendants were found guilty and condemned to death. The following year, their sentences were reduced to life in prison after capital punishment was outlawed in California. Over the following decades, Manson maintained his sinister celebrity. Turned down for parole a dozen times, he died of colon cancer in 2017 at eighty years of age, almost all of them spent behind bars.

# #76 *ESQUIRE* MAGAZINE COVER

## The MacDonald Family Massacre

**(1970)**

*According to Jeffrey MacDonald, his family was slaughtered by drug-crazed hippies in a nearly exact replay of the Sharon Tate massacre. Investigators grew yet more suspicious when they found an* Esquire *magazine with a cover story on the Manson murders.*

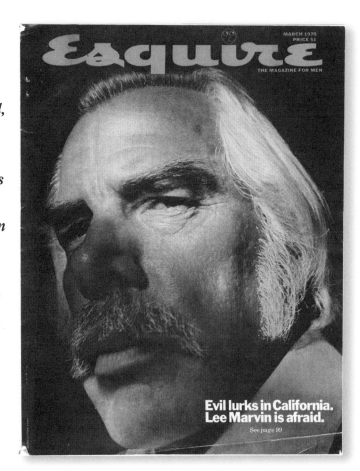

A case that has generated heated controversy for more than half a century, the "Fatal Vision" murders (as they were called after a book about them used it as the title) took place early in the morning of February 17, 1970. At a few minutes shy of 4:00 a.m., military police at Fort Bragg, North Carolina, were summoned by a gasping phone call to the home of Dr. Jeffrey MacDonald, a Princeton-educated physician who had volunteered for the Green Berets. "We've been stabbed," he gasped. "People are dying." When the military police arrived, they found that the tidy garden apartment had been turned into an abattoir.

As one journalist reported, MacDonald's twenty-five-year-old pregnant wife, Colette, "had been stabbed with a knife a total of sixteen times in the chest and neck—and twenty-one more times in the chest with an ice pick driven in to the hilt. She'd also been struck at least six times in the head with a club." Her five-year-old daughter, Kimberley, "had been struck in the head with a club at least six times. . . . She had also been stabbed in the neck with a knife several times." The younger child, two-year-old Kristen, "had a total of thirty-two stab wounds."

In contrast to this frenzied overkill, MacDonald himself had suffered relatively minor injuries, the most serious of which was a small wound between two of his ribs that partially collapsed one lung.

Brought to the medical clinic, MacDonald claimed that, after falling asleep on the living room couch, he was awakened in the middle of the night by screams from his wife and older daughter. Opening his eyes, he saw four figures looming above him: a Black man in a fatigue jacket, two white men, and a stringy-haired blonde woman in a floppy hat who

was chanting, "Acid is groovy, kill the pigs." Leaping to his feet, MacDonald engaged in a fierce battle with the Black man, who repeatedly stabbed him with an ice pick and clubbed him into unconsciousness. When MacDonald came to, he discovered that Colette and the kids had been slaughtered and that one of the perpetrators had scrawled the word "PIG" in blood on the headboard of the marital bed.

Investigators quickly became suspicious of this story. Besides the forensic evidence—none of which proved consistent with MacDonald's account—there were his superficial injuries, which, as one doctor later put it, were entirely "compatible with self-infliction." The living room where a life-and-death struggle between the combat-trained physician and his armed assailant allegedly took place was in remarkably good shape. And then there were the uncanny similarities between MacDonald's tale and an article on the Manson murders in the March 1970 issue of *Esquire* magazine that was found in the living room.

Reconstructing the crime from the blood splatter patterns and other clues, investigators speculated that MacDonald—who, it emerged, had been cheating on his wife—had gotten into an argument with Colette that escalated into violence when she struck him with a hairbrush. Flying into a rage, MacDonald grabbed a heavy piece of wood he'd been using for home repairs and savagely clubbed both Colette and his daughter Kimberly, who had evidently come into the bedroom to see about the commotion. He finished the job by stabbing them both to death. To make it appear as though a Manson-like massacre had taken place, he murdered his toddler Kristen and used Collette's blood to inscribe the word "PIG" on the headboard. Then he carefully

The above suspects wanted in connection with the Aggravated Assault & Murder of Colette MacDonald-26, and daughters, Kimberly-6, Kristen Jean-2, also, the Aggravated Assault of Capt. Jeffrey MacDonald on February 17, 1970, inside residence on Ft. Bragg, N.C.

*Police sketches of the four alleged killers, based on MacDonald's descriptions.*

inflicted a few wounds on himself, including the neat incision in his chest.

Three months later, MacDonald was brought before an army tribunal. Among the character witnesses called to testify on his behalf was his father-in-law, Freddy Kassab, who tearfully declared, "If I ever have another daughter, I'd still want the same son-in-law." MacDonald's lawyer also learned of a local seventeen-year-old drug addict named Helena Stoeckley, known to go around in a blonde wig and floppy hat, who had reputedly been seen in a car with three men around the time of the murders and who, when questioned, conceded that she might have been in the MacDonalds' home on that night, though she couldn't be sure since she was so stoned on mescaline. On October 13, 1970, all charges against MacDonald were dismissed by the presiding colonel, who recommended "that appropriate civilian authorities be requested to investigate the alibi of Helena Stoeckley." Two months later, MacDonald received an honorable discharge.

Just a few days after returning to civilian life, MacDonald made an appearance on Dick Cavett's late night talk show where he mostly complained about how he'd been treated by army investigators, barely mentioning his slaughtered family. Watching at home was Freddy Kassab, who was so outraged that he embarked on his own investigation of the murders. Before long, he became convinced that MacDonald was guilty.

Over the following years, while MacDonald threw himself into a life of swinging 1970s bachelorhood, Kassab relentlessly pursued the case against his son-in-law. Thanks in large part to his tireless efforts, MacDonald was eventually indicted for the murders of his wife and two daughters and brought to trial in July 1979.

Trial investigators located Helena Stoeckley, who, in the intervening years, had told conflicting stories to various acquaintances regarding her whereabouts on the night of the murders. Called as a witness, Stoeckley—whose drug consumption at the time of the killings included the nearly daily intake of heroin, liquid opium, marijuana, hashish, LSD, mescaline, barbiturates, and angel dust—had no memory of where she had been that night but insisted that she had never participated in the slaughter, never been inside the MacDonald home, and never even laid eyes on MacDonald himself until she had entered the courtroom that morning to testify.

Testifying on his own behalf, MacDonald alternated between extravagant displays of uncontrolled sobbing and caustic, condescending responses to the prosecuting attorney. Confronted with the discrepancies between his own accounts of the crime and the physical evidence, MacDonald was unable to offer any plausible explanations.

One of the most damning pieces of evidence was the blue pajama top that MacDonald had worn on the fatal night and had been found on Colette's upper body, where—so MacDonald claimed—he had tenderly draped it after discovering her savaged corpse. There were more than forty small holes in the garment. According to MacDonald, they were the result of his ferocious struggle with the Black attacker. Forensic experts, however, were able to show that, when the garment was folded in the way that it had been laid atop Colette's chest, there were only twenty-one holes, which exactly matched the twenty-one puncture wounds made by the ice pick: In short, MacDonald had not used his pajama top to cover the terrible wounds on his wife's body made by her supposed assailants, but had placed it over her chest before stabbing her himself.

At the conclusion of the seven-week trial, it took the jury six and a half hours of deliberation to arrive at a verdict. MacDonald was found guilty of second-degree murder in the deaths of Colette and Kimberly and murder in the first degree in the case of Kristen (whose slaying, the jurors believed, was a "calculated act, designed to support his cover story" that his family had died in a Manson-like massacre by drug-crazed hippies). He was sentenced to three consecutive life terms in prison. MacDonald's lawyers filed a series of appeals, one of which succeeded in getting the conviction overturned and earning MacDonald a brief respite from prison. Before long, however, the Supreme Court had reversed the lower court's ruling and MacDonald returned to prison where, despite unrelenting efforts by his lawyers and staunch supporters, he would remain for the next forty years.

In the spring of 2021, MacDonald, seventy-seven years old and in deteriorating health, made a final effort to win parole under a federal compassionate release law. The request was denied.

# #77 FORENSIC BUST OF JOHN LIST

## The Family Annihilator

**(1971)**

*For nearly two decades, John List got away with a horrific crime. Then investigators brought in world-renowned forensic sculptor Frank Bender to do a facial reconstruction of the fugitive.*

J ohn List falls into the category of mass murderers known as "family annihilators." They are typically middle-aged men perceived by their neighbors as loving husbands, devoted fathers, and good providers who—overcome with an intolerable sense of failure—slay their families, presumably to spare them from hardship and shame.

Born in 1925 and the only child of stern German American parents, List was a devout Lutheran and a Sunday school teacher, earned a master's degree in accounting at the University of Michigan before enlisting in the army, and served honorably during both World War II and the Korean War. In 1951, while stationed at Fort Eustis, Virginia, he met and married a woman named Helen Taylor, the widow of an infantryman killed in action in Korea.

Leaving the military the following year, List embarked on a successful accounting career. By 1965, he had become the vice president and comptroller of a New Jersey bank, a position that allowed him to afford a nineteen-room mansion in the town of Westfield, where he lived with his wife, three children, and elderly mother.

Just six years later, however, his life began to unravel when his bank closed and he found himself unemployed. Concealing the humiliating truth from his family, he left home each morning as if going to work, spent the day looking for a job or poring over newspapers in the local train station, then returned at his usual hour. Adding to his extreme stress was the increasingly erratic behavior of his wife, who, in addition to her longtime alcoholism, was exhibiting the effects of tertiary syphilis, contracted from her first husband.

His children also seemed to be going astray, particularly his teenaged daughter, Patricia, who was thinking of becoming an actor—a godless occupation in List's view—and hanging around high school friends who dressed (in his estimation) like "cheap sluts" and were known to smoke the Devil's Weed, marijuana. "I was concerned that she and the boys would drift away from the church," he later explained. "Finally, I broke and killed them."

On the morning of November 9, 1971, after seeing his children off to school, he shot his wife in the back of the head while she was drinking coffee in the kitchen. His eighty-four-year-old mother, who occupied an attic apartment, was preparing her breakfast when List came upstairs, gave her a kiss on the cheek, and shot her in the left eye. He then emptied his mother's savings account at the bank, returned home, and fixed himself lunch. When Patricia and her thirteen-year-old brother, Frederick, returned from school, he shot each in the back of the head. His fifteen-year-old son, John Jr., was playing in a soccer game, so List drove over to watch. Afterward, he brought John Jr. home and put a bullet in the back of his head. The boy did not die easily. List shot him repeatedly until he stopped moving.

Except for his mother—whose corpse was too heavy to lug downstairs—the bodies were laid out on sleeping bags in the ballroom. He briefly considered taking his own life but quickly dismissed the idea since, as he later explained, he was sure his family "would all go to heaven" and, given God's all-merciful nature, there was a chance that he would be forgiven and be reunited with them in the afterlife. If he died by suicide, however, he would "a hundred percent, automatically go to hell."

The next morning, he drove to JFK airport in New York. A month would pass before suspicious neighbors contacted the police and the atrocities were discovered. Searching the house, investigators discovered a five-page letter addressed to the family's pastor, in which List freely confessed to the murders.

Not long afterward, List's car was found abandoned at the airport. New Jersey investigators and FBI agents launched a massive hunt for the fugitive both in the US and overseas. But John List had vanished without a trace.

In the spring of 1989, nearly eighteen years after List's disappearance, Frank Bender—a forensic sculptor renowned in law enforcement circles for his ability to re-create the likenesses of long-dead, unidentified murder victims from their fleshless skulls—received an unusual commission. The producers of the television show *America's Most Wanted*, who were planning to do a segment on the List case, hired him to produce a plaster bust of the fugitive as he would appear at his current age, sixty-four. The resulting sculpture of a balding jowly man with thick black eyeglasses proved to be so uncannily accurate that when the program aired on May 21, a Denver viewer named named Wanda Flanery, was stunned by its resemblance to a former neighbor, a mild-mannered accountant she knew as Robert Clark, who had recently moved to Virginia with his wife, Delores. Less than two weeks later, List was arrested at his Richmond accounting firm.

Despite fingerprint evidence to the contrary, he steadfastly denied that he was John List. Eventually the truth emerged. Using the alias Robert Clark—the name of a college classmate—he had made his way out west by bus, settling in Denver where he lived in a trailer park and got a job as a night cook at a Holiday Inn. Gradually, he had worked his way back to the kind of respectable life he had led before committing mass murder: joining a church; marrying a shy, religious woman; starting his own business as an accountant and tax consultant. Even he couldn't believe his good luck. "I didn't really think I would get away with it for more than a week or two," he admitted. "I decided to stay free as long as I could. I might have had it in my mind to turn myself in, but I never gave it serious consideration. . . . I was enjoying my life."

At the end of his seven-day trial in early April 1990, he was convicted of five counts of first-degree murder. Addressing the judge at his sentencing hearing, he took no responsibility for his terrible crimes. "Because of my mental state at the time," he declared, "I was unaccountable for what happened." Given five consecutive life sentences without the possibility of parole, he remained immured in Trenton State Prison until his death from pneumonia in March 2008 at age eighty-two.

# #78 JOHN WAYNE GACY'S BUSINESS CARD

## "The Killer Clown"

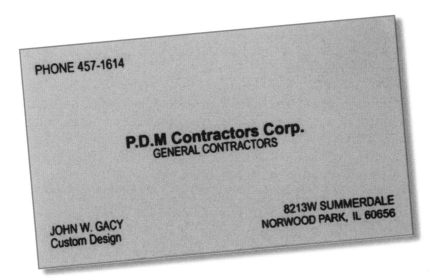

PHONE 457-1614

**P.D.M Contractors Corp.**
GENERAL CONTRACTORS

JOHN W. GACY
Custom Design

8213W SUMMERDALE
NORWOOD PARK, IL 60656

**(1972–1978)**

*The ability of serial killers to hide their malevolent natures behind masks of respectability is one of their most unnerving characteristics. Few have epitomized this chilling duality more than the monstrous sex-killer John Wayne Gacy.*

Thanks largely to Stephen King's *It*, the evil clown has joined the mummy, the werewolf, the vampire, and the zombie in the pantheon of pop culture monsters. King's child-killing Pennywise is, of course, pure make-believe, sprung from his creator's singularly dark and fertile imagination. Infinitely more disturbing was the actual "Killer Clown," John Wayne Gacy.

Born in 1942, he was named after America's reigning icon of rugged masculinity by a father who clearly hoped that his son would grow up to be a "real man," then proceeded to subject him to relentless physical abuse and humiliation. Constantly derided as a "sissy," John grew up to be a pudgy hypochondriac whose homosexual drives were a source of profound self-loathing. In an attempt to appear "normal," he cultivated a gruff, swaggering air and hurried into an early marriage, settling down in Waterloo, Iowa, where he ran a Kentucky Fried Chicken franchise and joined the local Jaycees. Even while leading an outwardly respectable life, however, he was busily molesting underage boys, including the son of a fellow Jaycee. Arrested in 1968 for sodomy, he was hit with a ten-year jail term, though he proved to be such a model prisoner that he was paroled after just eighteen months.

Divorced from his first wife—who had filed papers on the day of his sentencing—he relocated to Chicago, where he married again, moved into a suburban ranch house, and started a successful contracting business. A good neighbor always willing to lend a hand, he hosted annual summertime parties attended by hundreds of guests, devoted himself to local politics and charitable causes, and loved to entertain children in hospitals and orphanages in the guise of "Pogo," a boisterous clown with a candy-colored costume and a red-painted, bat-wing smile. At the same time, this apparent pillar of the community was secretly perpetrating some of the most horrific serial murders in the annals of American crime.

Though some of his victims were acquaintances or employees, most were street hustlers and runaways. Gacy—sometimes posing as a cop—would snare his prey at the bus station or in the local gay district. Back in his house, he would lock the young man in handcuffs, then spend hours sodomizing and torturing him before slowly strangling him to death.

These atrocities, which began in 1972, went on for six years until the disappearance of a fifteen-year-old boy named Robert Piest in December 1978. A bright, ambitious student who worked after school as a stock boy in a pharmacy, Piest told his mother that he was leaving the drugstore early to see Gacy about a job. When he failed to return home, his parents notified the police, who put a tracer on Gacy and learned about his sodomy conviction ten years earlier.

Before long, Gacy was under arrest. Conducting a search of his house, investigators came upon suspicious and increasingly ominous bits of evidence, including personal items—jewelry, clothes, wallets—that clearly belonged to adolescent boys. They also found something else: A trapdoor in a living room closet opened into a flooded crawl space that turned out to contain the decomposed remains of twenty-nine young men, so putrefied that many were impossible to identify. Four other bodies, as Gacy eventually revealed, had been dumped in a nearby river, bringing the murder count to thirty-three. Authorities would spend decades attempting to put names to the exhumed victims. When one of them was identified in the fall of 2021 through DNA evidence and genealogical databases, the news made the *New York Times*.

Sentenced to death in 1980, Gacy spent fourteen years awaiting execution. During that time, he turned out scores of grotesquely cheery paintings, many of circus clowns and Disney characters. These became coveted collectibles among a certain group of true crime connoisseurs, selling for thousands of dollars. Just after midnight on May 10, 1994, he was executed by lethal injection. His last words were "Kiss my ass."

*Gacy's creepy self-portraits as Pogo the Clown have become coveted objects by collectors of macabre art.*

# #79 TED BUNDY'S VW BEETLE

## Ted Bundy

**(1974–1978)**

*With its passenger seat and inner door handle removed, Ted Bundy's 1968 Volkswagen Beetle became a death trap for the young women lured inside.*

If there is such a thing as a quintessential serial killer—a bright, personable, upstanding young man whose shiny exterior masks a creature of unspeakable evil—then Ted Bundy certainly qualifies. A genuine Jekyll and Hyde, he led an outwardly exemplary life as a clean-cut law student, civic-minded citizen, and caring partner, even while conducting a horrific homicidal career that took the lives of at least thirty girls and women.

Born in 1946 to an unwed mother, he was raised to believe that his mother was his sister and his grandparents were his father and mother. Though he professed to have only fond memories of his early home life, his grandfather appears to have been a virulent racist and petty tyrant who reportedly possessed a large collection of violent hard-core pornography that the young Bundy had access to. Unsubstantiated rumors also claim that his grandfather was, in fact, his biological dad—that Ted was the product of incestuous rape.

By the time he entered school, Bundy was already aware that he was not like other children. Watching his classmates, he didn't understand "what made people want to be friends . . . what underlay social interactions." Devoid of a conscience, he viewed other people as little more than objects to be manipulated for his own gratifications. Eventually, by closely studying his peers, he learned to mimic normal human behavior, becoming so adept at this play-acting that for rest of his life even those closest to him failed to perceive his monstrous nature.

Though it is possible that Bundy began killing as early as age fourteen—when an eight-year-old Tacoma girl was abducted from her bedroom a few blocks away from Bundy's home and never seen again—his appalling career began in earnest in January 1974 when he broke into the basement home of an eighteen-year-old University of Washington coed, bludgeoned her skull with a metal rod yanked from her bedframe, then rammed the rod into her vagina. Somehow, she survived. The same could not be said for seven other young women who crossed paths with Bundy in the succeeding months. Some vanished at night while walking to or from their dormitories or sorority houses. Two were lured from a crowded beach in broad daylight on the same afternoon by a good-looking young man wearing an arm sling who asked for their help in unloading a sailboat from the roof of his car.

Accepted into the University of Utah in August 1974, he moved to Salt Lake City where he divided his time between law studies and lust-murder, slaughtering a string of young women, including the teenage daughter of a local police chief. Bundy later confessed that he sometimes returned to the remote, wilderness spots where he had dumped his victims and had sex with their corpses. Occasionally he severed their heads and brought them back to his apartment as trophies. During this period, he also made forays into Colorado where at least five other young women died at his hands.

He was arrested in August 1975 after a Utah highway patrol officer stopped him for erratic driving and discovered a cache of suspicious items in his car, including an ice pick, a mask made of pantyhose, and handcuffs. Picked out of a lineup by a young woman he had tried to abduct the year before, he was found guilty of aggravated kidnapping, sentenced to a stiff term in the Utah State Penitentiary, then extradited to Colorado in January 1977 to stand trial for murder.

Opting to serve as his own attorney, he managed to escape by jumping from a second-story window of the Aspen courthouse. He

*Ignoring the old courtroom adage—"He who represents himself has a fool for a client"—Bundy, with his usual cockiness, chose to act as his own defense lawyer.*

was recaptured six days later but escaped again in December, squeezing through a hole in the ceiling of his cell that he had painstakingly made with a smuggled hacksaw. This time, he headed for Tallahassee, Florida, where, in the early morning hours of January 15, 1978—one week after his arrival—he snuck into a sorority house and, in a demoniacal frenzy, set upon four sleeping coeds, killing two and gravely wounding the others. In one case, Bundy chewed off the nipples of his victim and left deep bite wounds in her buttock that forensic experts were later able to match to castings of his teeth.

A month later, after committing one final outrage—the abduction-murder of a twelve-year-old schoolgirl—he was arrested while driving a stolen car. Again, he acted as his own defense lawyer. Found guilty and sentenced to death, he managed to delay his execution for a decade until January 24, 1989. The night before he went to the chair, he confessed to thirty murders in seven states, though some students of the case believe that the total is much higher—that Bundy had slaughtered so many young women even he couldn't remember them all.

# #80 **PRESCRIPTION SLIP**

## "Dr. Death"

**(1974–1998)**

*Some serial murderers seek out careers as health care workers because the job offers convenient ways to exercise their dark intentions without arousing suspicion. One of the most notorious was British physician Harold Shipman, whose victims are thought to number in the hundreds.*

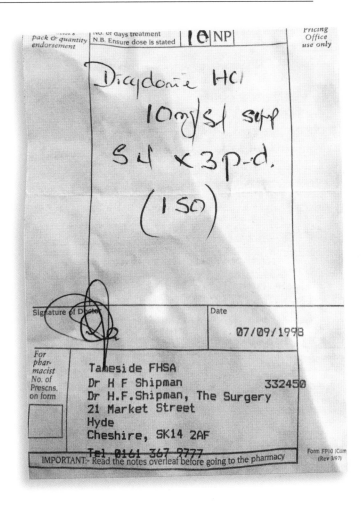

Gaining total control over another human being and dispensing death at their whim fills serial killers with an exhilarating sense of omnipotence. Because the medical profession offers its practitioners the regular opportunity to make godlike, life-or-death decisions, some serial killers have pursued careers as physicians. And because their victims are people who are ill to begin with, such psychopaths can get away with murder for many years—sometimes for decades—without arousing suspicion. Perhaps the most notorious of this breed was the British physician Harold Frederick Shipman, often referred to as the world's most prolific serial killer.

The roots of his psychopathology are impossible to pinpoint, though some have traced them to his quasi-incestuous relationship with his doting mother, who instilled in him an overweening sense of his own superiority. Students of the case agree that her lingering death from cancer when he was seventeen had a profound effect on his life. The caring attention he gave her during her illness—coming straight home from school so he could serve her tea, sit with her, and tend to her needs— helped forge the kindly bedside manner that would later endear him to his patients. And the sight of the family physician administering morphine injections to ease her final agonies is said to have played a formative role in his later lethal career, introducing him to the properties of the drug that would become his murder weapon of choice.

In 1974, four years out of medical school, Shipman, then twenty-six, joined a practice in the West Yorkshire town of Todmorden. It was there that the seemingly irreproachable, hard-working young physician began exhibiting signs of psychological trouble. After experiencing a series of blackouts, Shipman told his colleagues that he was an epileptic, an explanation they accepted until it was discovered that he had been forging prescriptions for a morphine-like painkiller called pethidine and injecting himself with it. Arrested for forgery and stealing drugs, he was hit with a sizable fine and forced out of the practice. At the time, no one seemed to notice the unusually high death rate among his patients, three of whom—elderly widows in reasonably stable health—died suddenly on the same day after house calls by the dedicated young doctor.

After a six-month stint in rehab, Shipman was soon back on the job. By 1977, he and his family had moved to Hyde, a town in Greater Manchester, where he quickly established himself as a highly respected member of the community and a much beloved general practitioner. Over the next twenty-one years, first as a member of a medical center, then after setting up his own private practice, he murdered a staggering number of patients, the vast majority of them elderly women. Though some of his victims were put to death during office visits, most were killed at home. His MO in the latter instances was always the same. He would pay an unexpected house call on a fairly healthy

*A lethal dose of the powerful painkiller diamorphine was Shipman's go-to murder method.*

patient, inject her with the powerful opioid diamorphine, then hurry away. Later—often summoned by a frantic call from a relative who had discovered the corpse—he would return and sign the death certificate, attributing the unexpected death to natural causes.

Suspicions about Shipman first arose in 1997 when the local undertaker, Alan Massey, sensed that, as he put it, "something was not quite right." For one thing, he was called upon to provide his services for the doctor's dead patients with surprising frequency. There was also the bizarre fact that their bodies were almost invariably found fully clothed and seated in their favorite easy chairs or resting on a settee. Though Shipman managed to reassure Massey that "there was no cause for concern," the undertaker's daughter, Deborah, was not so easily persuaded and made her concerns known to another local physician, Dr. Susan Booth. Booth, who had suspicions of her own, shared them with a colleague, Dr. Linda Reynolds, who alerted the South Manchester coroner. Before long, a police investigation was underway.

Though aware that authorities had begun looking into his records, Shipman could not stop killing. Indeed, by then, his homicidal mania had grown so extreme that he was sometimes doing away with his patients at the rate of one a day.

The unparalleled career of "Dr. Death" (as he was soon to be known by the world) finally came to an end in June 1998, when he killed Kathleen Grundy, an unusually fit octogenarian and former mayor of Hyde, then brazenly forged a will in her name that left him her entire fortune of nearly £400,000. As soon as Grundy's solicitor daughter, Angela, set eyes on the document, she saw it was fake and contacted the police, who already had Shipman in their sights. Before long, Grundy's corpse was exhumed and autopsied. When lethal amounts of diamorphine were discovered, Shipman was arrested.

He was tried and convicted of murdering fifteen of his patients, though the actual total is estimated at roughly 250. On January 13, 2004, four years after entering prison, Harold Shipman hanged himself in his cell.

# #81 DAVID BERKOWITZ'S HYMNAL

## "Son of Sam"

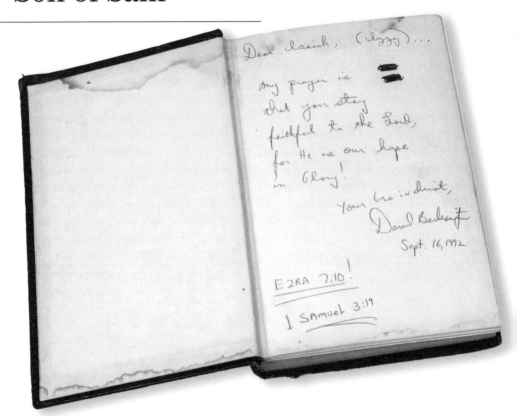

**(1976–1977)**

*Ten years into his imprisonment for the serial murders that terrorized New York City, the former "Son of Sam" claimed to have undergone a religious conversion, becoming a born-again Christian. He now styles himself "Son of Hope."*

The power of a lone madman to terrorize an entire city was vividly illustrated between the summers of 1976 and 1977 when the adult population of New York lived in fear of a night-prowling boogeyman initially dubbed the ".44-Caliber Killer." He struck first on the night of July 29, shooting two young women seated in a parked car in the Bronx, killing one. Nine more random shootings would occur over the following year. Though young people in cars—often dating couples—would continue to be his targets of choice, he also shot a pair of teenaged girls chatting on a stoop and a nineteen-year-old Columbia University student as she walked home from school. Before his rampage was over, a total of six young New Yorkers were dead and seven more severely wounded.

At the scene of one double murder, police found a long, ranting note from the killer that would supply him with a new and enduring nickname. "I am the 'Son of Sam,'" it read in part. "I am a little 'brat.'" Another, addressed to famed newspaper columnist Jimmy Breslin, declared that "Sam's a thirsty lad and he won't let me stop killing until he gets his fill of blood." Like the famous Jack the Ripper letter with the return address "From Hell," the message to Breslin began with a greeting "from the gutters of N.Y.C., which are filled with dog manure, vomit, stale wine, urine, and blood."

The massive manhunt for "Sam" finally came to an end, as such things often do, through pure happenstance. On the night of his final murder, a woman out walking her dog noticed a policeman ticketing an illegally parked car. Moments later, she spotted a young man with a "dark object" in one hand get into the automobile and drive away. A few days later, she contacted the police, who promptly traced the summons through their computer and learned that it had been left on the windshield of a Ford sedan registered to a Yonkers resident, David Berkowitz. The following day, Yonkers police tracked down Berkowitz's car. Inside, they found a small arsenal of weapons that the killer was planning to deploy in an apocalyptic act of carnage, a kamikaze assault on a Long Island disco.

A pudgy-faced postal worker who had been raised by adoptive Jewish parents in the Bronx, Berkowitz turned out to be a grotesque combination of psychotic and "incel," or involuntary celibate: a delusional madman and virulent misogynist who believed that a neighbor named Sam Carr was transmitting commandments to kill through his pet Labrador retriever, and who targeted attractive young women as a way of taking revenge for a lifetime of sexual rejection.

Despite his manifest derangement, Berkowitz was found mentally fit to stand trial. He was eventually sentenced in 1978 to three hundred years in a supermax prison, where, after undergoing a religious conversion, he adopted a new nickname—"Son of Hope"—and began contributing essays on his newfound faith to Evangelical websites.

# #82 TED KACZYNSKI'S TYPEWRITER

## "The Unabomber"

**(1978–1995)**

*Though Ted Kaczynski's crimes were the work of an unhinged personality, many of the ideas put forth in his antitechnology manifesto have been embraced by radical environmentalists.*

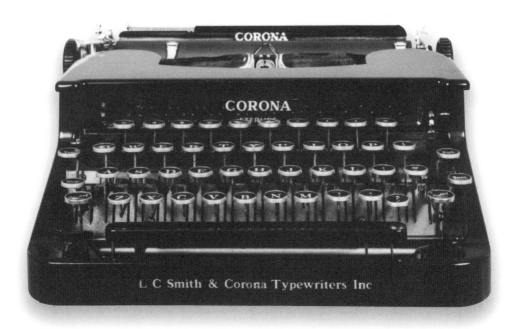

With a recorded IQ of 167, Ted Kaczynski was a math prodigy who skipped two grades in school, entered Harvard at sixteen, and—after receiving his doctorate from the University of Michigan in 1967 at the age of twenty-five—joined the math faculty at University of California, Berkley, the youngest person ever appointed to a tenure-track professorship at the institution. He was also a paranoid schizophrenic who developed a fanatical hatred of modern Western civilization.

Resigning from his academic position in 1969, he retreated to the wilds of Montana, built a hermit's cabin in the woods, and launched a one-man war against the technological forces he blamed for all of society's ills. He began with relatively minor acts of vandalism, but his campaign took a more violent turn in 1978 when he began targeting figures from the worlds of science and technology who, in his unhinged view, represented the evils of the "industrial system" that (as he would later write) had reduced "human beings . . . to engineered products and mere cogs in the social machine." In May of that year, a suspicious package directed to an engineering professor at Northwestern University was opened by a security guard, who suffered minor injuries to one hand when the crude homemade bomb it contained exploded.

Over the course of the next eighteen years, Kaczynski mailed or hand-delivered more than a dozen increasingly sophisticated parcel bombs to science professors, engineering students, computer salesmen, and corporate executives, including the president of United Airlines. Many suffered severe injuries—loss of fingers and hands, partial blindness, shrapnel wounds to their faces and bodies. Dubbed the "Unabomber" by the FBI (an acronymic nickname deriving from "University and Airline Bomber"), Kaczynski became the object of the one of the longest and costliest manhunts in the agency's history.

Not long after his final outrage—the 1995 murder of Gilbert B. Murray, chief lobbyist for a forest-products trade group who was killed when he opened a package addressed to his predecessor—Kaczynski mailed a typed, thirty-five-thousand-word essay to both the *New York Times* and the *Washington Post*, offering to "desist from terrorism" if the papers published it in full. Titled "Industrial Society and Its Future," the "Manifesto" (as it came to be called) was a detailed, heavily footnoted screed about the dehumanizing effects of modern technology. In the hope that some reader might recognize the author, the FBI, with the approval of United States Attorney General Janet Reno, authorized its publication.

The strategy worked. In February 1996, Kaczynski's brother David informed the FBI that the manifesto bore the hallmarks of his sibling's writing style and crackpot ideas. Two months later, on April 3, Kaczynski was arrested in his cabin, where FBI agents found a mountain of incriminating evidence, including a live bomb and the original copy of the manifesto, along with the typewriter on which it had been transcribed. Indicted on more than a dozen federal charges, he pleaded guilty on all counts to avoid the death penalty and was sentenced to life imprisonment without parole.

# #83 GARY HEIDNIK'S CHURCH MEMBERSHIP CARD

## Gary Heidnik

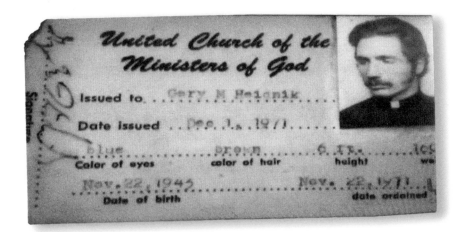

**(1986–1987)**
*Self-appointed bishop of a church he founded in 1971,*
*Gary Heidnik attracted a congregation of fifty members*
*who would come to his house to hear him preach, unaware*
*that a half dozen women were chained up in his basement*
*"horror dungeon."*

Born in a Cleveland suburb in 1943, Gary Heidnik was the product of a broken home. He suffered extreme humiliation at the hands of his father who, among other abuses, dealt with his son's bed-wetting by forcing him to hang his soiled sheets out the window for the whole neighborhood to see. His mother was an alcoholic who abandoned the family when Gary was two and ultimately died by suicide.

Despite his superior intelligence (his IQ was measured at 148), he was a high school dropout, joining the army at seventeen. Within two years of his enlistment, he had begun to manifest the severe psychological problems that would afflict him for the rest of his life. Diagnosed with schizoid personality disorder during a stay in a military hospital, he was discharged in October 1962. Over the next twenty-five years, he would be in and out of psychiatric institutions twenty-one times and survive two dozen suicide attempts.

During his more lucid periods, Heidnik applied himself to a variety of pursuits. He trained as a practical nurse and found work at a Veterans Administration hospital, though he lasted only a few months before being fired for "poor attendance and a bad attitude." With the savings from his army pension, he purchased a run-down three-story house in Philadelphia and became a landlord. He also found Jesus. In 1971, he incorporated the United Church of the Ministers of God, elected himself bishop, and attracted a handful of followers who contributed $1,500 to the operation. Heidnik—who was something of a financial whiz—invested the funds in the stock market and, within ten years, built up a half-million-dollar portfolio.

Heidnik's first serious run-in with the law occurred in 1978, when he locked his girlfriend's intellectually disabled sister in his basement, raped, and sodomized her. Indicted on a string of charges, including kidnapping, false imprisonment, and involuntary deviant sexual intercourse, he was sentenced to three to seven years in the penitentiary. He ended up serving four years, most of it in various mental institutions. During much of that period, he refused to talk, insisting that "the Devil had shoved a cookie down his throat."

Following his release, he married a Filipino mail-order bride, who abandoned him three months later, having tired of being beaten, anally raped, and forced to watch him have sex with sex workers. Shortly after her departure, Heidnik became obsessed with a plan to create a "baby factory" in the basement of his house. Between Thanksgiving 1986 and the following May, he abducted five victims—most of them young Black intellectually disabled women—and held them captive in what the tabloids would eventually describe as his "horror dungeon." They were subjected to torture, beatings, and daily rape, and fed a diet of bread and oatmeal, with an occasional dog biscuit treat. When one of the women died after being chained to a pipe by her wrists for a week, Heidnik dragged her body upstairs, dismembered it with a power saw, cooked her head in a saucepan, roasted her rib cage in the oven, and ground up her flesh in a food processor. Then he mixed the ground meat with dog food and force-fed it to the others. Another member of his "horror harem" died after being thrown into a water-filled pit and electrocuted with a live wire.

In April 1987, Heidnik was arrested after one of his captives managed to elude his clutches and alert the police. At his arraignment, he offered one of the more novel defenses in the annals of American jurisprudence, claiming that the women were in the basement at the time he moved in. Convicted of two counts of first-degree murder and sentenced to death, he was executed by lethal injection on July 6, 1999.

# #84 WRAPPER FROM CANDY FACTORY WHERE JEFFREY DAHMER WORKED

## "The Milwaukee Cannibal"

**(1987–1991)**

*For six years, between 1985 and 1991, Jeffrey Dahmer held down a job at Milwaukee's Ambrosia Chocolate factory while conducting a secret life as one of history's most appalling sex-killers.*

J effrey Dahmer was enamored of dead things from an early age. Instead of comic books and baseball cards, he collected roadkill, stripping the carcasses down to the bones, which he liked to bleach and place in a bucket so he could enjoy the clicking sounds they made when he rattled them around.

Dahmer committed his first murder at the age of eighteen, when—after picking up a young hitchhiker and bringing him home for sex—he bludgeoned the young man to death with a barbell, then dismembered the body and buried the parts in the woods. Then his bloodlust remained dormant until he reached twenty-seven. After a stint in the army, he moved to Milwaukee where he found work in the Ambrosia Chocolate Factory and lived with his grandmother. On the night of September 15, 1987, he picked up a young man named Steven Toumi in a gay bar. The two repaired to a hotel room where Dahmer beat and strangled Toumi to death in an alcoholic stupor.

The following year, Dahmer killed his next victim, Jamie Doxtator, a fourteen-year-old boy he picked up outside the same bar. Dahmer took Doxtator to his grandmother's house, drugged him with sleeping pills after sex, then strangled him, dismembered him, and disposed of the remains in the trash, though he kept the boy's skull as a ghoulish souvenir after scraping it clean of flesh. A few months later, he murdered again, this time having sex with the corpse before disposing of it.

Moving into his own apartment, Dahmer plunged into a life of ever-escalating atrocity: cannibalism, necrophilia (including sex with his victims' intestines), the ritualistic preservation of body parts. In at least one instance, he drilled a hole in the skull of a drugged teenager and injected his brain with muriatic acid in an attempt to turn him into a "sex zombie." Thirteen men and boys ranging in age from fourteen to thirty-two—many of them minorities—met unspeakable ends in what would become known as Dahmer's chamber of horrors.

The end of the carnage came on a muggy night in late July 1991, when two Milwaukee patrolmen spotted a dazed Black man stumbling toward them, a pair of handcuffs dangling from one wrist. Flagging down their squad car, he gestured wildly toward Dahmer's building and stammered out a tale of attempted murder. What the officers found left them reeling in disbelief.

Seven skulls and five complete skeletons were stashed around the apartment, along with miscellaneous remains: bone fragments, decomposed hands, genitalia in a lobster pot. The drawers of the bedroom were crammed with Polaroids of body parts and mutilated corpses—seventy-four photos in all. A fifty-seven-gallon drum contained three dismembered torsos dissolving in acid. The refrigerator and freezer were stocked with decapitated heads, arm muscles, and an assortment of viscera: intestines, lungs, livers, kidneys, and a heart that Dahmer later said he was saving to "eat later." The police also found bottles of acid, chloroform, and formaldehyde, along with three electric saws.

The revelation of Dahmer's unspeakable deeds sent shock waves across the country. At his 1992 trial, his attorney argued that the very nature of Dahmer's enormities was proof of his madness. The jury, however, rejected the insanity defense and found him guilty. He was sentenced to 941 years in prison. During his final statement, Dahmer expressed a desire to die. His wish came true on November 28, 1994, when he was bludgeoned to death by a fellow inmate while cleaning a bathroom.

# #85 LAURIE DANN'S GUN LICENSE

## "The Winnetka Killer"

**(1988)**

*According to a research group that tracks such grim data, 98 percent of US mass shootings since 1966 have been carried out by men. Laurie Dann was one of the deadly exceptions.*

W hen we think of the perpetrators of mass school shootings, we tend to picture angry young men. But in 1988, gunshots rang out in a second-grade classroom in Illinois and the shooter was a woman.

Her name was Laurie Wasserman Dann. Born in 1957 in an affluent suburb of Chicago, she had what most accounts describe as an "unremarkable" childhood. An indifferent student in high school, she attended a succession of colleges without ever earning a degree. She then got engaged to a pre-med student named Steve Witt, who—unable to deal with her extreme possessiveness—broke off the relationship.

Moving back to Chicago in 1980, Laurie took a job as a cocktail waitress at a country club, where she met and fell in love with Russell Dann, a handsome, athletic young man who worked in his family's insurance business. Even during their courtship Russell noticed certain peculiarities in Laurie's behavior—her habit of opening the car door at stoplights and tapping her foot on the ground, her refusal to close kitchen cabinets or pick up dropped utensils, the way she would tiptoe around her parents' living room carpet, as though terrified of setting her foot on it. These OCD symptoms—which he initially dismissed as "harmless superstitions"— grew more extreme after their marriage in September 1982. Though given to scrubbing her hands dozens of times a day, she scattered trash around the house, stuck spending money in the freezer, and stored canned food in the dishwasher. Her car, as acquaintances observed, "looked like the home of a bag lady."

At her husband's pleading, she began to see a psychiatrist but terminated treatment in March 1984. The following year, she and Russell separated. By then, Laurie's mental condition had deteriorated even further. She located her former college boyfriend, Steve Witt, now doing his residency at a New York City hospital, and began harassing him by phone, as well as putting in anonymous calls to administrators accusing him of having raped her in the emergency room. She also filed complaints with the police, claiming that Russell had broken into her parents' apartment and vandalized it and had placed a Molotov cocktail in her home. In September 1986, someone—undoubtedly Laurie, though her guilt could never be proved—snuck into Russell's apartment while he slept and stabbed him in the chest with an ice pick, just missing his heart. Not long afterward, she walked into a Glenview gun shop and purchased a Smith & Wesson .357 Magnum.

In 1987, Laurie hired herself out as a babysitter. Though some parents found her "sweet and nice," others returned from outings to discover that their sofas had been slashed, carpets cut up, freezers plundered of food. By early 1988, Laurie was living in a student dormitory in Madison, Wisconsin, where she became known as the "psycho elevator lady" for her habit of aimlessly riding the elevator all night. She would leave raw meat under the seat cushions in the TV room, wander the halls naked, and sleep in the garbage room wrapped in a plastic trash bag. She made anonymous calls to former babysitting clients who had accused her of theft, telling one terrified mother, "Your children are going to die." On May 16, she left Madison and drove back to Glencoe, Illinois. By then, she had put together a list of people she intended to kill.

Early on Friday, May 20, she drove to the suburban homes of a half dozen former babysitting clients, leaving packages of tainted kiddie snacks on their doorsteps: Rice Krispies treats and boxed fruit drinks doctored with arsenic she had stolen from a science lab in Madison. Proceeding to the home of another family—the Rushes, long-time babysitting clients whose young sons, Patrick and Carl, were crazy about her—she loaded the boys into her car, telling their mother that she intended to take them to a carnival in nearby Evanston. Instead, she drove them to a Highland Park elementary school, where—so she mistakenly believed—the two sons of her former sister-in-law, Susie Taylor, were enrolled. After tossing a Molotov cocktail into the building, she headed for a nearby daycare center attended by Taylor's daughter and attempted to set it ablaze with a can of gasoline. Dropping the Rushe children back home, she then drove to another elementary school in nearby Winnetka. Inside, she followed a little boy into a bathroom and shot him in the chest, then burst into a second-grade classroom and fired at five other children, killing one and critically wounding the rest.

Fleeing in her car, she crashed into a tree and took refuge in the home of a family named Andrews, holding them hostage for hours. Twenty-year-old Philip Andrews tried to wrestle Laurie's gun away from her and was shot in the chest. He managed to stagger outside, where he collapsed on the lawn. By then, the house was surrounded by police. Speaking through a bullhorn, Laurie's father begged her to surrender. Receiving no response, an assault team burst inside the house. They found her in a second-floor bedroom, dead from a bullet to the head.

# #86 RAT MAN DRAWINGS

## "The Otaku Killer"

**(1988)**

*Because they lead such double lives, serial killers often imagine that, like comic book characters, they have superhuman alter egos. In the warped mind of sociopathic comic book fanatic Tsutomu Miyazaki, the true perpetrator of his atrocities was his evil Other Self, "The Rat Man."*

At around three o'clock on the sweltering afternoon of August 22, 1988, in the Japanese prefecture of Saitama, a four-year-old girl named Mari Konno left her apartment to visit a friend. She sported a page-boy haircut and wore a pink-trimmed T-shirt with a picture of a cat, black shorts with white stripes down the sides, and a pair of pink sandals.

As she made her way through the sprawling apartment complex, a car pulled up beside her. The driver emerged and—asking Konno if she would like to get out of the heat and go someplace cool—held out a hand. Both his hands looked strange, with grotesquely elongated fingers that would later be compared to the ratlike claw of the silent-movie vampire Nosferatu. Konno, however, was undisturbed. Taking him by one of his taloned hands, she got into the car. Witnesses later testified to seeing the little girl walking in a remote wooded area with a young man with a round, pudgy face, curly hair, and dressed in white slacks and a white summer sweater.

A few days after Konno's disappearance, her parents received a postcard with an ominous message: "There are devils about." The police—by then engaged in a massive search for the missing girl—dismissed the card as the work of a crank. Only later would they learn that it had been sent by Konno's abductor: a sadistic, pedophiliac sex-killer named Tsutomu Miyazaki.

Born premature in August 1962, he came into the world with badly deformed hands, the result of a condition that fused the joints together. He was an unusually bright child, but his classmates' constant teasing caused him to withdraw into a world of fantasy, fed by his obsessive interest in manga and anime, often featuring scenes of hard-core bloodshed and titillating sex. In his isolation and all-consuming interest in violent comics and cartoons, he fell into the category of "otaku," the Japanese equivalent of what Western culture calls a geek. Miyazaki, however, was not just a socially maladjusted fanboy. Like other budding serial killers, he enjoyed torturing animals, including a cat that he confessed to having boiled alive and his own pet dog, which he garroted with a wire. As he matured into adolescence, he began collecting pornographic videotapes, many involving children. The only person in his life who seemed to care for him was his grandfather. When the old man died, Miyazaki ate some of his cremated bones.

Miyazaki struck a second time, on October 3, 1988. Once again, he lured a schoolgirl into his car—seven-year-old Masami Yoshizawa. Driving to the scene of his previous outrage, he strangled her, stripped her naked, and sexually assaulted the corpse before fleeing with her clothing. Another large-scale manhunt failed to turn up a trace of the missing girl.

Four-year-old Erika Namba was the next to die. She was abducted in the late afternoon of December 12 as she walked home from a friend's house. Miyazaki drove the sobbing child to a remote parking area, forced her to undress, then snapped photos of her naked body before strangling her.

As he drove away with the corpse stowed in his trunk, he veered off the road and got stuck in a drainage ditch. Realizing that he would have to call for assistance, he removed the body and dumped it in a nearby woods. It was found two days later. Its discovery convinced police that the still-missing girls, Mari Konno and Masami Yoshizawa, were undoubtedly dead and that a serial murderer was on the loose. Intensified efforts to locate the bodies, however, came to nothing; the search for their killer was equally fruitless.

Reveling, like others of his breed, in sadistic power games, Miyazaki mailed another taunting postcard on December 20, this time to Erika Namba's parents. Assembled from cut-and-pasted characters from magazines and newspapers, it read: "Erika. Cold. Cough. Throat. Rest. Dead."

While police were conducting their sweeping manhunt, Miyazaki had gone back to the spot where he had left Konno's body, brought the decomposed corpse back home, and—after cutting off her hands and feet and stashing them in his closet—incinerated the rest in his furnace. Then he boxed up the cremains.

Early on the morning of February 6, 1989, as Konno's father left his apartment on the way to work, he found the box on his doorstep. Along with a pile of ashes, charred bone fragments, and ten baby teeth, it contained photos of a little girl's shorts, underwear, and sandals, and a note reading: "Mari. Bones. Cremated. Investigate. Prove."

Miyazaki, however, was not done with Mari Konno's parents. At the funeral for his daughter on March 11, 1989—seven months after she vanished—her father made a piteous plea for the killer to return the rest of her remains. When he and his wife returned home from the ceremony, they found another letter from "Yuko Imada," the name Miyazaki used, waiting for them, this one describing in gruesome detail the condition of Mari's decomposing body.

On June 6, Miyazaki committed his fourth atrocity. He came upon five-year-year-old Ayako Nomoto playing by herself in a park and, after persuading her to pose for some photographs, led her to his car. It wasn't until he offered her a stick of gum that she noticed his hands and said something about how funny they looked. Flying into a rage, Miyazaki strangled her to death and stashed her body in the trunk. He then drove home and smuggled the corpse into his house, where he photographed it in pornographic positions, and eventually hacked it apart, roasting the hands in his backyard and devouring the flesh.

The end came for Miyazaki less than two months later, on July 23. Trolling for victims, he came upon two little sisters and cajoled the younger one into following him to a riverbank, where he got her to strip and began shooting pornographic photos. In the meantime, the older, nine-year-old sister had run home and alerted her father, who hurried to the spot and began grappling with Miyazaki. Though Miyazaki managed to break free, he soon found himself in the hands of the police. He eventually confessed to all four murders.

When detectives searched his apartment, they found nearly six thousand ultraviolent videotapes and comic books. The discovery created an uproar among the Japanese public, who blamed Miyazaki's atrocities on "otaku" culture (in the same way that moral crusaders in the US view violent video games as a leading cause of juvenile crime). Branded the "Otaku Killer" by the press, he was put on trial in March 1990 and spent much of the time drawing cartoons of a character called "Rat Man," a supposed alter ego who he claimed was responsible for the crimes. Between appeals and prolonged examinations by mental health experts, seven years passed before Miyazaki was sentenced to death and another eleven before he was hanged.

# #87 IVAN MILAT ACTION FIGURE

## "The Backpacker Murders"

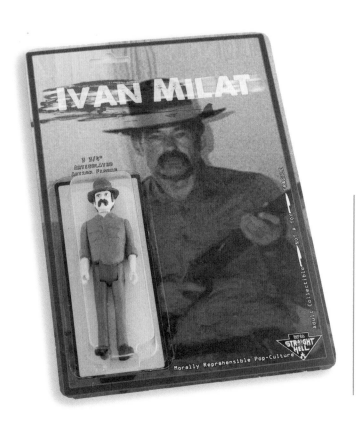

**(1989–1992)**

*Perpetrator of some of the ghastliest crimes in Australian history, Ivan Milat has achieved the kind of dark celebrity sometimes bestowed on human monsters.*

Among aficionados of hard-core horror, the 2005 movie *Wolf Creek*—in which a trio of young backpackers in the Australian outback fall prey to a sadistic psycho-killer—stands as a grueling exemplar of the genre known as "torture porn." What makes the film even more titillating to its admirers is the fact that it was partly inspired by a real-life case, that of the so-called Backpacker Killer, Ivan Milat.

Born in New South Wales, Australia, in 1944, the fifth of fourteen children, Milat showed signs of antisocial personality disorder (today's preferred term for psychopathy) from an early age. By his teens he was already in trouble with the law for a series of home burglaries. In his twenties, he did four stints behind bars for breaking and entering, stealing, and car theft.

His crimes became more vicious in 1971, when he picked up two eighteen-year-old female hitchhikers, drove them to a remote spot in the woods, and raped one of them at knifepoint. Charged with abduction and rape, he faked his suicide and fled to New Zealand. About two years later, after running afoul of the law, he returned to Australia, where he was promptly re-arrested and put on trial. Subjected to a particularly nasty cross-examination by Milat's attorney, the rape victim recanted her original testimony and Milat walked free.

For the next two decades, he led a relatively respectable life as a married man, father, and employee of the Department of Transport and Main Roads. In 1987, however, having suffered increasingly violent abuse at the hands of her husband, his wife fled the marriage.

Two years later, young backpackers began to disappear.

In late December 1990, Deborah Everist and James Gibson, both nineteen, were thumbing rides from Sydney to an outdoor festival when they vanished. Two years later, a twenty-one-year-old German tourist, Simone Schmidl, left Sydney to hitchhike to Melbourne, where she planned to rendezvous with her mother. She never arrived. Two more German hitchhikers, twenty-two-year-old Gabor Neugebauer and his twenty-one-year-old girlfriend, Anja Habschied, disappeared in December 1991. The following April, Caroline Clarke and Joanne Walters—young British women on vacation—also went missing.

Clarke and Walters were the first to be found. In mid-September 1992, two runners in Belanglo State Forest, about eighty-five miles south of Sydney, came upon their decomposed remains. Walters had been stabbed nearly three dozen times in the chest and back. Clarke had been shot ten times while blindfolded and stabbed multiple times in the chest. Both had been sexually assaulted.

In October 1993, a local man collecting firewood in a particularly remote area of the forest unearthed Gibson's skeletal remains, lying in a fetal position in a shallow grave. Everist's were uncovered close by. Both had been subjected to the same unbridled savagery as the two British women. A month later, police searchers scouring the forest found the skeletons of the remaining three victims.

A special task force was created to hunt for the serial murderer, and the government offered a reward of a half-million dollars for information leading to his arrest. The case was covered by news organizations throughout the United Kingdom. It was an Englishman named Paul Onions who, after reading stories about the so-called Backpacker Killer in the British tabloids, finally helped bring the two-year manhunt to an end.

*Hunter of humans Ivan Milat poses with one of his weapons.*

In January 1990, Onions had been back-packing around Australia when he got a lift from a mustachioed man who introduced himself as "Bill." Near a turnoff to the Belanglo State Forest, the man suddenly pulled to the side of the road, drew a revolver, and announced, "This is a robbery." Onions, an ex-navy man, leapt from the car and ran, bullets whizzing past his head. Onions was saved by another driver, who brought him to the nearest police station.

Convinced that the man who attacked him was the "Backpacker Killer," Onions contacted police in Australia, who flew him from England in early May 1994. By that time, Ivan Milat was a person of interest in the case, investigators having discovered his long criminal record and his arrest and trial for abduction and rape twenty years earlier. It was also known that he sometimes went by the nickname "Bill." Shown photographs of thirteen suspects, including Milat, Onions positively identified him as his would-be killer.

Two weeks later, on May 22, a squad of fifty police officers raided Milat's home, where they discovered an arsenal of weapons, including a rifle that matched the type used on his victims, and a trove of their belongings: tents, sleeping bags, backpacks, clothing, and more.

Tried in July 1996, Milat was found guilty of murdering the seven backpackers and sentenced to life for each of the homicides. In the course of his incarceration he survived several suicide attempts, once by swallowing razor blades, staples, and part of a nail clipper and once by swallowing a metal spring from the flushing mechanism of his toilet. He died of esophageal and stomach cancer in October 2019 at the age of seventy-four.

# #88 DANNY ROLLING'S ARTWORK

## "The Gainesville Ripper"

**(1990)**

*Artwork by serial killers is a distinct category of murderabilia. While some imprisoned sex-killers specialize in images that are at odds with their malevolent natures, Danny Rolling flaunted his diabolical fantasies in his jailhouse drawings.*

Danny Rolling :< 4-21-96 ☆

Like so many sociopathic killers, Danny Rolling suffered a nightmarish childhood, in his case at the hands of a sadistic policeman father who subjected him to relentless abuse and humiliation. It began when the boy first started to crawl. Displeased at the infant for pulling himself across the floor in an ungainly manner, the senior Rolling grabbed his son by a leg and banged him against a wall. Over the following years, he subjected Danny to regular whippings. At one point, irritated by the behavior of Danny's beloved dog, he beat the animal so savagely that it died in the young boy's arms. By early adolescence, Danny was heavily into alcohol and drugs and had survived several suicide attempts. He had also become a Peeping Tom, a compulsion that would later evolve into housebreaking, rape, and ultimately sex-murder.

In 1971, the seventeen-year-old Rolling joined the air force but was discharged within two years for drug possession and disobeying orders. Returning to his family home in Shreveport, Louisiana, he made a short-lived attempt to reform his life by joining a Pentecostal church, where he met and married another congregant, Omatha Ann Halko. Owing to his increasingly erratic behavior—disappearing for days, threatening her with a shotgun, resuming his voyeuristic habits—she left him three years later.

Over the next decade, from 1978 through 1988, he committed a string of armed robberies in Alabama, Georgia, and Louisiana and did time in various prisons. In November 1989, sixteen months after his final parole, while living back in Shreveport, he broke into the home of a local family, the Grissoms. He stabbed three of them to death with a KA-BAR knife: fifty-five-year-old Tom Grissom, his eight-year-old grandson, Sean, and his twenty-four-year-old daughter, Julie, who had been raped, douched with vinegar, and posed obscenely on her bed.

A fight with Rolling's father the following May escalated into a gun battle that left the old man with two bullet wounds to the stomach and one in the forehead. Fleeing Shreveport, Rolling made his way to Kansas City, Kansas, committing rapes and robberies along the way, then headed back east where, in August 1990, he set up camp in a wooded area not far from the campus of the University of Florida in Gainesville.

On August 24, Christina Powell and Sonja Larson, seventeen-year-old roommates, were found raped, butchered, and posed in their student apartment. The killer had broken in while they slept, bound and gagged them with duct tape, then raped and savaged them with a foot-long military KA-BAR knife. Afterward, he had mutilated the corpses and arranged them in obscene poses.

The next night, he struck again. This time the victim was eighteen-year-old Christa Hoyt, a sophomore at Santa Fe College, whom he raped and then killed in a frenzy of violence, stabbing her to death, slicing off her nipples, and cutting her open from breastbone to groin. He then decapitated the corpse, placing the head on a shelf before fleeing the scene. The savagery of the crime would earn him the tabloid nickname, the "Gainesville Ripper."

Panic gripped the community. Hundreds of students fled the state. Many who remained traveled in groups and avoided being alone.

Though twenty-three-year-old Tracey Paules shared in the general unease, she was not overly concerned. Her roommate, also twenty-three, was Manuel Taboada, a strapping six-foot-three-inch senior who weighed over two hundred pounds. With Manny around, no harm would befall her. Or so she believed.

In the early morning hours of August 27, the Ripper broke into their apartment while they slept. Taboada awoke to find himself under attack by the knife-wielding maniac. Though the young man put up a ferocious struggle, he was no match for the Ripper's blade, suffering thirty-one wounds.

Awakened by the commotion, Paules—as court documents later recorded—

> **opened her door to investigate...
> Seeing [the blood-drenched assailant],
> she ran back into her bedroom,
> locking the door. [Rolling] kicked
> it in and was on her. He taped her
> hands behind her back and taped
> her mouth. He removed her T-shirt
> and raped her, turned her over on
> her stomach, and stabbed her three
> times in the back. She died quickly.
> Eight to ten seconds, and it was over.
> He removed the tape and dragged
> her into the hallway, went into the
> bathroom, wet a washcloth, wiped
> the blood from her face, and raped
> her again. He douched her out with
> a kitchen cleanser and left.**

With the city in a panic, police intensified their search for the sex-killer. Suspicion fell heavily on a local man named Edward Humphrey—a chronic troublemaker with a history of violently erratic behavior. But the real killer, Danny Rolling, was miles away.

After the slaughter in Gainesville, Rolling headed for Ocala, where, on September 8,

he was captured after robbing a supermarket at gunpoint. At first, the police didn't realize that they had bagged the Ripper. Further investigation into his background, however, revealed that he was wanted in Shreveport for the attempted murder of his father. Authorities also learned of the horrific triple homicide in Shreveport during the time Rolling was living there, a crime that bore marked similarities to the Gainesville horrors.

An examination of evidence gathered from the campsite where Rolling had stayed after arriving in Gainesville produced overwhelming physical evidence linking him to the murders of the five college students, including a pubic hair that—thanks to DNA analysis—was matched with one of the victims. Before long, Rolling had confessed.

At his 1994 trial, his lawyer tried to persuade the jury that Rolling deserved sympathy because of his brutal upbringing. Whatever sympathy they might have felt for the mistreatment he had suffered as a child failed to mitigate their outrage at the atrocities he had committed as an adult. On April 23, 1994, he was sentenced to death for five counts of murder. A dozen years would pass before that sentence was carried out. At around 5:00 p.m. on October 25, 2006, Rolling was wheeled into the death chamber. Asked if he had any last statement, he broke into song. He was still singing as the fluids were pumped into his arm. Thirteen minutes later, he was pronounced dead.

# #89 ROBERT PICKTON'S CHAINSAW

## "The Pig Farm Killer"

22070

**(1991–2001)**
*Female victims dismembered by chainsaw, their body parts fed to pigs for disposal, is the stuff of hard-core "slasher" movies. Robert Pickton turned that nightmare into reality.*

A common variety of serial murderer, dating back to the days of Jack the Ripper, is the so-called "harlot killer." Driven by a profound loathing and fear of female sexuality, this type of homicidal maniac preys primarily, often exclusively, on sex workers: highly vulnerable women easy to snare and overpower, and often so socially marginalized that the world barely notices when they disappear.

Between 1991 and 2001, dozens of Canadian sex workers who worked a seamy stretch of downtown Vancouver vanished from the streets. It wasn't until 1998 that the police, pressured into action by family members of the missing, created a task force. Their investigation eventually led them to a reprobate named Robert Pickton.

Born in 1949 and brought up on a pig farm less than twenty miles outside of Vancouver, Pickton—whose standards of personal hygiene were roughly the same as those of his swine—inherited the place with his brother following the death of their parents. Letting the farm go to seed, they focused their energies on running an anything-goes nightspot called the Piggy Palace: a converted barn where strippers, prostitutes, Hells Angels, drug addicts, and assorted ne'er-do-wells could enjoy music, drugs, unprotected sex, and the occasional cockfight. Security was reportedly provided by a vicious six-hundred-pound boar that patrolled the property.

Tipped off that Pickton had a large stash of illegal weapons on the premises, police raided the farm in February 2002 and turned up a mountain of evidence linking him to several dozen of the missing women. Subsequent searches of the property uncovered assorted body parts, heads, and a freezer packed with ground human flesh that Pickton allegedly mixed with pork and sold to consumers. These ghastly remains represented only a fraction of the victims Pickton claimed to have killed. The corpses of others, so he boasted, had been fed to his pigs.

Tried and found guilty of six counts of second-degree murder, he was sentenced to the maximum punishment under Canadian law: life imprisonment with no possibility of parole for twenty-five years. Exactly how many women met death at his hands is unknown. Pickton himself confessed to forty-nine murders, lamenting the fact he had fallen one short of his goal of fifty.

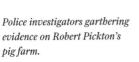

*Police investigators garthering evidence on Robert Pickton's pig farm.*

# #90 SUSAN SMITH SELF-PORTRAIT

## "The Modern-Day Medea"

Love ya!
Susan '04

**(1994)**
*Had it been drawn by a kindergartener, this crayoned self-portrait would seem charming. As the product of an adult woman who committed the horrific crime of murdering her own children, it is indescribably creepy.*

At around nine o'clock on the night of October 25, 1995, the McCloud family of Union, South Carolina, was startled by a frantic pounding on their front door. They opened it to find a hysterical young woman on their porch, screaming about a Black man taking her car with her kids inside it. When the police arrived, the overwrought woman— a local resident, twenty-three-year-old Susan Smith—spilled out a harrowing tale.

At about six that evening, she sobbed, she had gone shopping at Walmart with her two sons: Michael, age three, and Alex, his fourteen-month-old brother. After wandering the aisles with them for three hours, she had strapped them into the rear child seats of her 1990 Mazda Protege, then headed for the home of a high school friend. As she sat waiting at a red light on a deserted street in the town of Monarch Mill, the unlocked passenger door swung open and a young Black man—badly out of breath as though fleeing a crime—jumped in beside her, pointed a gun at her head, and commanded her to drive. After seven miles or so, he told her to pull over, ordered her out of the car, and slid behind the wheel. "Let me take my babies!" she begged. Saying that it would take too long to unbuckle them, he promised not to hurt them and sped off, leaving her screaming in the road.

The story broke that same night on local TV and radio stations. By the next morning, it was front-page news across the nation. The nation's heart went out to the distraught mother, who initially went into seclusion. She eventually emerged with her estranged husband, David, at her side, appearing on network morning programs to make tearful pleas for her little ones' safe return. Even as the search for the children continued, however, investigators were beginning to have serious doubts about her story.

Smith described the carjacker as a Black man escaping a crime scene—but no crimes had been reported in the area that night. And if it were true—if he really *was* making a desperate getaway—why bring along two white babies? Smith also claimed that he had jumped into her car while she was stopped at a red light with no one else around. But that particular traffic light only turned red if another car approached the intersection from a different direction. If Smith had really been stopped at the light, another driver would surely have witnessed the crime. Moreover, why hadn't the carjacker taken her to some remote spot where she wouldn't have been able to summon help so readily?

There was also the matter of Smith's behavior in the days following the ostensible abduction. She didn't appear to cry and within twenty-four hours of her children's disappearance invariably referred to them in the past tense. Just as odd was her tendency to dwell on her own response to the tragedy— how she couldn't eat, couldn't sleep.

Police began a covert investigation into Smith's background. Soon they learned that, earlier in the fall, while working as a secretary at a local textile plant, she had become romantically involved with the owner's handsome son, Tom Findlay, widely regarded as the town's most eligible bachelor. Smith's dream of becoming the wife of the wealthy young man was abruptly shattered, however, when she received a "Dear John" letter from him explaining that, as much as he cared for her, he was not prepared to take on the responsibility of raising another man's children. When police interviewed Findlay, he provided them with a copy of the break-up letter, which he had composed on his computer. It had been sent to Smith on Tuesday, October 18—one week before the supposed kidnapping.

More persuaded than ever that Smith's story was a fabrication, police began to subject her to intensive questioning. Results of two polygraph tests clearly indicated that she was lying. Finally, on November 3, under increasing pressure from investigators, Smith cracked. Her two-page confession would transform her from an object of widespread sympathy into the nation's most reviled woman.

\*\*\*

Police divers had already searched John D. Long Lake on the theory that the carjacker might have ditched the stolen vehicle in its dark, murky waters. But they had only swum out about thirty feet from the shore. Now, armed with more precise information from Smith, they found the car nearly one hundred feet from the boat ramp upside down on the muddy bottom, its windows sealed, the little boys still strapped into their car seats. Autopsy results would later establish that the boys had been alive when their mother sent them into the lake and may have suffered inside the sealed car for as long as forty minutes before drowning.

When news of the discovery broke, the people of Union sent up a collective howl of fury. Members of the Black community had particular reason to feel aggrieved. "For nine days," as *New York Post* opinion columnist Andrea Peyser put it, "every Black man aged seventeen to fifty felt as he was under suspicion."

The aftermath and subsequent trial revealed that Smith was, in fact, an intensely troubled young woman who had been traumatized by the suicide of her beloved father when she was six and had survived two suicide attempts of her own while still in her teens. She had also been sexually molested by her stepfather, who had continued to conduct a sexual relationship with her into her adulthood.

At her trial in July 1995, her defense lawyer argued that Smith had severe depression and that the murders were a nonfatal suicide in which Smith planned to drown herself as well as her sons. In the end, however, jurors were more convinced by the emotional arguments of the prosecution, who insisted that Smith had perpetrated an unthinkable atrocity, "eliminat[ing] her toddlers so that she could have a chance at a life with Tom Findlay, the man she said she loved."

Though the prosecution sought the death penalty, Smith was sentenced to life in prison, where, in the decades since her incarceration, she has managed to make the news on several occasions for her habit of having sex with her prison guards.

# #91 ANDREW CUNANAN'S HOUSEBOAT HIDEOUT

## Andrew Cunanan and the Versace Murder

**(1997)**

*The search for cross-country spree killer Andrew Cunanan—one of the largest manhunts in US history—came to an end on this Miami Beach houseboat.*

orn in 1969, Andrew Cunanan grew up in an upscale suburb of San Diego, the son of a stockbroker father accused of embezzlement who fled to his native Philippines to avoid arrest. By the time his father left, Cunanan—who was openly gay in high school—had already settled in San Francisco's Castro District, where, though unemployed, he maintained a flashy lifestyle thanks to the largesse of a succession of older, wealthy men, who were drawn to both his polished charm and his zest for BDSM sex.

In the fall of 1996, Cunanan's world came apart after he was dumped by his latest sugar daddy. Virtually overnight, he went from a life of comfort and glamour to a sordid, hand-to-mouth existence, barely supporting himself by peddling drugs (and reportedly consuming them, along with alcohol, in increasing quantities). The following April, he flew from California to Minneapolis. Two nights after his arrival, he killed his first victim, a friend named Jeffrey Trail with whom he'd had a falling out, bludgeoning Trail to death with two dozen hammer blows to his head. Five days later, on May 1, he used Trail's handgun to pump several .40-caliber bullets into the head of David Madson, the former boyfriend Cunanan had once described as "the love of my life."

Fleeing in Madson's Jeep, Cunanan made his way to Chicago, where he somehow gained entrance to the home of a seventy-two-year-old real estate mogul named Lee Miglin, whom he'd never met before. For reasons unknown, he subjected Miglin to a horrific form of torture, wrapping his head in duct tape with breathing space at the nose, then stabbing him repeatedly with pruning shears before cutting open his throat with a gardening saw.

Heading east in Miglin's Lexus, Cunanan next killed a forty-five-year-old cemetery caretaker named William Reese in Pennsville, New Jersey, shooting the victim in the head with the pistol he had used to slay Madson, then making off in Reese's Chevy pickup. The date was May 9. In less than two weeks, the one-time party boy had brutally murdered four men.

News reports about Cunanan had earned him a spot on the FBI's "Ten Most-Wanted List." In the meantime, he made his way south, ultimately arriving in Miami Beach, where he checked into a down-at-the-heels hotel on May 12. For two months, Cunanan left his room mainly at night to hit the glitzy gay clubs of South Beach. During the days, he holed up, eating takeout pizza and subs, and whiling away his time with TV, fashion magazines, and S&M pornography.

In early June, he drove to South Beach, parking just two blocks away from the palatial residence of the celebrated fashion designer Gianni Versace. Cunanan had nothing personal against the fashion icon; it was more likely the designer embodied all the glamour and celebrity Cunanan himself coveted.

At around 8:30 a.m. on July 15, Versace—following his usual morning routine—left his mansion and strolled a few blocks away to a café where he purchased coffee and a handful of magazines. A few minutes later, he was back home. As he was opening the ornate wrought-iron front gates, Cunanan strode up and shot him twice in the head with a 40-caliber pistol.

As the fifty-year-old Versace collapsed onto the stone steps of his palazzo, his companion, Antonio D'Amico, rushed outside and pursued the assassin, who swung around, aimed his gun at D'Amico and waved him away without firing. Then Cunanan dashed into a nearby parking garage. It was there that investigators found the Chevy pickup that had been stolen from the New Jersey cemetery worker, William Reese. Inside the truck were bloody clothes and a US passport in the name of Andrew Phillip Cunanan.

Cunanan was now the object of one of the biggest manhunts in US history. Sightings poured in from every contiguous state, but he never left South Beach. Eight days after the Versace shooting, Fernando Carreira—the seventy-one-year-old caretaker of a houseboat docked in a Miami Beach marina—entered the vessel and found evidence of an intruder. Hurrying outside to call the police, he heard a single shot. After nearly five tense hours of police watching and waiting, they fired tear-gas cannisters into the vessel and shouted "Come out! Come out!" A few minutes later, a SWAT team entered the boat. They found Cunanan, dressed only in boxer shorts, sprawled faceup on a bed. He had shot himself in the mouth with the .40-caliber handgun that lay on his stomach.

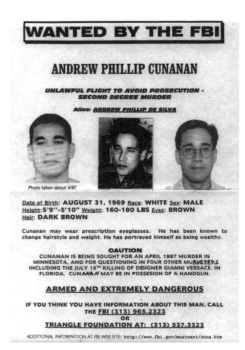

*Cunanan briefly made the FBI's Most Wanted list.*

# #92 LOGGING CHAIN

## The Torture-Murder of James Byrd Jr.

**(1998)**

*To the great shame of the US, the noose has become a symbol of the racist brutality inflicted on Black Americans. However, not every lynching has been done with a rope. The horrendous lynching of James Byrd Jr. was committed with a chain like this one.*

G rowing up in the East Texas town of Jasper in the 1970s and '80s, John William King showed no signs of racial prejudice. As a child, he had sleepovers at the homes of Black friends and one of his closest pals was a Black kid who shared his passion for computer games.

For unknown reasons—possibly the death of his doting mother, or the discovery that he was adopted, or his dead-end existence in a town that had known better days contributed—King's life began to unravel in his early teens. Dropping out of high school, he worked at a series of menial jobs while getting into regular trouble with the law for crimes ranging from disorderly conduct to burglary. In and out of various institutions, he landed in a prison notorious for the brutality of its inmates, where survival depended on membership in a gang. King joined—and ultimately became the leader of—a group called the Confederate Knights of America, imbibing its white supremacist philosophy. By the time he was paroled in July 1997, he was covered in racist tattoos, including images of Woody Woodpecker in Klansman garb and a Black man dangling from a tree limb. Even his Zippo cigarette lighter bore a KKK insignia, along with Nazi storm trooper symbols and the words *Sieg Heil*.

King was living back in Jasper when he received an unexpected visit from former jail mate and fellow CKA member Lawrence Russell Brewer in May 1998. The two spent their time partying with underage girls, burglarizing local businesses, and looking for ways to make trouble. At around 2:00 a.m. on Sunday, June 7, 1998, the two hell-raising ex-cons, along with King's roommate Shawn Berry, were driving around in the latter's pickup when they happened upon James Byrd Jr., a Black man walking unsteadily by the side of the road. A hard-drinking forty-nine-year-old with a lengthy rap sheet of his own, Byrd was stumbling home after a late-night party with friends. Berry, who was driving and who knew Byrd by sight, offered the inebriated man a lift. Byrd climbed into the truck bed, where a thirty-foot logging chain lay coiled beside him.

Livid at his friend for "picking up a fucking" Black man (though he used a different term), King declared his intention to "scare the shit" out of Byrd. As events would prove, however, he had a far more monstrous plan in mind.

At around eight that Sunday morning, Cedric Green was driving down Huff Creek Road, which cut through piney woods and dead-ended at a little church. As he came over a hill, Green spotted something that he took, at first, for a deer carcass. Looking closer, he saw that it was a hideously mangled human body, missing its head and one arm.

Police were soon on the scene. Not long afterward, a report came in that a woman who lived nearby had discovered human remains—head, right shoulder, and right arm—in a gulley next to her driveway. From other evidence—a trail of blood and human tissue that ran the length of Huff Creek Road, scattered articles of clothing, a set of dentures, and more—it became clear that the victim had been dragged to his death.

His identity was established when one of the lawmen found a wallet with a driver's license and Social Security card in the name of James Byrd Jr. Not far from wallet, the officers found something else: a Zippo cigarette lighter inscribed with the name "Possum"— Bill King's prison nickname—and bearing markings that turned out to be Ku Klux Klan and Nazi storm trooper symbols. They also came upon a torque wrench with the name "Berry" crudely etched into the handle.

King, Berry, and Brewer were soon in custody. The story that emerged from their testimony and forensic evidence was almost too grisly to believe. After driving Byrd to the remote road out of town, they beat him, defecated and urinated on him, then chained him by the ankles to the truck and started driving. The autopsy report on his injuries made it clear that Byrd had been subjected to unimaginable torture:

**Nearly all of Byrd's anterior ribs were fractured. He suffered massive brush burn abrasions over most of his body. Both testicles were missing and gravel was found in the scrotal sac. Both knees and part of his feet had been ground down, his left cheek was ground to the jawbone, and his buttocks were ground down to the scrotum and lower spine. Some of his toes were missing and others were fractured. Large lacerations of the legs exposed muscle.**

The forensic pathologist who conducted the postmortem concluded that—until his head and upper extremity were torn away from the rest of his body—James Byrd had been alive and conscious throughout the ordeal.

In the following months, Jasper—a town that had prided itself on it supposedly enlightened racial attitudes—became notorious as the site of one of the most horrific lynchings in the nation's history. News media descended on the town in droves for Byrd's June 13 funeral. Among the speakers were Jesse Jackson, Al Sharpton, and Secretary of Transportation Rodney Slater, who read a letter from President Clinton. Basketball star Dennis Rodman covered the cost of the $30,000 burial.

Far from displaying remorse for the atrocity, King took pride in it. In a note to Brewer written while awaiting trial, he assured his "bro" that "regardless of the outcome of this, we have made history and shall die proudly remembered." He signed off: "Much Aryan Love." Brewer, too, remained unrepentant, declaring that he would "do it all over again." Both men received death sentences and were executed by lethal injection, Brewer in September 2011, and King in April 2019. Berry, whose attorney convinced the jury that his client was an unwilling participant in the crime, escaped the death penalty and was sentenced to life in prison with the possibility of parole in 2039.

# #93 **WOODEN RAIL FENCE**

## The Martyrdom of Matthew Shepard

**(1998)**

*For many gay rights activists, the split-rail fence on which the martyred Matthew Shephard was tortured, bound, and left to die possesses the sacred quality of the True Cross.*

Though homophobic attacks were so common in 1998 that the FBI recorded nearly 1,300 of them, the murder of Matthew Shepard was an atrocity of such resonant, tragic symbolism that it immediately entered the national consciousness.

On the night of October 6, 1998, Shepard—a slight, delicate-featured, twenty-one-year-old student at the University of Wyoming in Laramie—was seen leaving a local watering hole with two other young men, Aaron McKinney and Russell Henderson, initially described as strangers he had just met that evening. Eighteen hours later, a cyclist biking through a remote area came upon what he took to be a Halloween scarecrow lashed to a wooden fence. Looking closer, he saw that the figure's face was masked in blood, except for two pale streaks running down the cheeks—the tracks of the dying victim's tears. Still alive but in a coma from the savage pistol-whipping he had suffered, Shepard lingered in the hospital for six days before succumbing to his injuries

Under arrest, McKinney and Henderson—two aimless lowlifes with police records dating back to their teens—claimed that, recognizing Shepard as an easy mark, they had lured him into their truck by pretending to be gay. Driving him to the outskirts of the city, they had tied him to the fence, robbed him, then shattered his skull with a dozen blows from McKinney's .357 Magnum, set him on fire, and left him to die in the freezing prairie night. Both men were eventually sentenced to life sentences without the possibility of parole.

The initial news accounts of the atrocity stated that the "shy," "gentle," "boyishly idealistic" Shepard had been slain by two gay-hating "rednecks" who then "crucified" him.

Subsequent research into the case has offered a more complicated picture, with evidence emerging that Shepard and McKinney were acquaintances—and possibly occasional sex partners. There have also been indications that Shepard—who, after being gang-raped during a high school trip to Morocco, had turned to drugs and alcohol as a way of managing his PTSD—was, like McKinney, a crystal meth user, and that his death was related to his possession of a large shipment of the drug.

None of that, of course, mitigates the horror of what was done to him. In the years since he suffered his agonizing death, he has become a powerful symbol for the gay-rights movement, inspiring movies, television shows, and plays—most notably, *The Laramie Project*, which has been performed all over the world. Most significantly, his murder, along with that of James Byrd Jr., led to the passage of a major federal hate crimes law.

# #94 WEAPONS BELONGING TO ERIC HARRIS AND DYLAN KLEBOLD

## The Columbine Massacre

**(1999)**

*Though the Columbine massacre was not America's first mass school shooting, it ushered in an era when such atrocities have become terrifyingly common.*

In the spring of 1999, America first heard a name that would soon become a byword for a frightening new phenomenon, the mass school shooting: Columbine.

Situated in the foothills of the Rockies in the Denver suburb of Littleton, Columbine High School was the site of the massacre. Its perpetrators were two seniors, Eric Harris and Dylan Klebold. In the aftermath of their rampage, the media portrayed the pair as social outcasts, possibly gay, who belonged to a Goth-style clique called the "Trench Coat Mafia" and were specifically targeting the jocks who had bullied them. The truth, however, was very different. Far from being a dorky misfit, Eric Harris—the driving force behind the massacre—was a cool, self-possessed charmer who smoked, partied, and cultivated an edgy "military chic" look. He was an avid fan of baseball, liked to drink with his buddies, and was successful with girls.

He was also a textbook psychopath. Outwardly normal, with a bright and engaging personality, behind his "mask of sanity" he was a cunning, manipulative, and utterly remorseless, and secretly exulted in his (supposed) superiority to the mere mortals around him.

A math prodigy and computer whiz from a loving, affluent household, Dylan Klebold also appeared to be a normal high schooler; he excelled at fantasy league baseball, had an after-school job at a pizza shop, and—despite his almost painful shyness—was dating a bright, attractive girl whom he proudly squired to the senior prom. He was also an extreme depressive who, beginning in the spring of his sophomore year, began pouring out his tormented musings in a journal discovered after his death. Alternating between spiritual introspection and expressions of abject self-loathing, the entries are those of a desperately unhappy adolescent.

Eric Harris also recorded his thoughts, both on a website and in a journal. "I feel like God," he ranted. "I am higher than almost everyone else in terms of human intelligence." The rest of humanity was composed of nothing but "pathetic fuckheads" too dense to perceive the hollowness of their own zombielike existence or to appreciate his dazzling insights into the true meaning of life. "Fuck mercy, fuck justice, fuck morals, fuck rules, fuck laws. All you fuckers should die! DIE!"

Harris began putting his antisocial fantasies into action in his sophomore year when, with Klebold as an eager accomplice, he embarked on a series of so-called "missions": petty crimes and misdemeanors that escalated from malicious acts of property damage to the break-in of an unoccupied van, an offense that landed them in police custody. But these small-time infractions were just a warm-up to the enormity that Harris, in typically grandiose fashion, called Judgment Day.

Preparations began a year in advance: producing explosives, assembling an arsenal, plotting an onslaught with military precision. After diverting police and firefighters with a decoy bomb planted several miles from the school, Harris and Klebold, armed to the teeth, would blow up the crowded cafeteria with two other propane bombs, then—having positioned themselves on a hillside outside the main entrance—mow down fleeing survivors of the blast. Finally, after the crowds of first responders, frantic parents, and local reporters had rushed to the scene, the killers' parked cars, rigged with more time bombs, would explode, wiping out everyone in the vicinity.

They might have reached that awful goal had Harris known more about explosives. At around 11:15 a.m. on Judgment Day—Tuesday, April 20—the pair brazenly carried two duffel bags, each containing a twenty-pound time-bomb, into the cafeteria and set them down by the lunch tables. They then headed back outside and waited for the fireworks to begin. When the bombs failed to detonate, they pulled out their weapons and advanced on the school, firing first at some students lounging outside, then heading into the building. Over the next forty-nine minutes, they rampaged through the school, shooting randomly at fellow students and teachers, tossing homemade pipe bombs, exchanging exultant cries—"This is awesome!" "This is what we always wanted to do!"—as they went. The bulk of their victims—ten people out of an eventual thirteen fatalities—were slaughtered in the library, where, at 12:08 p.m., the murderers ended their own lives with simultaneous blasts to their heads.

Though the Columbine killers intended something far worse, they still managed to perpetrate the deadliest school shooting in American history up to that point. They also left a terrifying legacy. In the years since, the country has been plagued by a string of these enormities, among them the 2012 bloodbath at Sandy Hook Elementary School in Newtown, Connecticut, when a profoundly disturbed misfit named Adam Lanza gunned down twenty first-graders, along with six adult staff members; the 2018 massacre at Marjory Stoneman Douglas High School which claimed the lives of seventeen victims; and the 2022 Uvalde Elementary school shooting, which took the lives of nineteen children and two teachers.

In terms of sheer body count, the most appalling of them all occurred in April 2007, when college senior Seung-Hui Cho, armed with two semiautomatic handguns, shot and killed thirty-two people and wounded seventeen more at Virginia Tech University. Before embarking on his murderous spree, Cho produced a rambling rationalization of his crimes in the form of a videotaped "manifesto." Among Cho's self-professed motives was his admiration for the homicidal pair he saw as heroic models: his brother "martyrs" (as he called them) Eric Harris and Dylan Klebold.

# #95 ARMIN MEIWES'S SHIRT SWATCH

## "The Man-Eater of Rotenburg"

**(2001)**
*Armin Meiwes's crime was not only appalling in itself. It was made even more so by the enthusiastic participation of his victim.*

Born in the German city of Essen in 1961, Armin Meiwes was a lonely, socially isolated boy. By the time he was ten, he was daydreaming about butchering and devouring his classmates as a way of "assimilating" them so that, as he put it, they would "stay with [him] forever." As an adolescent, those fantasies became sexualized. He would masturbate while imagining that he was slicing open male schoolmates and consuming their entrails.

Following military service, he found work as a computer technician while living with his mother in a rambling forty-room manor house in a village a few miles from the city of Rotenburg. At night, he would devote himself to a grotesque hobby: using photos clipped from gay porn magazines, naked Ken dolls, and bodies molded out of marzipan to create nightmarish computer images of men being disemboweled, dismembered, and prepped for grilling.

The turning point came when, following the death of his mother in September 1999, he plunged into the dark online world of sado-masochistic chat rooms and discovered an entire subculture of like-minded fetishists who shared his cannibalistic fantasies. To his delight, an astonishing number expressed a wish to be killed and eaten. Using the pseudonym "Antrophagus," Meiwes began running an ad: "I'm looking for young men between eighteen and thirty years to slaughter. If you have a normally built body, then come to me. I'll butcher you and eat your delectable flesh."

Meiwes's depraved dream came true in February 2001, when he made contact with a forty-three-year-old microelectronics engineer named Bernd Brandes who had posted his own ad in a cannibal forum, offering himself as a meal—a "meat deliverer," as he put it. After exchanging a series of graphic sext messages in which Meiwes promised to fulfill Brandes's long-held desire to be eaten alive, the pair settled on a date for their ghastly liaison.

Brandes arrived, as scheduled, on Friday, March 9. His butchering began that evening after he swallowed twenty sleeping pills and a half-bottle of schnapps. After setting up a video camera to tape the proceedings, Meiwes amputated Brandes's penis with a kitchen knife, seasoned it with salt, pepper, and garlic and fried it. Both men then tried to eat it but found it too "chewy."

By then, Brandes was bleeding heavily and shaking with cold. Meiwes ran a hot bath where the mutilated man could comfortably bleed to death, then retreated to his bedroom to while away the time with a Star Trek novel. The following morning, he placed the still-living Brandes on his homemade butcher's table, cut his throat, then hung him upside down from a meat hook, gutted and beheaded him, and carved his flesh into steaks that he stored in a freezer and consumed over the next eighteen months.

Bursting with pride over his atrocity, Meiwes posted details on a cannibal chat room under the pseudonym "Franky." A visitor to the site alerted the police, who tracked down Meiwes and arrested him in December 2002. He was brought to trial just over a year later. Since there were no German laws against cannibalism and since Meiwes's victim had volunteered to be killed, he was convicted of manslaughter and sentenced to eight and a half years behind bars. Outrage over the leniency of the sentence led to a retrial in 2006. This time, the "Man-Eater of Rotenburg" was sentenced to life imprisonment.

# #96 SCOTT PETERSON'S BOAT

## The Murder of Laci Peterson

**(2002)**

*Though the exact circumstances of Laci Peterson's murder remain shrouded in mystery, there seems little doubt that her corpse was dumped out of this boat.*

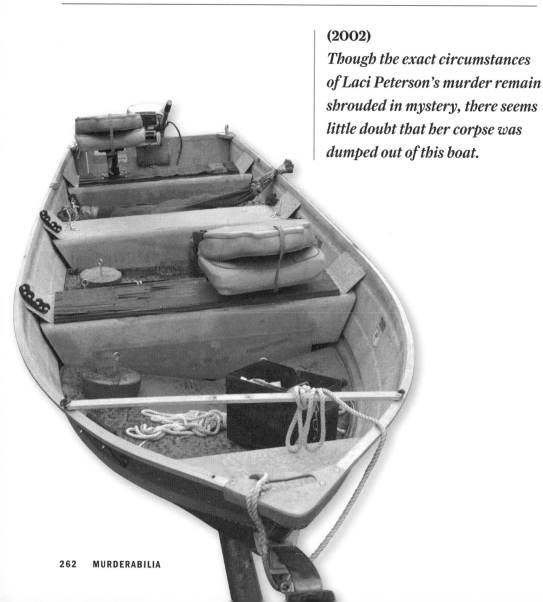

When college sophomore Laci Rocha met Scott Peterson in a California café, she was smitten at first sight. Convinced that they would end up together, she telephoned her mother and announced: "I have met the man I am going to marry." With his virile good looks and million-watt smile, Scott's exterior belied the reality that he was a cold-blooded sociopath.

Like others of his breed, Scott Peterson was remarkably good at mimicking normal human behavior—at fashioning what psychologist Hervey Cleckley has famously called a "mask of sanity." To those who knew him growing up, Scott seemed a model youth: smart, well-behaved, with a puppy-dog eagerness to please. The girls he dated in high school found him courtly and romantic. Even then, however, there were warning signs of an underlying disorder: He repeatedly lied about his achievements, casually cheated on his supposedly steady girlfriends, and displayed a bizarre lack of emotion when caught red-handed in a deception.

Following a storybook wedding and a Tahitian honeymoon in the summer of 1997, the Petersons opened a small restaurant in San Luis Obispo, then, three years later, moved to Modesto, where Scott took a job as a salesman for a fertilizer company, while Laci worked as a substitute elementary school teacher. They purchased a three-bedroom fixer-upper and transformed it into a suburban showplace. When Laci became pregnant in the summer of 2002 with a son they decided to name Conner, all of Laci's domestic dreams appeared to have come true, including a nursery with a nautical theme, complete with a "Welcome Aboard" life preserver hung over the crib.

Even as he played the role of excitedly expectant father, however, Scott was leading a secret life with another woman. Her name was Amber Frey. They had begun their relationship in the third week of November, when Frey—a slender, blonde, twenty-seven-year-old massage therapist and single mother—accepted a date with the ostensibly unmarried Scott. Swept off her feet by Peterson's seductive charm, she fell into bed with him after their first date and was soon involved in an affair so intense that, as author Marilee Strong observes in *Erased: Missing Women, Murdered Wives*, "it was more like a parallel marriage."

When, in the first week of December, she heard from an acquaintance that Scott was no bachelor, she confronted him and demanded an explanation. Sobbing, he admitted that he had in fact been married but had "lost his wife," leading her to believe that he as a widower. It was, of course, another of his brazen lies. But by then, he was already planning to make it come true.

At around 5:30 p.m. on December 24, 2002, Laci Peterson's mother, Sharon Rocha—at home preparing Christmas Eve dinner for her family—received an alarming phone call from her son-in-law. He had just returned home from a day of fishing and discovered that Laci was missing. Dispatched to the Peterson home, police questioned Scott, whose demeanor struck them as odd. Despite his conviction that his wife had fallen victim to foul play, his responses seemed, as one of them noted, "casual and nonchalant . . . bored, tired, and devoid of urgency." His alibi—that, on a cold, rainy Christmas Eve morning, he had spontaneously decided to drive ninety miles to the San Francisco Bay to do some sturgeon fishing—seemed both implausible and full of inconsistencies.

Over the following weeks, hundreds of law officers and civilian volunteers scoured the parks and rural areas around Modesto for the missing woman. Rewards, ultimately amounting to half a million dollars, were offered for information leading to her safe return. Missing persons flyers were distributed, a command center was established at a local hotel, candlelight vigils were held, and a website was launched.

For a while Laci's family stood behind Scott, while officials grew suspicious. All that changed in January, when Amber Frey came forward and revealed that she had been Scott's lover. Scott appeared on *Good Morning America*, shamefacedly admitting to his affair but insisting that he had nothing to do with Laci's disappearance. Shortly after learning of Scott's adultery, Laci's brother, Brent Rocha, announced that he was "no longer supporting him."

On successive days in the second week of April, the putrefied corpses of a three-and-a-half-pound baby and a headless woman—the torso clad in bra and maternity pants—washed ashore near the spot where Scott had "gone fishing" on Christmas Eve. DNA tests conclusively proved that the remains were those of Laci Peterson and her nearly full-term fetus, evidently expelled from the ruptured womb of the mother by the build-up of abdominal gasses produced during decomposition—a ghastly phenomenon known as "coffin birth."

A few days later, Scott was arrested in San Diego, twenty miles from the Mexican border. He had disguised his appearance, having grown a goatee that he had bleached—along with eyebrows and hair—to a weird orange hue. He told the arresting officers that he was on his way to play golf, though that hardly accounted for the survivalist stockpile found in his car, a cache that included an entire wardrobe, nearly fifteen thousand dollars in cash, and a supply of Viagra.

At his five-month trial, which began in June 2004, Peterson was represented by high-profile attorney, Mark Geragos, whose various arguments failed to bear up against the testimony of Amber Frey, whose descriptions of Scott's lovey-dovey phones calls to her even as hundreds of concerned citizens frantically searched for his missing wife effectively sealed his doom.

On November 12, 2004, the jury found Scott Peterson guilty of first-degree murder. He was formally sentenced to death on March 16, 2005, and immediately transported to San Quentin State Prison. In December 2021, he was resentenced to life in prison without the possibility of parole. Like so many sociopaths, he continues to maintain his innocence, as do his unflaggingly loyal family members who maintain an appeal website that offers a reward of $250,000 for information that would lead to his release.

# #97 JOHN ALLEN MUHAMMED'S BUSHMASTER RIFLE

## The Beltway Snipers

**(2002)**

*It was the sheer randomness of the Beltway Sniper murders that ignited such widespread public panic.*

A man of such changeable moods that acquaintances sometimes called him "the chameleon," John Allen Muhammad could be gentle and charming one moment and frighteningly hostile the next. Born John Allen Williams in 1960, he spent seventeen years in the military, serving in the Gulf War and distinguishing himself as a sharpshooter.

By the time he returned to civilian life in 1994, he had joined the Nation of Islam and was married to his second wife, Mildred. Moving to Tacoma , Washington, with their three children, they opened a car repair business that failed a short time later. His frequent infidelities led to the breakdown of their marriage. In 1999, Mildred filed for divorce and was granted custody of the children. Muhammad promptly purchased a Bushmaster XM15-E2S rifle, informed Mildred that she was "not going to raise my children," and threatened to kill her. Though she got an order of protection, she allowed him to visit the children. In March 2000, he picked up the children after school and absconded with them to the Caribbean island of Antigua.

During his time in Antigua, Muhammad supplemented his income as a car repairman and housepainter by selling forged visas and work permits to would-be immigrants desperate to get into the United States. One of these was a Jamaican-born woman, Una James, mother of a son named Lee Boyd Malvo.

An exceptionally bright child, well-loved by everyone who knew him, Malvo suffered from his constantly uprooted existence. Wrenched from his father at an early age, he was in search of a surrogate. In 1999, at age fifteen, he found John Allen Muhammad.

It wasn't long before Malvo had moved in with Muhammad. In thrall to the man he began calling "Dad," Lee began working out every day, acquired a new interest in firearms, and became a convert to the Nation of Islam.

When Antiguan authorities got wind of Muhammad's immigration-papers scam in the spring of 2001, he headed back to the States with his three children and Malvo. With the help of authorities, Muhammad's ex-wife, Mildred, located and reclaimed possession of their three children and whisked them off to Washington, DC.

Some would claim that it was the loss of his children that caused Muhammad to "snap." Whatever the case, in the following months, he grew increasingly bitter toward white America, expressing open admiration for the 9/11 terrorists. The military-style regimen he devised for Malvo now included intensive rifle practice at a gun range and daily training in sniper techniques. In February 2002, the two men set off on a murderous odyssey that would eventually paralyze the nation's capital.

On the sixteenth of that month, as a test of Malvo's readiness and resolve, Muhammad, who had a grudge against a woman named Isa Nichols, sent the boy to her house with orders to knock on the door and shoot the woman who answered. As it happened, Nichols's twenty-one-year-old niece, Keenya Cook, opened the front door. Malvo raised his .45-caliber pistol and killed her with a single shot to the face.

Over the next eight months, the deadly pair moved around the United States, traveling mostly by bus and committing a string of shootings in states ranging from California to Texas to Florida. Along the way, they purchased a used blue Chevrolet Caprice, in the rear of which Muhammad created a hidden sniper's perch by cutting a hole in the trunk just above the license plate, removing part of the back seat, and building a small platform for a rifle tripod.

The killing spree that would earn them international notoriety began on the evening of October 2, 2002, when a fifty-five-year-old man was fatally shot in a supermarket parking lot in Wheaton, Maryland. The following day, four more random shootings around Maryland and one in Washington, DC, would claim the lives of five innocent victims, among them a landscaper mowing a lawn, a part-time taxicab driver filling up at a gas station, and a retired carpenter out for a stroll. Eight more people doing mundane activities—pumping gas, loading up their cars after shopping, walking across restaurant parking lots—would be shot in the following two and a half weeks, five of them fatally.

The shootings by the killers—now known alternately as the "DC Snipers" and the "Beltway Snipers"—generated widespread fear. Over a significant stretch of the mid-Atlantic region, people were terrified to gas up their vehicles, send their children to school, or run everyday errands.

A coalition of law enforcement agencies launched a massive hunt for the killers. Toying with their pursuers, Muhammad left a series of messages at different crime scenes, including an inscribed Tarot card with the instruction "Call me God" and a note vowing to continue the slaughter unless a ten-million-dollar payment was deposited into a Bank of America account.

On October 17, an anonymous caller phoned the police and boasted of having pulled off a murder-robbery in Montgomery, Alabama. A fingerprint obtained at that crime scene was matched to Lee Boyd Malvo. FBI agents in Tacoma quickly learned of Malvo's connection to John Allen Muhammad. It wasn't long before investigators established that Muhammad had purchased both a Bushmaster semiautomatic rifle and a 1990 blue Caprice like the one several eyewitnesses had seen at shooting sites.

The climax came on October 24, when the snipers' car was spotted at a rest stop in Maryland. A small army of SWAT teams, members of the FBI's Hostage Rescue Team, and other paramilitary units descended on the vehicle, only to find the suspects peacefully asleep. The two men surrendered without a struggle.

Convicted of murder in November 2003, Muhammad was sentenced to death and executed by lethal injection six years later. Malvo, sentenced to life without parole, remains incarcerated in Red Onion State Prison in Virginia, where, in March 2020, he got married.

# #98 "GRIM SLEEPER" BILLBOARD

## The "Grim Sleeper" Murders

**(1985–1988, 2002–2007)**

*In the hunt for the serial killer dubbed "The Grim Sleeper," billboards showed police sketches of the suspect and offered a large reward. After the murderer's capture, the billboards paid tribute to his eleven victims.*

**M**urderers who prey only on sex workers are so common that they constitute their own criminal category: "harlot killers," a term that dates back to the most infamous of them all, Jack the Ripper. In that sense, there was nothing especially unique about Lonnie Franklin Jr.—nothing except for the long hiatus between his two murder sprees, a period of dormancy that earned him his nickname: the "Grim Sleeper."

Born in Los Angeles in August 1952, he was a troublemaker by age sixteen, when he was expelled from high school for beating up a classmate. A few years later, while posted in Germany during a stint in the army, he and two buddies abducted a seventeen-year-old girl and gang-raped her at knifepoint.

Dishonorably discharged, he returned to his old neighborhood in South Central Los Angeles, got married, fathered two children, and, after briefly working as a security guard and garbage man, supported himself as a backyard car mechanic. He was also obsessed with sex and conducted simultaneous adulterous affairs with various girlfriends while regularly patronizing sex workers.

His sadistic drive to sexually dominate women took a lethal turn in August 1985 when he murdered a twenty-nine-year-old cocktail waitress, shooting her three times in the chest with a .25-caliber handgun and dumping her corpse in a South Central alley. One year later, almost to the day, the body of a thirty-four-year-old Black sex worker, sexually assaulted and killed in the same way, was found partially hidden beneath a fetid mattress in another alley.

By the time another victim turned up in January 1987, Los Angeles police were aware that they had a serial killer on their hands. Even as a special task force conducted an intensive manhunt for the "Southside Slayer" (as he was originally dubbed), women continued to die. By the fall of 1988, four more Black sex workers had been raped, shot to death, and discarded like trash. And then, in November of that year, the killings ceased.

Thirteen years later, the naked corpse of a fifteen-year-old foster-care-runaway-turned-sex worker was found in a South Central alleyway. When DNA evidence linked her to one of the earlier victims, it became clear that the 1980s "Southside Slayer" had emerged from hibernation. Now given the nickname the "Grim Sleeper" by a journalist, he committed two more homicides, one in July 2003, the other on the first day of 2007, bringing his confirmed total to ten.

The break finally came with the use of a new forensic tool: the familial DNA search, which allows police to run tests on close relatives of criminal suspects. In March 2010, lab technicians matched DNA from the Grim Sleeper murders to that of a twenty-nine-year-old man recently arrested on a felony firearms charge: Christopher John Franklin. Christopher had been a toddler at the time of the Sleeper's first murder spree. His father, however—Lonnie Franklin Jr.—closely resembled the description of the serial killer provided by the only woman to survive one of his attacks. Assigned to covertly follow Lonnie, a team of undercover agents managed to retrieve his DNA from a partially eaten pizza slice he left behind. When a positive match came in, Lonnie found himself under arrest.

Charged with ten murders (though suspected of as many as twenty-five), Lonnie Franklin Jr. was convicted on all counts and sentenced to death in June 2016. He was still awaiting execution when he was found dead in his cell on San Quentin's death row in March 2020.

# #99 REMAINS OF PRESSURE COOKER BOMB

## The Boston Marathon Bombing

**(2013)**

*Inspired by jihadist websites, one-time "party guy" Tamerlan Tsarnaev enlisted his younger brother's help in committing the worst terrorist attack on American soil since 9/11.*

In April 2002, Anzor and Zubeidat Tsarnaev—natives of Chechnya fleeing persecution in their homeland—sought asylum in the United States. They brought with them their younger son, Dzhokhar, then nine years old, leaving his teenaged brother, Tamerlan, in the care of an uncle in Kyrgyzstan. One year later, Tamerlan joined his family in Cambridge, Massachusetts, where they had settled.

After graduating with mediocre grades from a prestigious Cambridge high school, Tamerlan enrolled at Bunker Hill Community College but dropped out after three semesters to pursue his passion: boxing. A talented heavyweight who won several regional Golden Gloves championships, he aspired to fight in the Olympics. His hopes were wrecked when he was arrested after hitting his girlfriend during an argument. Though the case was dismissed when she declined to file charges, the arrest made him ineligible for citizenship for five years, thus disqualifying him for a place on the US Olympic boxing team.

Around this time, Tamerlan morphed from a pot-smoking, "fun-loving party guy" (as one friend described him) into a devout Muslim, renouncing drugs and alcohol, growing a beard, and swapping his designer jeans for traditional Muslim garb. He also became increasingly radicalized. In heated diatribes against the West, he derided the Bible as a "cheap copy of the Quran," claimed the 9/11 attacks were engineered by the US as an excuse to persecute Muslims, and regularly visited jihadi websites.

Tipped off by Russian intelligence sources that Tamerlan had become a follower of Islamic extremism, the FBI opened an investigation in March 2011 but closed it after finding nothing to link him to terrorism. On September 11 of that year—the tenth

anniversary of the 9/11 attacks—two Jewish acquaintances of Tamerlan's, along with their roommate, were slaughtered in Waltham, Massachusetts, their throats cut to the bone and—in the case of the Jewish victims—their penises sliced off. Though the case remains officially unsolved, subsequent evidence pointed to Tamerlan as one of the perpetrators. In January 2012, Tamerlan left for a visit with relatives in Russia, where he reportedly attempted to join jihadi fighters. When he returned home in July, he created a YouTube channel that posted links to militant Islamic websites; he also became an avid reader of the online al-Qaeda magazine, *Inspire*, whose first issue contained an article called "How to Make a Bomb in the Kitchen of Your Mom."

\*\*\*

Known as "Jahar" to his buddies, Tamerlan's kid brother, Dzhokhar, was, by all accounts, a typical American teen. Soft-spoken, sleepy-eyed, and laid-back, he had the usual interests of his cohort: girls, hip-hop, TV shows like *The Walking Dead* and *Game of Thrones*, and smoking pot. He attended the University of Massachusetts Dartmouth on a scholarship with the vague idea of becoming an engineer but spent most of his time hanging out, getting high, and earning spending money by dealing weed. During his three semesters of college, he failed seven classes and had a cumulative GPA of 1.094.

By early 2012, he had fallen under the radical sway of his idolized older brother. Previously nonchalant about religious matters, he now declared that the Prophet Muhammad was his "role model," immersed himself in militant Islamic propaganda, and insisted to friends that some terrorist attacks were justified "because of what the US does in other countries." Their parents having returned to Chechnya, he and Tamerlan now occupied the family's Cambridge apartment by themselves. In the early months of 2013, Tamerlan, following the instructions he had found in *Inspire*, began assembling the parts for two homemade bombs. He also acquired a 9mm semiautomatic handgun and several boxes of ammunition.

* * *

A beloved tradition dating back to 1897, the Boston Marathon is held on the third Monday of April. At around 2:30 p.m. on April 15, 2013, while exultant runners crossed the finish line, security cameras recorded two young men—one in a black cap, dark hooded coat, and sunglasses, the other in a beige hoodie and white cap worn backward—moving through the crowd. Both were carrying black nylon backpacks. Around fifteen minutes later, they strolled away—this time, without their backpacks.

Moments later, two homemade, shrapnel-filled, pressure cooker bombs detonated fourteen seconds apart near the finish line. Three people were killed, one of them an eight-year-old boy. Hundreds of others suffered injuries of varying degrees of severity, from broken bones and ruptured eardrums to mangled or severed limbs. That evening, while panic swept the city, President Obama appeared on television, vowing to "find out who did this" and subject them to "the full weight of justice."

Over the next few days, the Boston police conducted a massive hunt for the terrorists. On Thursday, April 18—seeking to enlist the public's help—the FBI released the surveillance images of the suspects, soon to be identified as Tamerlan and Dzhokhar Tsarnaev.

The brothers decided to flee Boston for New York City. As they headed out of Cambridge, they came upon an MIT police officer in his squad car, shot him six times—twice in the head—and tried, unsuccessfully, to steal his service pistol from its locked holster. Soon after, they carjacked a Mercedes SUV and kidnapped the driver, who managed to escape when the brothers stopped for gas and frantically called 911 to report the two young men who had bragged about committing the marathon bombings and shooting the MIT police officer.

An APB went out immediately. Spotted shortly afterward by a Watertown cop, Tamerlan came to stop in a leafy residential neighborhood. Calmly stepping from the vehicle, gun in hand, he began firing at his pursuer, who immediately radioed for help, which soon arrived. A ferocious, eight-minute battle ensued, with Tamerlan blasting away while Dzhokhar hurled pipe bombs at the lawmen. Though hit multiple times by police fire, Tamerlan didn't go down until he was tackled to the ground. As the cops struggled to subdue him, Dzhokhar leaped into the SUV, spun a U-turn, and drove toward the huddle of police officers who were wrestling to handcuff his brother. As the cops leapt out of the way, the SUV rolled over Tamerlan and dragged him several yards before speeding into the night. Rushed to the hospital, Tamerlan died of gunshot wounds and the injuries inflicted when his brother ran over him.

While the local populace sheltered in place, thousands of lawmen—including state police, members of the Massachusetts National Guard, SWAT teams, and FBI agents—scoured Watertown for the fugitive. At around six o'clock that evening—April 19—a retired phone company employee named David Henneberry looked out a window into his backyard and saw that the plastic tarp protecting his dry-docked powerboat had been displaced. He investigated and was startled to see a body curled up on the blood-splattered deck. Dashing back into the house, he called 911.

In short order, the boat was surrounded by a phalanx of heavily armed cops along with members of the FBI Hostage Rescue Team. During a ninety-minute standoff, police tried to dislodge the fugitive with gunfire, stun grenades, and an armored tanklike vehicle, the BearCat, that repeatedly rammed the vessel. As SWAT team members advanced on the boat, the badly wounded Dzhokhar finally emerged and was taken to the same hospital where twenty-six survivors of the carnage he and his brother had perpetrated were still being treated. Police later found a blood-stained, penciled manifesto the young terrorist had scrawled while hiding in the boat. "The US Government is killing our innocent civilians," it read in part, "I can't see such evil go unpunished."

Tried in the spring of 2015 on thirty charges, including four counts of murder, Dzhokhar was found guilty and sentenced to death. In July 2020, a three-judge panel reversed the sentence on appeal, sending the case to the US Supreme Court, which, in March 2022, reversed the appeals court finding and upheld the death sentence.

# #100 SOIL FROM THE SLENDER MAN STABBING SITE

## The Slender Man Stabbing

**(2014)**

*Originating as an internet meme, the fictitious Slender Man took on a life of his own, ultimately infiltrating the susceptible minds of two mentally unstable schoolgirls with lethal results.*

Beginning in 2009, a nightmarish creature began haunting the internet: A grotesquely tall and skinny male figure in a black suit and tie, he had a featureless white face, long, dangling arms, and was sometimes pictured with tentacles growing out of his back. His name was Slender Man.

A thirty-year-old elementary school teacher named Eric Knudsen concocted him as part of an online challenge to invent a new paranormal image, and Slender Man soon took on a life of his own, generating an elaborate mythology about his origins, powers, and sinister designs, most of which involved doing harm to young children. He was also said to possess a form of mind control that made his followers do his evil bidding.

In the spring of 2014, three twelve-year-old girls—Morgan Geyser, Anissa Weier, and Payton "Bella" Leutner, sixth graders at Horning Middle School in Waukesha, Wisconsin—celebrated Geyser's birthday with a sleepover at her house. The next morning, they went to a nearby park, where Geyser and Weier suggested that they play hide-and-seek in the woods bordering the playground.

No sooner had the trio entered the forest than, at Weier's signal, Geyser reached beneath her jacket, drew a steak knife she had taken from her kitchen, and set upon Leutner, stabbing her in the arms, legs, and chest—nineteen times in all. One wound missed a major artery by less than a millimeter; another punctured her diaphragm and cut into her liver and stomach. Weier and Geyser, who had been planning the attack for months, left their victim to die.

Miraculously, Leutner somehow survived. Discovered by a passing bicyclist as she crawled from the woods, she was rushed to the hospital, underwent immediate life-saving surgery, and provided police with a description of her assailants. Later that afternoon, Geyser and Weier were arrested as they were heading out of town.

Convinced of the reality of Slender Man, the preteens saw themselves as "proxies." Killing their friend, Weier calmly explained to police, was a way to "prove ourselves worthy to Slender." Their destination at the time of their arrest was Nicolet National Forest in northern Wisconsin, where Slender Man supposedly dwelled. The two girls were planning to live with him.

Charged with attempted first-degree homicide, Morgan Geyser was found "not guilty by reason of mental disease or defect" and sentenced to forty years in a state mental hospital. Anissa Weier pleaded guilty to being a party to attempted second-degree murder and was sentenced to twenty-five years in a different psychiatric institute. In July 2021, having been evaluated by a trio of doctors who concluded that she no longer posed a threat to herself and others, she was granted conditional release.

*The myth of Slender Man only grew when two 12-year-olds attempted to kill a classmate to prove themselves worthy to him.*

# Books Consulted

For a complete list of sources used for this work, please visit: workman.com/murderabilia.

# Photo Credits

**INTERIOR (alphabetical order):**
**Alamy:** Allstar Picture Library Limited: p. 163; Paul Briden: p. 116; Everett Collection Inc: p. 182; FLHC NV5: p. 47; Ken Hawkins: p. 220; © Keystone Pictures USA/ZUMAPRESS.com/Alamy Live News: p. 146; Montana Photographer: p. 64; Niday Picture Library: p. 97; PA Images: p. 150; PictureLux/The Hollywood Archive: p. 173; Reuters: p. 249; Smith Archive: pp. 126, 138; SuperStock: p. 99; The History Collection: p. 142. **AP Images:** Associated Press: p. 199; Chris Gardner, Pool: p. 265; *The Indianapolis Star*, Rob Goebel: p. 194; Steve C. Wilson: p. 218. **Archive.org:** Christian Kunkel: p. 35. **Eric Harvey Brown:** pp. 18, 25, 32, 46, 62, 86, 102, 132, 136, 206, 224, 238, 274. **Chicago History Museum:** DN-0001079, *Chicago Daily News* collection: p. 56. **Joel Comen:** p. 201. **Courtesy of Handy Family Collection:** p. 42. **Courtesy of the Author:** pp. 3, 6, 7, 17, 19, 22, 26, 27, 28, 41, 54, 68, 69, 71, 72, 76, 78, 84, 90, 93, 96, 100 (top and bottom), 104, 106, 108, 109 (top and bottom), 114, 128, 130, 140, 144, 149, 160, 165, 168, 176, 178, 183, 193, 208, 215, 221, 228, 230, 232, 246, 252, 260. **Countway Library, Harvard:** pp. 20, 21. **Fall River Historical Society:** pp. 50, 52. **Flickr:** Office of Public Affairs: p. 226; Steven R. Shook: p. 1. **Getty Images:** Archive Photos: p. 157; Bettmann: pp. 67, 111, 158, 167, 171, 180, 203; BIPS/Hulton Archive: p. 161; Chicago History Museum/Archive Photos: p. 98; Corbis Historical: pp. 151, 245; Steve Eichner/WireImage: p. 217; International News Photo/Archive Photos: p. 156; Mark Leffingwell/Digital First Media/Boulder Daily Camera: p. 257; Kevin Moloney/Hulton Archive: p. 255; *New York Daily News*: p. 101; *New York Daily News* Archive: p. 107; Popperfoto: p. 112; Mario Ruiz/The Chronicle Collection: p. 212; Sheridan Libraries/Levy/Gado: p. 34; The *Washington Post*: p. 198. **Herkimer County Historical Society:** p. 66. **Illinois State Archives:** p. 61. **Library Company of Philadelphia:** p. 24. **Los Angeles Public Library:** Los Angeles Herald Examiner Photo Collection: p. 175. **Metropolitan Police:** p. 148. **Murderpedia:** p. 244. **Museum of Modern Art:** The Judith Rothschild Foundation Contemporary Drawings Collection Gift: p. 154. **Museums of Western Colorado:** p. 39. **New York Public Library Digital Collection:** p. 15. **Portsmouth Athenaeum:** p. 33. **Reuters:** Dominick Reuter: p. 270. **Science Source Images:** Dr P. Marazzi/Science Source: p. 222. **San Diego State University:** Special Collections & University Archives: p. 75. **Shutterstock:** Austral Int: p. 240; Casper/AP: p. 196; Mark Guthrie: p. 186; imageBROKER: p. 170; Bill Ray/The LIFE Picture Collection: p. 190; Paul Sakuma/AP: p. 262; Todd Squires: p. 275; Nick Ut/AP: p. 268. **Surgeons Hall Museums, The Royal College of Surgeons of Edinburgh:** pp. 8, 10. **The Mental Shed:** Charlie Hintz: p. 80. **Travis County Archives:** p. 43. **University of North Carolina at Chapel Hill:** Wilson Special Collections Library: pp. 118, 120. **Wikimedia Commons:** The following image is used under a Creative Commons Attribution CC BY-SA 2.0 Generic License (creativecommons.org/licenses/by-sa/2.0/deed.en) and belongs to the following Wikimedia Commons user: gargantuan: p. 134. **Wikimedia Commons:** The following image is used under a Creative Commons Attribution CC BY-SA 3.0 Germany License (creativecommons.org/licenses/by-sa/3.0/de/deed.en) and belongs to the following Wikimedia Commons user: German Federal Archive: p. 82. **Wikimedia Commons:** The following image is used under a Creative Commons Attribution CC BY-SA 3.0 Unported License (creativecommons.org/licenses/by-sa/3.0/deed.en) and belongs to the following Wikimedia Commons user: ORTS email: p. 241. **Public Domain:** Attys: p. 110; Billmckern: p. 30; Gallica Digital Library: pp. 57, 88; Lake City, Colorado National Historic District: p. 37; NYC JD: p. 12; Obsidian Soul: p. 251; Realart: p. 94.

# Index

Page numbers in *italics* refer to illustrations or their captions.

## A

"Acid Bath Murderer," 3, 148–150
action figures, *186*
Adams, Florence, 63
Adams, Katherine, 63
Adams, Mr. and Mrs. William, 5–7
Adams, Samuel, 19
Agron, Salvador, 178–179, *178*
Ahakuelo, Benny, 125
Albermann, Gertrude, 83–84
Ambrosia Chocolate Factory, 230, 231
*American Tragedy, An* (Dreiser), 66
*America's Most Wanted*, 214
Amurao, Corazon, 197
*And a Child Shall Lead Them* (Coleman), *201*
Anderson, John, 16
Andrassy, Edward, 135
Andrews, Philip, 234
ankle camera, *106*
anti-Hawaiian cartoon, *124*
Arizona State Asylum for the Insane, 123
artwork
  Gacy's, *217*
  Miyazaki's, *235*
  Rolling's, *240*
  Smith's, *246*
Attenborough, Richard, *163*
autoerotic asphyxiation, 171
autopsy report, 43–45, *43*

## B

"Backpacker Murders," 238–240
*Badlands*, 173
Bailey, F. Lee, 167, 185
Baniszewski, Gertrude, 194–195, *195*
Barker, Lex, 176, 177
Barnet, Henry Crossman, 63
Barnum, P. T., 2–3
Barrow, Clyde, 3, 116–117
Bath School Disaster, 2, 108–109, *109*

Baxter, Willie, *26*
Beatles, 207
*Beautiful Cigar Girl, The* (Ingraham), 15–17, *15*
Behavioral Science Unit, FBI, 145
Bell, Charles Steele, 131
Bell, Charlotte Jane, 72
Bell, Mary, 200–202
Bell, Shannon, 38–40
Bell's painting, *201*
belongings, victim's, *238*
Beltway Snipers, 265–267, *265*
Bender, Frank, 212, 214
Bender family, 28–31, *30*
Benedict, Harriet, 67
Bennett, Keith, 187
Berkowitz, David, 224–225
Berry, Shawn, 253–254
bestiality, 81
Bialk, Frank, 61
Bicknese, Diedrich, 60
Bicknese, Louisa, 60
billboard, "Grim Sleeper," *268*
"Black Dahlia," 135, 156–157, *156*
"Black Museum," 3
Blackwell bathtub, *78*
Bloch, Robert, 169
Bloody Benders, 28–31
*Blue Dahlia, The*, 157
"Bluebeard," *57*
boat, Peterson's, *262*
Boddy, Lucinda, 44
body snatchers, 9
Bonnie and Clyde, 3, *3*, 116–117
Booth, Susan, 223
boots, Schmid's, *190*
Borden, Abby, 51–53
Borden, Andrew, 51–53
Borden, Emma, 51, 52, 53
Borden, Lizzie, 3, 50–53, *50*, *52*
Boston Marathon bombing, 270–273
Boston Strangler, 183–185
Bowen, Seabury, 51–52, 53
Brady, Ian, 186–187, *186*
Bragg, Charley, 155
Brandes, Bernd, 261
Breslin, Jimmy, 225
Brewer, Shawn, 252–254

Bridgeford, Shirley Ann, 172
Bridgewater State Hospital, 185
"Bring Back Our Darling," 34–36
broadsides, 5
Brown, Beresford, 162, 164
Brown, Frances, 152, 153
Brown, Grace, 66–67, *67*
Brown, Martin, 200–202
Bruns, Richie, 192–193
Brussel, James A., 145
Bryan Pearl, 2
Budd, Edward, 111
Budd, Grace, 111, *111*, 112
Budlick, Maria, 84
Bugs, The, 185
Bundy, Ted, 1, 218–220, *220*
Burke, William, 3, 8–11, *8*, *10*
"burking," 10
Burnham, Alice, 79
Bushmaster XM15-E2S, 265–267, *265*
business/calling cards, *100*, 215
Byrd, James, Jr., 252–254, 256
Byrnes, Frank, 138, 139

## C

Cabazon, Jean "Frenchy," 39
Cacioppo, Virginia, 143
cadavers, dissecting, 9, 11
Cagney, James, 106–107
Cain, James M., 107
Camden Massacre, 158–160
cannibalism, 37–40, 112–113, 142–143, 229, 230–231, 261
"Capeman" murders, 178–179
Capone, Al, 114–115, *114*
Capote, Truman, 180, 182
Carey, Cornelius, 23–24
Carr, Sam, 225
Carreira, Fernando, 251
Cavett, Dick, 210
Central State Hospital for the Criminally Insane, 169
chainsaw, Pickton's, *244*
Chang, Henry, 125
Chesebrough, Blanche, 63
chloroform, 86–87, *86*
Cho, Seung-Hui, 259
Christie, John Reginald Halliday, 162–164